Dangerous Prayers *from*

THE COURTS OF HEAVEN

that Destroy Evil Altars

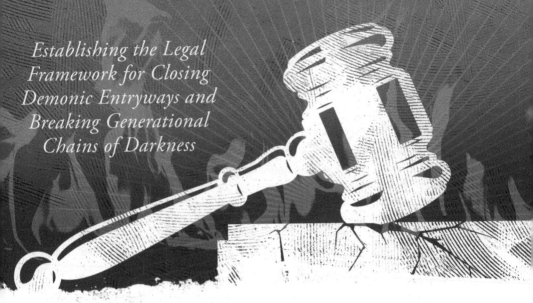

Establishing the Legal Framework for Closing Demonic Entryways and Breaking Generational Chains of Darkness

Dangerous Prayers *from*

THE COURTS OF HEAVEN

that Destroy Evil Altars

Supernatural Keys for Silencing Evil Altars Permanently

Dr. Francis Myles

DESTINY IMAGE® PUBLISHERS, INC.

P.O. Box 310, Shippensburg, PA 17257-0310

"Promoting Inspired Lives."

This book and all other Destiny Image and Destiny Image Fiction books are available at Christian bookstores and distributors worldwide.

Cover design by Eileen Rockwell.

For more information on foreign distributors, call 717-532-3040.

Reach us on the Internet: www.destinyimage.com.

ISBN 13 TP: 978-0-7684-5758-2

ISBN 13 eBook: 978-0-7684-5759-9

ISBN 13 HC: 978-0-7684-5761-2

ISBN 13 LP: 978-0-7684-5760-5

For Worldwide Distribution.

1 2 3 4 5 6 7 8 / 25 24 23 22 21

Contents

Preface

Therefore, confess your sins to one another [your false steps, your offenses], and pray for one another, that you may be healed and restored. The heartfelt and persistent prayer of a righteous man (believer) can accomplish much [when put into action and made effective by God—it is dynamic and can have tremendous power].

—James 5:16

The unmistakable testimony of scripture is that prayer works, anytime and everywhere. This statement might bother some people who have been praying for years with no tangible results. However, the Scriptures say, "let every man be a liar and God be true" (see Rom. 3:4). From Genesis to Revelation, God has not changed His primary form of communication with mankind. It is through the vehicle of prayer. Jesus lends His support to the importance of prayer when He declares, in the eighteenth chapter of Luke's Gospel, *"men always ought to pray and not lose heart"* (Luke 18:1 NKJV). The reality is that God always answers prayer, even when it seems as though the heavens above us are closed and God is silent.

In my study of prayer for more than two decades I have come to the sobering conclusion that most prayers are not answered because they're prayed from the wrong spiritual disposition. In other words, they are prayed amiss! This is why I decided after many years of constant prodding from my wife to write a book on prayer. I will demonstrate to you that all New

Testament praying is categorized in three different realms of prayer. Unfortunately, many Christians only know one or two of these realms of prayer. One of the biggest missing links in the global prayer movement is how to pray effectively from the Courts of Heaven. The absence of this prayer link has resulted in much unanswered prayer.

Thankfully, that mystery is revealed and solved in this powerful book. I chose to call this book *Dangerous Prayers from the Courts of Heaven that Destroy Evil Altars* because I have loaded this book with powerful and strategic prayers that are designed to help you hit the mark. I wrote this prayer book with the hundreds of thousands of people in mind who are suffering from the tyranny and frustration of unanswered prayers. To be honest, some Christians stopped praying and threw in the towel a long time ago. If the truth be told, many Christians do not pray much except at meals. Some people don't know how to pray effectively because they don't know what to say in the place of prayer. This book solves these challenges for disfranchised Christians everywhere and in every sphere.

I have divided this book into two sections. Section One lays a biblical foundation for how to pray and explains the three realms of prayer that all believers have access to. The second section of this book is what I call the book of *dangerous prayers*. The section is loaded with well-designed prayers for securing spiritual breakthroughs in any area of your life. I double dare you to share this book with your friends and family. Are you ready to walk into a season of answered prayers? Let's get the ball rolling!

Yours for Messiah's Kingdom,
Dr. Francis Myles
Author, *Issuing Divine Restraining Orders from the Courts of Heaven*
Presiding prelate, Kingdom Invasion Network and
Francis Myles International

SECTION ONE

Prerequisites

Chapter One

Men Ought to Pray Always!

Now Jesus was telling the disciples a parable to make the point that
at all times they ought to pray and not give up and lose heart.
—**Luke 18:1**

To say the subject of prayer is an important aspect of living in the Kingdom is truly an understatement—it's more like prayer is to spiritual life what oxygen is to the human body! Knowing this essential relationship between prayer and living effectively in the Kingdom of God, Jesus declares, "Men ought to pray at all times and not lose heart!" With this one blanket statement Jesus forever endorsed prayer, everywhere and under all circumstances, as the primary means for engaging God and releasing answers to life's most perplexing problems. My late spiritual mentor Dr. Myles Munroe in his bestselling book on prayer defines prayer as such: "Prayer is an earthly license for heavenly interference." E.M. Bounds declares, "Without prayer man cannot and without prayer God will not!" You will fully understand this last statement in the next chapter.

Jesus' life on earth is a classic example of a man totally dependent on divine resources that are available to anyone willing to pay the price to wait on God in the place of prayer. To this end the writer of the book of Hebrews describes Jesus' earthly prayer life as follows:

*In the days of His earthly life, Jesus offered up both [specific]
petitions and [urgent] supplications [for that which He*

needed] with fervent crying and tears to the One who was [always] able to save Him from death, and He was heard because of His reverent submission toward God [His sinlessness and His unfailing determination to do the Father's will] (Hebrews 5:7).

However, simply saying that "people ought to pray" trivializes what has become for many Christians a source of tremendous pain and frustration. "Dr. Myles, what are you talking about?" you might ask. I am referencing thousands of well-meaning Christians around the world who pray regularly with occasional times of fasting only to be confronted with what seems like an invisible wall of "unanswered prayer." They are the reason I wrote the book of *Dangerous Prayers*.

Breaking Through the Wall of Unanswered Prayer

So I say to you, ask and keep on asking, and it will be given to you; seek and keep on seeking, and you will find; knock and keep on knocking, and the door will be opened to you. For everyone who keeps on asking [persistently], receives; and he who keeps on seeking [persistently], finds; and to him who keeps on knocking [persistently], the door will be opened (Luke 11:9-10).

In the above passage of scripture, the Lord Jesus is dealing head-on with the problem of "unanswered prayer." Jesus as the God-man knows firsthand the frustration that ensues from the hearts of genuine seekers of truth and His Kingdom who don't seem to break through the seemingly invisible barrier to their prayers. To this group of spiritual seekers Jesus tenderly says, "Keep on asking, keep on seeking, and keep on knocking" and eventually the door to the supernatural, a higher realm of revelation and answered prayer will be opened.

Jesus is showing us in this passage that the dilemma of "unanswered prayer" lies not in God's unwillingness to meet the desperate needs of these spiritual seekers but in a *missing spiritual ingredient* that can unlock the realm of answered prayer. In my study of the subject of prayer for many years, it's clear to me more than ever that what, how, and from where you pray has far more to do with the lack of answered prayers than what you need! This book is designed to provide answers to this prayer triangle! All the activation prayers at the end of this book were designed with the passionate goal of getting thousands of "unanswered prayers" answered! The promise the Lord has given me for this book is that hundreds of thousands of people will find answers to prayer and to some of life's most perplexing problems.

Three Realms of Prayer

One of the greatest joys of my life is my friendship with my dear friend Robert Henderson. In my humble opinion Robert is one of the apostolic fathers God has raised to champion the revelation on the Courts of Heaven. His latest book, *Father, Friend, and Judge*, lays another important foundation stone in this unfolding revelation on prayer. Robert has helped deepen my own understanding of the Courts of Heaven. Prayer is such an important spiritual technology for engaging the supernatural power of God, so understanding it in its different realms and forms is critical to getting the spiritual breakthroughs we desperately need.

> *It happened that while Jesus was praying in a certain place, after He finished, one of His disciples said to Him, "Lord, teach us to pray just as John also taught his disciples"* (Luke 11:1).

The eleventh chapter of Luke's Gospel opens up with a question about prayer from one of Jesus' disciples. I am so glad this unnamed disciple was moved by the Holy Spirit to ask it. The Bible tells us that Jesus was in His customary place of prayer when this very observant disciple posed his request, "*Lord, teach us to pray just as John also taught his disciples.*" I quickly took notice of the fact that Jesus never corrected the disciple's assumption that effective prayer could be taught. This is a huge piece of revelation and it ought to give hope to all of us who feel like strangers with nothing to say in the place of prayer. I remember when I got in saved in 1989. I loved God dearly, but prayer was a huge challenge to say the least. Thankfully, I met a prayer warrior who also became my pastor who taught me how to pray longer than five minutes!

However, my current level of praying and understanding of how the realm of answered prayer works is far more superior today than it was in 1989. By reading this prayer book, you are getting the benefit of years of study and reflection on the subject of prayer. Responding to His disciples' request, "Lord, teach us to pray just as John also taught his disciples," Jesus answers the question by categorizing prayer in three important but distinct realms. Each of these realms of prayer has a different focus and spiritual disposition. It's important to note that these realms of prayer are not in an ascending order of importance; they are all equally important but different in the spiritual activity and disposition required to be successful in these realms of prayer.

First Realm of Prayer: Approaching God as Father

> *He said to them, "When you pray, say: 'Father, hallowed be Your name. Your kingdom come. Give us each day our daily bread. And forgive us our sins, for we ourselves also forgive*

everyone who is indebted to us [who has offended or wronged us]. And lead us not into temptation [but rescue us from evil" (Luke 11:2-4).

When Jesus began teaching on prayer, He started by opening up the first realm of prayer. He said, *"When you pray, say: 'Father.'"* The statement was pretty obvious. In this realm of prayer Jesus commands us to approach God as Father. This suggests that in this realm or dimension of prayer the person praying must already be born again in order to claim such an intimate relationship with the heavenly Father. It goes without saying that this first realm of prayer requires an intimate relationship with the heavenly Father. God is the creator of everyone on earth, but He is not the heavenly Father of everyone on earth. This is because the right to become a child of God is only given to those who have accepted Jesus as their personal Lord and Savior. This is what the scripture has to say about this issue in John 1:12:

> But to as many as did receive and welcome Him, He gave the right [the authority, the privilege] to become children of God, that is, to those who believe in (adhere to, trust in, and rely on) His name.

In this realm or dimension of prayer, we start by presenting our request to God the Father after we have worshiped Him and acknowledged the greatness of His holy name. It's definitely a realm of prayer fueled by total devotion to God the Father! It is in this realm of prayer where we are encouraged to ask for God's Kingdom to invade our life. It is in this realm of prayer where we approach God specifically to provide for "our daily bread and forgive us of our sins." In this realm of prayer, Jesus seems to suggest that unforgiveness toward others can be a huge hindrance to having our prayers answered. This realm of prayer is very personal. It's not about us praying for others; it's about building an intimate relationship with our heavenly Father while getting our personal needs met. A lot of prayer is answered in this realm. I have personally benefited a lot from this realm of prayer. However, if you do not experience answered prayer in this realm, your situation might require a different realm or dimension of prayer. So, we will now move on to the second realm or dimension of prayer.

Second Realm of Prayer: Approaching God as Friend

Then He said to them, "Suppose one of you has a friend, and goes to him at midnight and says, 'Friend, lend me three loaves [of bread]; for a friend of mine who is on a journey has just come to visit me, and I have nothing to serve him'; and from inside he answers, 'Do not bother me; the door has already been shut and my children and I are in bed; I cannot get up and give you anything.' I tell you, even though he will not get up and give him anything just because he is his friend, yet because of his persistence and boldness he will get up and give him whatever he needs" (Luke 11:5-8).

Jesus seamlessly moves on to the next dimension of prayer. Jesus introduces us to this second realm of prayer with this statement: "*Suppose one of you has a friend.*" Notice that in this second realm of prayer, Jesus never uses the word *Father* once! Instead, He shifts to another important word, *friend*, meaning that this realm of prayer is where we approach God as Friend and not as Father. The reason becomes abundantly obvious. Jesus tells us about a friend in need who approaches another friend at midnight. The word *midnight* suggests a crisis of some sort, because no one visits anybody's home to simply fraternize or have coffee at midnight. It would be very awkward to go to the house of anybody at midnight just to have coffee or tea. So this second realm of prayer deals with "others in crisis" who need your spiritual assistance in order to obtain a spiritual breakthrough for themselves.

Jesus continues to unravel the mystery behind this second realm of prayer by pointing to the fact that the "friend" who was approached at midnight also went to see another "more powerful friend" who had the resources needed by the person seeking help. *The picture becomes abundantly clear—this realm of prayer is the realm of intercession, where we stand in the gap for others.* In the realm of intercession, we don't pray for our personal needs; instead, we leverage our relationship (friendship) with God in order to meet the needs of others. It's truly a selfless act of love. I have personally benefited in terms of answered prayer because I went to seasoned intercessors about an urgent need and they went before the Lord on my behalf until I received my deliverance. Jesus also shows us that in this second realm of prayer, the primary spiritual currency is *friendship with God and persistence in prayer.* However, I have been saved long enough to know that not every prayer is answered by God in this realm of prayer. For the longest time, before I discovered the third realm of prayer I was perplexed and frustrated by the apparent lack of answers to genuine times of intercession. This leads us to the third dimension of prayer. I also want you to take note of the fact that the prayers in this book are based upon this third and final realm of prayer.

Third Realm of Prayer: Approaching God as Judge

Now Jesus was telling the disciples a parable to make the point that at all times they ought to pray and not give up and lose heart, saying, "In a certain city there was a judge who did not fear God and had no respect for man. There was a [desperate] widow in that city and she kept coming to him and saying, 'Give me justice and legal protection from my adversary.' For a time he would not; but later he said to himself, 'Even though I do not fear God nor respect man, yet because this widow continues to bother me, I will give her justice and legal protection;

otherwise by continually coming she [will be an intolerable annoyance and she] will wear me out."' Then the Lord said, "Listen to what the unjust judge says! And will not [our just] God defend and avenge His elect [His chosen ones] who cry out to Him day and night? Will He delay [in providing justice] on their behalf? I tell you that He will defend and avenge them quickly. However, when the Son of Man comes, will He find [this kind of persistent] faith on the earth?" (Luke 18:1-8)

Jesus finally exposes us to the final and third realm of prayer in the eighteenth chapter of Luke's Gospel. In introducing us to this third realm of prayer, Jesus opens it up with this statement, "Men ought always to pray and not lose heart." This suggests that this final realm of prayer is for people who are on the verge of giving up or losing hope because the mountains of problems they face have been stubbornly resistant to the prayers they have prayed until now. Consequently, this third dimension of prayer is for any unanswered prayers originating from the first and second realms of prayer. This third realm of prayer is also the final court of appeal for anything legal in nature spiritually speaking. Jesus then moves on to tell us the story of a desperate window and a corrupt judge. He tells us that in a certain city there was a judge, a corrupt one at that, who did not fear God nor respect any man. This widow went to this corrupt judge and asked him to give her justice and legal protection from her adversary.

The word *adversary* used in the passage comes from the Greek word *antidikos*. This is where we get the prefix *anti*, meaning "against," and the word *dikos* means "rights." So an adversary is a person or entity who is violating your legal rights as a citizen. We immediately see that Jesus is placing prayer in this realm in a judicial context or framework. No one thinks of a judge and places them inside a church or corporate office. Judges belong to the courts or judiciary. In the story Jesus told, the corrupt judge was very reluctant to give the widow the justice and legal protection she deserved.

However, her persistency became a nuisance to him, so in order to save himself the trouble he reluctantly gave her justice and legal protection from her adversary.

The moral of the story is that by going to a judge, though he was corrupt and reluctant, the woman got the breakthrough she desperately needed. Her breakthrough, having come out of the court system, was legally binding within the judge's jurisdiction. What is also interesting is that in this third realm of prayer, the widow never addressed her adversary directly. She only talked to the judge—the whole time! It is interesting that in courts all over the world, the defendant or plaintiff is never allowed by the judge to address the prosecutor directly except through their attorneys. This is the critical difference between the realm of intercession and operating in the courts of heaven. In the former, intercessors can directly wrestle or tango with satan and his demonic cohorts, whereas in the latter it is strictly forbidden by judicial protocol.

Jesus finally flipped the story by talking about His heavenly Father and comparing Him to the corrupt judge. Then Jesus makes the case that if the corrupt judge delivered the window from her adversary, how much more will the heavenly Father, who is a superior and righteous Judge, deliver His dear children from their adversary (satan) in the Courts of Heaven? So essentially this third realm of prayer is where we approach God as Judge. The prayers that I have loaded in this book are based upon this third realm of prayer. I will show you how to overthrow evil altars not by wrestling with them in prayer but by effectively prosecuting them in the Courts of Heaven.

Spiritual Accelerant: Fasting

[But this kind of demon does not go out except by prayer and fasting] (Matthew 17:21).

> *Then he said to me, "Do not be afraid, Daniel, for from the first day that you set your heart on understanding this and on humbling yourself before your God, your words were heard, and I have come in response to your words. But the prince of the kingdom of Persia was standing in opposition to me for twenty-one days. Then, behold, Michael, one of the chief [of the celestial] princes, came to help me, for I had been left there with the kings of Persia"* (Daniel 10:12-13).

Before we conclude this chapter, I want to talk to you about one of the most powerful spiritual accelerants that can speed up your spiritual breakthrough once you understand the three realms of prayer and how to navigate them. Whenever there is a fire that burns down a building in the United States, firefighters are sent to the location of the fire. After they put it out, they start to look for the presence or absence of an accelerant. If they find one, they immediately report the matter to the police, because it means that an arsonist was involved in the start of the fire. So what is an accelerant? As a matter of definition, an "accelerant" is:

1. Something that speeds up a process.
2. A substance that accelerates the spread of fire or makes a fire more intense.

In the above passage of scripture when the disciples of Jesus could not cast out a demon, which was in a little boy, Jesus encouraged them to engage in a spiritual practice that would act as an accelerant to the whole process of walking in the power of God. The accelerant that Jesus suggested was *fasting*. We also see that when Daniel was looking for answers concerning the future of Israel and the Jewish people who were in captivity in Babylon, the Bible tells us that he went into a time of fasting for 21 days. An angel of God appeared in his room as a result. The angel made it clear to him that God had answered his prayer on the first day of his fasting. However, the angel had been delayed by demonic resistance in the heavenly realms by the principality over the country of Persia. But as Daniel kept on praying and fasting, the Lord sent the archangel Michael to the aid of the angel with a message to deliver to Daniel. It is clear that fasting was the accelerant in the process of getting Daniel's breakthrough. I want to encourage you to consider going into a time of fasting before you start praying the prayers that are in the second half of this book. I am so excited for you. You are going to experience an avalanche of answered prayers. To God be all the glory. Amen.

Life Application Section

Memory Verse

> *So I say to you, ask and keep on asking, and it will be given to you; seek and keep on seeking, and you will find; knock and keep on knocking, and the door will be opened to you. For everyone who keeps on asking [persistently], receives; and he who keeps on seeking [persistently], finds; and to him who keeps on knocking [persistently], the door will be opened* (Luke 11:9-10).

Reflections

1. What is the first realm of prayer?

   _____

   _____

   _____

   _____

2. Why did Jesus tell the story of the corrupt judge in Luke 18?

_____

_____

_____

_____

Chapter Two

The Law of
Dominion and Altars

The greatest discovery in life is the discovery of purpose. The late Dr. Myles Munroe declares, "Wherever purpose is not known abuse is inevitable." The genesis of God's purpose for creating the human race can be found in the first two chapters of Genesis. The Genesis account underscores God's inherent motivation for creating a physical planet called Earth and creating spirit children whom He collectively called "Adam." God then created physical bodies made of dirt to house these spirit beings so that they could become legal residents and guardians of the visible world. From the beginning, our physical world (earth) was designed to be a spiritual colony of the Kingdom of heaven. It was never designed to be a habitation of demons and every foul spirit.

> *Then God said, "Let Us make man in Our image, according to Our likeness; let them have dominion over the fish of the sea, over the birds of the air, and over the cattle, over all the earth and over every creeping thing that creeps on the earth." So God created man in His own image; in the image of God He created him; male and female He created them. Then God blessed them, and God said to them, "Be fruitful and multiply; fill the earth and subdue it; have dominion over the fish of the sea, over the birds of the air, and over every living thing that moves on the earth"* (Genesis 1:26-28 NKJV).

God's Big Idea

In Genesis 1:26-28, we are told that humankind was created by God to be an ambassadorial representative of God's invisible Kingdom on the visible planet, called Earth. Said simply, we were created to rule over the world of matter on behalf of the Kingdom of God. Our purpose on earth is intricately tied to fulfilling our prophetic assignment as official representatives of the Kingdom of God. Anything short of fulfilling our ambassadorial assignment of manifesting the Kingdom of God here on earth as it is in heaven is a gross violation of our purpose. We were created to manifest God's character and His Kingdom government here on earth.

Our Dominion Mandate

> *So God created man in His own image; in the image of God He created him; male and female He created them. Then God blessed them, and God said to them, "Be fruitful and multiply; fill the earth and subdue it; have dominion over the fish of the sea, over the birds of the air, and over every living thing that moves on the earth"* (Genesis 1:27-28 NKJV).

On the sixth day of creation, God created His master species, mankind! Created in both the image (God's own spiritual essence) and likeness (God's own DNA) of God, there was no other creature that could compete with man's special position as the son of God. However, it's the gift of dominion that God gave man that I am most interested in. God said "let them have dominion," which comes from the Hebrew word *mamlakah* which means "ruler, rulership or kingdom." According to God this dominion mandate upon mankind would rest on four pillars:

1. Being fruitful

2. Multiplying

3. Filling or replenishing the Earth

4. Subduing the Earth

The Implications of Our Dominion Mandate

> *Then God said, "Let Us make man in Our image, according to Our likeness; let them have dominion over the fish of the sea, over the birds of the air, and over the cattle, over all the earth and over every creeping thing that creeps on the earth"* (Genesis 1:26 NKJV).

The million-dollar question I want you to be asking yourself is, "What is the spiritual connection between idols, evil altars, and man's dominion mandate?" When God created Adam and Eve (the first humans) and gave them dominion over this planet, He made an irreversible decree that would impact God and every celestial (spirit) being in all of creation in a very meaningful manner. When God transferred dominion (rulership) of this planet to mankind, He deliberately excluded Himself and every celestial (angelic) being from the earth's legal authority structure.

He said "let them" have dominion. Please take note of the words "let them." Take note that this expression excludes God and angels, or spirit beings, from interfering in earthly affairs without the legal permission of a man. By using the expression "let them," God locked Himself out of influencing this world without man's permission. Why would He do that? For two main reasons:

1. God wanted His spirit children in bodies of dirt to rule and subdue the earth as kings and priests and ambassadors of His invisible Kingdom in our visible planet.

2. God, in His eternal love for us, already knew at the time of Adam's creation that lucifer and one third of His angels had already fallen from grace and were cast out of heaven. These malicious spirits were trapped in the second heaven in search of another realm of reality to rule. Being a loving Father, God did not want these fallen and malicious spirits to rule the planet He designed for mankind. So He locked them out, but He never threw away the keys. I wish He had! God simply placed the keys to loose (allow legal entry) or bind (deny access) in the hands of humans.

God, Idols, and Altars

For as I passed along and carefully observed your objects of worship, I came also upon an altar with this inscription, To the unknown god. Now what you are already worshiping as unknown, this I set forth to you. The God Who produced and formed the world and all things in it, being Lord of heaven and earth, does not dwell in handmade shrines. Neither is He served by human hands, as though He lacked anything, for it is He Himself Who gives life and breath and all things to all [people] (Acts 17:23-25 AMPC).

God had effectively and irrevocably locked Himself and all celestial beings out of earth's legal authority structure, so how could He legally get involved in the affairs of men? Like any good and loving parent, God did not create us (give birth to us) and then shrug His shoulders and say, "Well, you are on your own now, because I am leaving." God created us first and foremost for fellowship and then to dominate this planet on His behalf so earth can become a colony of Heaven. However, by the *Law of Dominion* God could only accomplish both by securing man's permission or cooperation.

The Law of Dominion simply states that *spirits without physical bodies of dirt are illegal on earth* unless they are functioning through a human. *This is an unbreakable law of God's Kingdom.* Suddenly, *prayer* becomes critically essential, because it becomes man's way of giving God the legal permission He needs to righteously interfere in the affairs of men. Essentially, the Law of Dominion transformed the earth into the world of men. This is why the Messiah had to become a man in order to rescue us legally from the law of sin and death.

As a result of the far-reaching implications of the Law of Dominion, God in His eternal genius devised a way for Himself and His holy angels to enter our physical planet legally. *God showed Adam how to build an altar,* when He killed an animal in the garden of Eden to atone for their sin. How else did the children of Adam, Cain and Abel, know how to build an altar (see Gen. 4)? *The altar, like an airport, would serve as a meeting place between divinity and humanity.* It would be a consecrated place where spirits can legally land at man's beckoning. Since the first altar in the garden of Eden was covered in the blood of atonement, the altar would also become a place of death, sacrifice, and redemption.

The altar would essentially function as a power station connecting two worlds—Heaven and earth or hell and earth! Mankind is the legal guardian of this planet, so the most important element at any altar is the human who attends to the altar. This person who serves as the attendant to the altar essentially becomes a servant of either God or the demonic entity that has been given legal authority to operate freely in the world of men. There is only one God, so any other entity from the kingdom of darkness that is given legal authority through an altar to operate in the world of men becomes the "idol" (demon-god) behind that altar. *Because all altars are essentially power stations, the attendant to the altar becomes supernaturally empowered by either God or the idol (demon-god) that is behind the altar.* Until the altar is demolished, God or the demon-gods behind evil altars will continue to operate freely in the world of men. This is essentially the spiritual connection between God, idols, and altars! This book is loaded with powerful prayers from the Courts of Heaven to uproot evil altars that are speaking against you while overthrowing the demonic spirits that are powering these evil altars!

Two Types of Altars

> *And in the course of time Cain brought to the Lord an offer-ing of the fruit of the ground. And Abel brought of the first-born of his flock and of the fat portions. And the Lord had respect and regard for Abel and for his offering, but for Cain and his offering He had no respect or regard. So Cain was exceedingly angry and indignant, and he looked sad and depressed* (Genesis 4:3-5 AMPC).

In scripture there are two basic types of altars—righteous and evil altars. The first time in scripture we are confronted with this distinction is in the fourth chapter of the book of Genesis. This is the time when the two sons of Adam, Cain and Abel, decided to build altars so they can offer their sacrifi-cial offerings to the Lord. According to scripture, Cain brought to the Lord an offering of the fruit of the ground. This means that Cain, who was an agricultural farmer, placed vegetables on his altar. On the other hand, Abel brought of the firstborn of his flock and of the fat portions. God's reaction to the offerings on the two altars is pretty telling.

God demonstrably rejected Cain's offering, while He demonstrably accepted and showered with favor Abel's sacrificial offering. Why did God reject Cain's offering? God had already cursed the ground in Genesis 3:17, *"And to Adam He said, Because you have listened and given heed to the voice of your wife and have eaten of the tree of which I commanded you, saying, You shall not eat of it, the ground is under a curse because of you; in sorrow and toil shall you eat [of the fruits] of it all the days of your life"* (AMPC). I am certain Adam had already told his sons that the Lord had already cursed the ground because of his sin. So why would Cain bring an offering from something that was already cursed in order to secure atonement for his sins?

Cain's behavior toward God gives face to the true nature of all evil altars! Like Cain, "evil altars" are driven by rebellion, pride, and the desire to give life to the "accursed thing." God's rejection of Cain's offering shows us that He is very selective of what's given to Him at a righteous altar. This separates God from idols (demon-gods) who will accept any "accursed thing" that is offered to them by their human attendants. Fallen angels and demon spirits are so desperate for expression in the world of men that they will accept any offering provided so they can gain access to the world of men. God, on the other hand, is sovereign, holy, and separate from sinners, so He cannot be manipulated by His human attendants to His altar. This is why He accepted Abel's offering, because Abel gave Him exactly what He required for the remission of sins—the blood of an innocent animal, from the best of the flock!

Consequentially, Cain became the biblical symbol for an evil and defiled altar. It's an altar built on evil, pride, defiance, rebellion, rage, jealousy, selfish ambition, and murder. The god behind Cain's evil altar was the idol of self and ultimately satan. This is why Cain resisted and argued with God. Look at this: *"And the Lord said to Cain, Where is Abel your brother? And he said, I do not know. Am I my brother's keeper?"* (Gen. 4:9 AMPC). Look at the arrogance in Cain's answer. Who talks to God with such insolence, pride, and arrogance? *Every person who is an attendant to an evil altar built for the idol or gods in their life.* This may explain why some Christ-professing Christians are so full of pride and arrogance—their hearts are full of idols and they are spiritually connected to an evil altar and many don't even know it! This book is about breaking the power of these malicious demon spirits and the evil altars they use to capture our souls.

Life Application Section

Memory Verse

> *You shall have no other gods before or besides Me. You shall not make yourself any graven image [to worship it] or any likeness of anything that is in the heavens above, or that is in the earth beneath, or that is in the water under the earth; you shall not bow down yourself to them or serve them; for I the Lord your God am a jealous God, visiting the iniquity of the fathers upon the children to the third and fourth generation of those who hate Me* (Exodus 20:3-5 AMPC).

Reflections

1. What is an evil altar?

_____

_____

_____

_____

2. How does satan use evil altars in our life to bring accusations against us in Court?

_____

_____

_____

_____

Chapter Three

The Battle of Altars

For our struggle is not against flesh and blood [contending only with physical opponents], but against the rulers, against the powers, against the world forces of this [present] darkness, against the spiritual forces of wickedness in the heavenly (supernatural) places.

—Ephesians 6:12

Now that we understand the far-reaching spiritual implications of the Law of Dominion, we are now ready to dive into the heart of this book. I have loaded this book with powerful prayers for overthrowing and uprooting evil altars that are speaking against your God-given destiny and finances. I chose to call this chapter "The Battle of Altars" because much of what we call spiritual warfare is truly the battle of altars. We have a truly interesting case study in the Bible that showcases the outworking of this principle. In the book of First Samuel the Philistines managed to capture the ark of God, which was the symbol of the abiding presence of God in Israel. Without a doubt, the ark of God was a mobile altar that traveled with the children of Israel wherever they went. The Bible tells us the Philistines brought the ark of God to the city of Ashdod. What follows is truly interesting in the study of spiritual warfare.

Two Opposing Altars

> *Then the Philistines took the ark of God, and they brought it from Ebenezer to Ashdod. They took the ark of God and brought it into the house of Dagon and set it beside [the image of] Dagon [their chief idol]. When the people of Ashdod got up early the next day, behold, Dagon had fallen on his face on the ground before the ark of the Lord. So they took Dagon and returned him to his place* (1 Samuel 5:1-3).

I am certain every follower of Messiah Jesus knows that the Bible says we are involved in a high-stakes spiritual warfare between the Kingdom of light and the forces of darkness. Recently, the Lord showed me that what we call spiritual warfare is nothing short of the spiritual battle that ensues when an altar from God's Kingdom of light is placed next to an altar from the kingdom of darkness. The close proximity of these spiritual power stations and the fact that no two altars can occupy the same space is what results in spiritual warfare. Have you ever wondered why some people at your new job displayed a passionate animosity toward you even though you were meeting them for the very first time? It's not personal. The answer lies in understanding the dynamics of spiritual altars. Whenever two individuals carrying two opposing altars come into contact with each other, the spirit of animosity between them is proof that their two altars are now engaged in a spiritual battle.

In the above passage of scripture, the Philistines brought the ark of God from Ebenezer to Ashdod. Upon their arrival, they took the ark of God into the house of Dagon, and they set the ark of God next to this idol. Dagon was an ancient Mesopotamian fertility god. When they woke up the following morning, Dagon was lying on the floor with his face looking at the ground. *The ark of God, which was the altar of the Lord in Israel, was pronouncing its supremacy over the idol of the Philistines.*

Have you ever wondered why some people rub your spirit the wrong way, even when they are offering you a pleasant smile? You could be discerning the evil altar in their soul that is fighting against the altar of the Lord in your soul. Unfortunately, this same phenomenon takes place between the bloodlines of believers who love the Lord Jesus but have evil altars their forefathers planted in their family bloodline that have never been torn down. This book contains a divine prescription for deliverance from the oppressive power of these evil altars.

The Superior Altar Always Takes the Day!

> *But when they arose early the next morning, behold, Dagon had again fallen on his face on the ground before the ark of the Lord, and [his] head and both the palms of his hands were lying cut off on the threshold; only the trunk of Dagon was left him. This is the reason neither the priests of Dagon nor any who come into Dagon's house tread on the threshold of Dagon in Ashdod to this day. But the hand of the Lord was heavy upon the people of Ashdod, and He caused [mice to spring up and there was] very deadly destruction and He smote the people with [very painful] tumors or boils, both Ashdod and its territory. When the men of Ashdod saw that it was so, they said, The ark of the God of Israel must not remain with us, for His hand is heavy on us and on Dagon our god (1 Samuel 5:4-7 AMPC).*

According to the law of altars, *whoever carries the superior altar takes the day!* What does this statement mean? It means that in order to be delivered from the power of an evil altar and the idol connected to it, we must strengthen the altar of the Lord in our life. The altar of the Lord in our life must become stronger than the idol and evil altar we are trying to destroy. The good news is that when we use prayers that appeal to *the Courts of Heaven* we automatically gain the *spiritual stature of the Courts of Heaven*. **The Courts of Heaven function above the power of every evil altar.** In the above passage of scripture when the Philistines brought the ark of God into the house of Dagon, they did not understand the law of altars. But God did! So He did not waste time but demonstrated to them in no uncertain terms that the altar of the ark of God was superior to the altar of the idol, Dagon. When the Philistines found Dagon lying prostrate before the ark of God, they did not get the message. So they propped up this worthless demon-god once more and set it next to the ark of God. Huge mistake! The second day when they returned, the image of the idol Dagon was lying on the floor and its head and both of its hands were broken beyond repair. *This time the Philistines got the message and they were terrified, because Dagon was their most powerful national god!*

The moral of the story is abundantly clear. *Whoever carries the superior altar takes the day!* If you want the Lord to deliver you from the power of the idols and evil altars that are erected in your soul or generational bloodline, you must make sure that you practice spiritual disciplines like prayer and fasting. Regular times of prayer and fasting will starve these idols and evil altars in your soul or bloodline. Fasting does not change God, but it does strengthen your spirit man! For instance, if the altar of sexual perversion in your life is stronger than the altar of sanctification, you will lose the fight for holiness to the devil. This is why there have been cases in the body of Christ when a person who was mightily used by God fell prey to the scourge of sexual scandal. This does not mean that these believers (including King David) who fell into sexual sin were not saved. Most importantly, it does not mean they do not love Jesus; it simply means that they failed to destroy the idol and evil altar of sexual perversion that was rooted in either their soul or bloodline. *Unfortunately for them, they allowed the altar of sexual perversion to become stronger than the altar of the Lord, so it took the day!*

Repairing the Broken Altar of the Lord

*So Ahab sent word to all the Israelites and assembled
the [pagan] prophets together at Mount Carmel. Elijah
approached all the people and said, "How long will you hes-
itate between two opinions? If the Lord is God, follow Him;
but if Baal, follow him." But the people [of Israel] did not
answer him [so much as] a word. Then Elijah said to the
people, "I alone remain a prophet of the Lord, while Baal's
prophets are 450 men. Now let them give us two oxen, and
let them choose one ox for themselves and cut it in pieces, and
lay it on the wood, but put no fire under it. I will prepare
the other ox and lay it on the wood, and I will not put a fire
under it. Then you call on the name of your god, and I will
call on the name of the Lord; and the god who answers by
fire, He is God." And all the people answered, "It is well spoken" (1 Kings 18:20-24).*

Until I discovered divine revelation on the law of altars, I used to think
that the ministry of Elijah was about calling fire down from heaven! So as
a young healing evangelist, I preached from the above passage of scripture
many times. My favorite message was, "The God who answers by fire, let
Him be God." We saw so many mighty miracles of the Holy Spirit as a result
of this message. However, my revelation of this passage deepened signifi-
cantly when I met my dear friend Tony Kemp. Tony Kemp had been given
a life-changing heavenly encounter in which he met with Elijah in heaven.
During this heavenly encounter, Elijah told Tony Kemp, "My ministry was
not about calling fire down from heaven; it was about rebuilding the broken
altar of the Lord." When Tony told me this, flashlights of revelation went
through my spirit. Then I saw it! The fire of God came down immediately
after Elijah repaired the broken altar of the Lord.

Then Elijah said to all the people, "Come near to me." So all
the people approached him. And he repaired and rebuilt the
[old] altar of the Lord that had been torn down [by Jezebel].
Then Elijah took twelve stones in accordance with the num-
ber of the tribes of the sons of Jacob, to whom the word of the
Lord had come, saying, "Israel shall be your name" (1 Kings
18:30-31).

As soon as the prophet Elijah repaired the broken altar of the Lord, this
ancient spiritual power station went into high gear, reestablishing the broken spiritual connection between heaven and the nation of Israel. As soon
as this happened, there was a visible demonstration in the form of fire falling from heaven to authenticate the integrity of the spiritual connection.
When the people of Israel saw the fire of God falling down from heaven,
they bowed themselves to the ground and began to worship the Lord. They
began to shout, "The Lord is God, the Lord is God!" In the meantime, the
false prophets of Jezebel who served at the altar of Baal were shaking in their
boots. It was not long before Elijah the prophet told the people to arrest
them and killed all of them on the same altar of Baal that they had given
themselves to. I encourage you to take inventory of the spiritual condition
of the altar of the Lord in your life before using the *dangerous prayers* in the
last section of this book.

Life Application Section

Memory Verse

You shall have no other gods before or besides Me. You shall
not make yourself any graven image [to worship it] or any
likeness of anything that is in the heavens above, or that is in

the earth beneath, or that is in the water under the earth; you shall not bow down yourself to them or serve them; for I the Lord your God am a jealous God, visiting the iniquity of the fathers upon the children to the third and fourth generation of those who hate Me (Exodus 20:3-5 AMPC).

Reflections

1. What kind of god was Dagon?

    _____

    _____

    _____

    _____

2. What does this expression mean, "The superior altar takes the day"?

    _____

    _____

    _____

    _____

Chapter Four

Operating in the Courts of Heaven

I kept looking until thrones were set up, and the Ancient of Days (God) took His seat; His garment was white as snow and the hair of His head like pure wool. His throne was flames of fire; Its wheels were a burning fire. A river of fire was flowing and coming out from before Him; a thousand thousands were attending Him, and ten thousand times ten thousand were standing before Him; the court was seated, and the books were opened.

—Daniel 7:9-10

One of the most important revelations that God is revealing and restoring to the global church is how to operate in the Courts of Heaven. For the most part, this revelation is bringing the body of Messiah around the world into a realm of breakthrough prayer like I have never seen before! I have personally benefited greatly in the area of answered prayer due to tapping into this revelation. The *dangerous prayers* loaded in the second section of this book are based upon entering the Courts of Heaven and contending with satan before the Righteous Judge to relinquish all the legal rights he has acquired against our God-given destiny due to our sin or generational iniquity.

As a matter of definition, a court of law is:

- a place where justice is administered.

- a judicial tribunal duly constituted for the hearing and determination of cases.

- a session of a judicial assembly.

So based upon the above definition, a court of law is a place where justice is administered; it consists of a judicial tribunal that hears and determines cases that come before the court. The word *court* also refers to moments in time when there is a judicial assembly to hear a case. Globally, court cases always involves four key players, namely:

1. The presiding judge, who is the highest officer of the court. He or she actually embodies the court. This is why no court is ever in session until the judge is seated. This is exactly what Daniel saw in his prophetic vision as the Ancient of Days took His judicial seat (see Dan. 7:9) in heaven's highest court.

2. The prosecutor, who prosecutes the case based upon evidence that he or she has gathered against the accused. By function, the prosecutor is the most adversarial member of the court. It's no wonder the Bible uses the word *adversary* to describe satan's primary activity against the saints! (See Zechariah 3:1-2.)

3. The advocate or defense attorney—he or she is the most passionate defender of the legal rights of the accused in the courtroom. Jesus is also called our "advocate" in First John 2:1-2. This is truly exhilarating! The selfless and suffering Servant of Isaiah 53, who completely fulfilled the Law and the writings of the prophets, is now our faithful advocate post-resurrection in the Courts of Heaven. How cool is that?

4. The defendant or accused—this is the person or entity who has been accused of committing a crime against the state. Because followers of Messiah Jesus are citizens of the Kingdom of God, the crimes satan brings against us in the Courts of Heaven are

crimes against the Kingdom of God and its righteous principles. It's interesting to me that Revelation 12:10 declares:

Then I heard a loud voice in heaven, saying, "Now the salvation, and the power, and the kingdom (dominion, reign) of our God, and the authority of His Christ have come; for the accuser of our [believing] brothers and sisters has been thrown down [at last], he who accuses them and keeps bringing charges [of sinful behavior] against them before our God day and night."

The passage makes it clear that satan's favorite activity against New Testament believers is to level *accusations* against them in the Courts of Heaven. Christians who don't know how to operate in the Courts of Heaven are being destroyed by satan's unanswered accusations because of their lack of knowledge (see Hos. 4:6)!

A Relentless Adversary

Be sober, be vigilant; because your adversary the devil walks about like a roaring lion, seeking whom he may devour (1 Peter 5:8 NKJV).

The word *adversary* used in the passage comes from the Greek word *antidikos*. The prefix *anti* means "against" and the word *dikos* means "rights." So an adversary is a person or entity who is violating your legal rights. Unfortunately, so many Christians are spiritually lazy. They don't understand how relentless and malicious our adversary, satan, really is when he brings charges against us in the Courts of Heaven. Satan knows that Jesus' finished work on the cross "crushed his head," so the only thing he relies upon to deny the saints victory is the unanswered accusations against us in the Courts of Heaven. *One of the most important things about lawsuits or courtroom trials is that whosoever shows up for court always wins.*

When I was writing my book *Issuing Divine Restraining Orders from the Courts of Heaven*, the Lord said to me, "Francis, satan is getting away with so many default judgments simply because My people do not show up for court." I was stunned! This means that the Holy Spirit has been trying to nudge us to come before the Court of Heaven, but due to ignorance or religious pride it's difficult for most of us to believe that we are guilty of violating one of the laws of God. While we lived in denial, satan found a legal opening to level accusations against us in the Courts of Heaven. This is why books like this and Brother Robert Henderson's books on the Courts of Heaven are very important to the body of Christ. In the above passage of scripture, Peter the apostle gives us a stern warning. He warns us to be sober and vigilant because our adversary the devil is walking about like a roaring lion, seeking whom he may devour. How does satan "devour" the saints of the Most High? It is through legal accusations he brings against us in the Courts of Heaven for violating the law of God, frustrating the grace of God, or disobeying the Holy Spirit. Even though grace is available for us in the Grace Court (see Heb. 4:16), if we don't show up for court to answer satan's accusations through the finished work of Jesus, the grace God has for us will profit us nothing. Please remember, "Unused grace is wasted grace!"

Give Me Justice!

> *Now Jesus was telling the disciples a parable to make the point that at all times they ought to pray and not give up and lose heart, saying, "In a certain city there was a judge who did not fear God and had no respect for man. There was a [desperate]*

widow in that city and she kept coming to him and saying, 'Give me justice and legal protection from my adversary.' For a time he would not; but later he said to himself, 'Even though I do not fear God nor respect man, yet because this widow continues to bother me, I will give her justice and legal protection; otherwise by continually coming she [will be an intolerable annoyance and she] will wear me out.'" Then the Lord said, "Listen to what the unjust judge says! And will not [our just] God defend and avenge His elect [His chosen ones] who cry out to Him day and night? Will He delay [in providing justice] on their behalf? I tell you that He will defend and avenge them quickly. However, when the Son of Man comes, will He find [this kind of persistent] faith on the earth?" (Luke 18:1-8)

In one form or another, we have already discussed the spiritual implications of the above passage of scripture. In Chapter One we talked about how Jesus in the above passage demonstrates to us that if all our prayers are failing or not breaking through, we need to change the venue we are praying from. In the above scenario, Jesus places prayer in a judicial or courtroom context. He tells us the story of a widow woman who lived in a city that fell under the jurisdiction of the unnamed corrupt judge. However, even though the judge was totally corrupt, the woman knew that he was the only one who occupied a seat of judicial authority in that city over her adversary. It would seem from the text that the adversary also lived within the corrupt judge's jurisdiction. Consequentially, his judgments had enough reach in them to stop the attacks of the widow's adversary. The woman's cry was for *justice and legal protection from her adversary.*

"Justice" has to do with the restoration of legal rights previously denied, while "legal protection" seems to imply that the woman, besides having her legal rights restored, also wanted the judge to issue a *permanent restraining order* against her adversary concerning any future infractions. The picture of the Courts of Heaven Jesus paints from this story is breathtaking. Jesus is in essence telling us that we can come before the Court of Heaven and prevail on God the Father, the Righteous Judge, to give us justice in the restoration of our covenantal rights. Additionally, we can also move on the Court of Heaven to issue an active divine restraining order against satan, our vigilant adversary. This is essentially what the *dangerous prayers* in the second half of this book are going to do for you.

The Curious Case of Job

> *Now there was a day when the sons of God (angels) came to present themselves before the Lord, and Satan (adversary, accuser) also came among them. The Lord said to Satan, "From where have you come?" Then Satan answered the Lord, "From roaming around on the earth and from walking around on it." The Lord said to Satan, "Have you considered and reflected on My servant Job? For there is none like him on the earth, a blameless and upright man, one who fears God [with reverence] and abstains from and turns away from evil [because he honors God]." Then Satan answered the Lord, "Does Job fear God for nothing? Have You not put a hedge [of protection] around him and his house and all that he has, on every side? You have blessed the work of his hands [and con-ferred prosperity and happiness upon him], and his possessions have increased in the land"* (Job 1:6-10).

Before I conclude this chapter, I want to talk about what I call the curi-ous case of Job. In my humble opinion, Job is one of the most interesting characters in the Bible. What is of note is that most biblical scholars believe that the book of Job is the oldest book in the Bible. This means that the book of Job was written before Moses wrote the book of Genesis. For the longest time before I understood how to operate in the Courts of Heaven, the above passage of scripture was difficult theologically for me to swallow. I knew from Jesus' own words that satan and one third of the angels who rebelled against God were forcibly cast out of heaven. This is what Jesus told us about this event in Luke 10:18: *"He said to them, 'I watched Satan fall from heaven like [a flash of] lightning.'"*

So imagine my deep surprise when I read Job 1:6: *"Now there was a day when the sons of God (angels) came to present themselves before the Lord, and Satan (adversary, accuser) also came among them."* Satan in heaven before the Lord! What, are you kidding me? What is he doing up there? I thought he was cast out of heaven? These questions bombarded my troubled theological mind. What was even more surprising is the Lord's reaction to satan's presence in heaven. Listen to this:

> *The Lord said to Satan, "From where have you come?" Then Satan answered the Lord, "From roaming around on the earth and from walking around on it"* (Job 1:7).

The question I was expecting God to ask satan was, "What are you doing in heaven?" This question would have meant that satan had *no legal right* to be in Heaven. But that is not the question God asked! Instead, He asked satan where on earth he was coming from. When I received the revelation of the Court of Heaven, everything fell into place!

The Holy Spirit said to me, "Francis, satan is an officer of the Courts of Heaven until the age of sin is concluded. How can you have a trial without a prosecutor?" Suddenly, I saw the jigsaw pieces fall in place. Revelation 12:10 also fell in place. The accuser of the brethren is a prosecutor in the Courts of Heaven, and his job is to bring charges against the inhabitants of the earth who are found guilty of sinning against God's Word and government. This is why satan was in the Court of Heaven. He had come to prosecute cases! I guess the children of men were violating the law of God. It's interesting to me that the devil, who tempts us to sin against God, is the one who also prosecutes us in the Courts of Heaven the moment we act on the temptation. What an irony!

Job's Hedge of Protection

The Lord said to Satan, "Have you considered and reflected on My servant Job? For there is none like him on the earth, a blameless and upright man, one who fears God [with reverence] and abstains from and turns away from evil [because he honors God]." Then Satan answered the Lord, "Does Job fear God for nothing? Have You not put a hedge [of protection] around him and his house and all that he has, on every side? You have blessed the work of his hands [and conferred prosperity and happiness upon him], and his possessions have increased in the land" (Job 1:8-10).

While satan was trying to present cases in the Courts of Heaven against the children of men, the Lord brought up the name of Job. God asked satan if he had considered and reflected on the lifestyle of His servant Job. What is quite interesting is satan's response to the Lord's question about Job. Satan said, *"Have You not put a hedge [of protection] around him and his house and all that he has, on every side?"* For the longest time, I used to think that the hedge of protection around Job's life was some supernatural wall of fire. I guess when you come from a Pentecostal background, every divine solution looks like fire to you.

However, I was blown away when I discovered that the Hebrew word for *hedge* is *skuwk*. The word *skuwk* actually means "a restraint." The Holy

Spirit showed me that the protection or hedge around Job that satan was referencing was actually a legal order of the Court that God had put in place to protect him and his family and all of his possessions. The Lord showed me that what was on Job's life was a divine restraining order that the Courts of Heaven had actually superimposed over his life, family, and property. This divine restraining order made it impossible for satan and his minions to attack Job. I have gone into great detail on the subject of divine restraining orders in my book *Issuing Divine Restraining Orders from the Courts of Heaven*. However, it suffices to say that the *dangerous prayers* that you will be going through in the second half of this book include divine restraining orders against evil altars. It's no wonder we call this book *Dangerous Prayers from the Courts of Heaven that Destroy Evil Altars*.

Life Application Section

Memory Verse

> *You shall have no other gods before or besides Me. You shall not make yourself any graven image [to worship it] or any likeness of anything that is in the heavens above, or that is in the earth beneath, or that is in the water under the earth; you shall not bow down yourself to them or serve them; for I the Lord your God am a jealous God, visiting the iniquity of the fathers upon the children to the third and fourth generation of those who hate Me* (Exodus 20:3-5 AMPC).

Reflections

1. What is Job's hedge of protection?

   _____

   _____

   _____

   _____

2. In Job 1:5-6, what was satan doing in heaven?

   _____

   _____

   _____

   _____

Chapter Five

Seven Drops of Blood

For the life of the flesh is in the blood, and I have given it to you on the altar to make atonement for your souls; for it is the blood that makes atonement, by reason of the life [which it represents].

—Leviticus 17:11

One of the most powerful weapons we have in our arsenal as citizens of the Kingdom of God is the nuclear power of the blood of Jesus the Messiah. The testimony of the blood of Jesus is especially powerful in the Courts of Heaven. *The blood of Jesus is one of the most powerful voices in the Courts of Heaven.* When the blood of Jesus speaks, both God and satan listen. That's why the writer of the book of Hebrews compares the blood of Jesus to the blood of Abel. While the blood of Abel cried for vengeance against Cain, the blood of Jesus Christ cries for mercy and forgiveness for both the sinner and saint alike. Here is what the Scriptures say in Hebrews 12:24: *"And to Jesus, the Mediator of a new covenant [uniting God and man], and to the sprinkled blood, which speaks [of mercy], a better and nobler and more gracious message than the blood of Abel [which cried out for vengeance]."*

This is why the book of dangerous prayers that we're about to get into incorporates the awesome power of the blood of Yeshua, in every prayer I crafted for your deliverance. The blood of Jesus represents the only man who completely fulfilled the righteous demands of the Law of Moses, so it is the best instrument to settle all of satan's accusations against us each time we are found guilty of breaking the law of God. When we repent and invoke the precious blood of Jesus, all our sins and transgressions are completely forgiven. They are washed away in the sea of His grace and mercy. This is the clear testimony of the book of First John 1:9:

> *If we [freely] admit that we have sinned and confess our sins, He is faithful and just [true to His own nature and promises], and will forgive our sins and cleanse us continually from all unrighteousness [our wrongdoing, everything not in conformity with His will and purpose].*

Altars Are Places of Blood

> *For the life of the flesh is in the blood, and I have given it to you on the altar to make atonement for your souls; for it is the blood that makes atonement, by reason of the life [which it represents]* (Leviticus 17:11).

One of the laws of altars states that "all altars are places of blood, because altars are places of sacrifice." This is why in both the old and new covenant the altar was clearly distinguished from every other instrument in the temple. *The altar was always stained with blood.* This is why God hates the shedding of innocent human blood, because He knows that all spiritual altars, whether demonic or divine, are powered by blood. More often than not, places of blood in society are the best places to start looking for an altar. This is why every clinic owned by Planned Parenthood is not just a clinic, it is actually an altar to the god Molech. *Molech* is the biblical name of a Canaanite god associated with child sacrifice. The clinics of Planned Parenthood are powerful altars to this ancient demonic god whether the proponents of this powerful organization know it or not. The Bible has already identified this demonic god's insatiable appetite for the blood of children. Regardless of the politically correct reason for the slaughter of millions of innocent babies in the name of a "woman's right to choose," the proponents of this barbaric practice are being animated by this ancient demon-god of the Canaanites! It's no wonder Solomon says there is nothing new under the sun, which has not already happened in previous generations (see Eccles. 1:8-10).

Leviticus 17:11 shows us that the life of the flesh is in the blood, and then God goes on to say, *"I have given it to you on the altar to make atonement for your souls; for it is the blood that makes atonement, by reason of the life [which it represents]."* This scripture clearly proves that altars are places of blood, and the blood poured on an altar can be exchanged for "life" in other areas. The more precious the blood that is poured out on an altar, the more powerful the divine exchanges that we can appropriate from it. Thankfully, there is no blood more precious than the blood Jesus shed for us. Jesus shed His blood in seven places; so we can use the blood sacrifice of Jesus on the seven places (altars) He shed it on to exact miracles, signs, and wonders that we desperately need. I will now show you the seven places (altars) where Jesus shed His blood and the seven corresponding evil altars that were destroyed in the process.

Seven Drops of Blood and the Battle of Altars

1. Sweat Drops of Blood

And being in agony [deeply distressed and anguished; almost to the point of death], He prayed more intently; and His sweat became like drops of blood, falling down on the ground (Luke 22:44).

The first time Jesus shed His blood was in the garden of Gethsemane just before He was crucified. In the garden of Gethsemane, there was an intense spiritual battle between Jesus' will and the will of His heavenly Father. Please remember that in the garden of Eden, Adam listened to the voice of his wife above the voice of God and ate from the forbidden tree. The consequences of his disobedience involved the loss of his ambassadorial status in the garden of Eden, and the ground became cursed with thorns and thistles. Part of the curse that came upon mankind due to the ground being cursed is that mankind would have to "sweat it out" in order to get his daily provisions from the earth. I call this the evil altar of "toiling and sweating."

> *Then to Adam the Lord God said, "Because you have listened [attentively] to the voice of your wife, and have eaten [fruit] from the tree about which I commanded you, saying, 'You shall not eat of it'; the ground is [now] under a curse because of you; in sorrow and toil you shall eat [the fruit] of it. All the days of your life. Both thorns and thistles it shall grow for you; and you shall eat the plants of the field.* **By the sweat of your face you will eat bread until you return to the ground,** *for from it you were taken; for you are dust, and to dust you shall return"* (Genesis 3:17-19).

In my many years of apostolic service to the Lord, I have observed that millions of people in our world are human attendants to the evil altar of "toiling and sweating." Nothing comes easy for them. Every inch of prosperity or progress comes with intense, grueling, and backbreaking effort. For most humans, the struggle to survive is so intense that an endless stream of strangers, including the television, are raising their children. Their grueling work schedule of 10- to 12-hour workdays leaves no room to spend quality time with their children. The evil altar of toiling and sweating makes sure they rise early in the morning before their children are up and then arrive late at night when their love-starved children are already in bed.

Day by day this rigorous ritual continues again and again! They comfort themselves by saying, "I am doing this for my children and when I retire I will spend more time with my children." However, when they are old and tired, they discover they have little in common with their children, except for DNA. *One of the dangerous prayers in this book is directed at destroying this altar of toiling and sweating.* When Jesus' sweat became droplets of blood and fell to the ground, the curse of Genesis 3:17 was broken off the ground. This means the altar of "toiling and sweating" for everything in our life can be broken permanently in Jesus' name.

2. *Struck on the Face with Fists and Rods*

> *But Jesus kept silent. And the high priest said to Him, "I call on You to swear a binding oath by the living God, that you tell us whether You are the Christ, the Son of God." Jesus said to him, "You have [in fact] said it; but more than that I tell you [regardless of what you do with Me now], in the future you will see [Me revealed as] the Son of Man seated at the right hand of Power, and coming on the clouds of heaven." Then the high priest tore his robes [in mock horror] and exclaimed, "He has blasphemed [by making Himself God's equal]! What further need have we of witnesses or evidence? See, you have now heard the blasphemy. What do you think?" They answered, "He deserves to be put to death." Then they spat in His face and struck Him with their fists; and some slapped Him* (Matthew 26:63-67).

The second time Jesus Christ shed His blood was when they struck Him on His face with fists and rods. Our face is our glory. It represents our self-image and self-worth. It's the first thing people see about you. It's no wonder both men and women (especially women) spend millions of dollars each year on face products (cosmetics). Consequentially, to be beaten on the face with fists and rods represents the spirit of slander. Slander is one of the most destructive forces that can be levelled at a person's reputation in order to paint them in a negative light. Many people go through life trying to arrest lies about them that are circulating in the public square. Slander is so dangerous to a person's life and reputation that many law-abiding nations have libel laws on their books to deal with the problem of slander. Jesus was beaten in the face to restore our glory and destroy the spirit of slander. *One of the dangerous prayers in this book deals with uprooting the altar of slander in your life.*

3. Hair of His Beard Pulled Out

The Lord God has opened My ear, and I have not been rebellious, nor have I turned back. I turned My back to those who strike Me, and My cheeks to those who pluck out the beard; I did not hide My face from insults and spitting (Isaiah 50:5-6).

The third time Jesus Christ shed His blood was when they plucked out His beard off His cheeks. The beard was a huge symbol of honor and respect to a Jew. So the best way to put a Jewish man to shame was to pluck out his beard. Consequentially, to have His beard plucked out of His cheeks represents the spirit of shame. Shame is one of the most destructive forces on a person's psyche, and many go through life camouflaging themselves with external cosmetics because of the constant shame they struggle with. Some of you who are reading this book were abandoned or sexually molested when you were young. Since then, you have struggled internally with the spirit of shame. Jesus had His beard plucked out of His cheeks to restore our personal glory and destroy the spirit of shame. *One of the dangerous prayers in this book deals with uprooting the altar of shame in your life.*

4. Scourged on His Back

So he set Barabbas free for them; but after having Jesus severely whipped (scourged), he handed Him over to be crucified (Matthew 27:26).

The fourth time Jesus Christ shed His blood was when Roman soldiers scourged His back. This was truly a horrible way to die. Jesus' back was scourged (whipped) thirty-nine times, creating 39 blood-soaked stripes on His back. Jesus' scourged back represents the removal of the spirit of infirmity or sickness. The prophet Isaiah says it this way, *"But He was wounded for our transgressions, He was crushed for our wickedness [our sin, our injustice, our wrongdoing]; the punishment [required] for our well-being fell on Him, and by His stripes (wounds) we are healed"* (Isa. 53:5). Some of you who are reading this book are dealing with a health challenge or know someone battling a long-standing sickness. I have news for you—Jesus healed you over 2,000 years ago through the stripes on His back. *One of the dangerous prayers in this book deals with uprooting the altar of infirmity or sickness in your life.*

5. *The Crown of Thorns Pressed into His Scalp*

And after twisting together a crown of thorns, they put it on His head, and put a reed in His right hand [as a scepter]. Kneeling before Him, they ridiculed Him, saying, "Hail (rejoice), King of the Jews!" (Matthew 27:29)

The fifth time Jesus Christ shed His blood was when the crown of thorns pressed into His scalp. The crown of thorns pressed into His scalp represents the curse of "thorns and thistles" that God pronounced on the ground after Adam and Eve sinned against God in the garden of Eden. This is what Genesis 3:17-18 says about this: *"The ground is [now] under a curse because of you; in sorrow and toil you shall eat [the fruit] of it all the days of your life. Both thorns and thistles it shall grow for you; and you shall eat the plants of the field."* Due to the curse that came on the ground, God told Adam that increase from the land will come at great difficulty. Consequentially, the "crown of thorns" represents the spirit of poverty and the powerlessness that is associated with being financially poor. The book of Proverbs 10:15 says, *"The rich man's wealth is his fortress; the ruin of the poor is their poverty."* Some of you who are reading this book have struggled with the spirit of poverty for most of your life. You are tired of living from paycheck to paycheck or on the verge of financial bankruptcy. The good news is that Jesus restored your financial glory and destroyed the spirit of poverty. *One of the dangerous prayers in this book deals with uprooting the altar of poverty and powerlessness in your life.*

6. Crucified: Nails in His Hands and Feet

And when they had crucified Him, they divided His clothes among them by casting lots (Matthew 27:35).

The sixth time Jesus Christ shed His blood was when they nailed His hands and feet. Hands and feet both represent balance and productivity; when Adam and Eve fell into sin there was an immediate imbalance in the relationship between *God and man, man to man, and man to earth!* This spiritual imbalance greatly affected man's productivity, since a relationship with God is the turbine of unending productivity. Jesus' crucifixion fixed this imbalance and restored man's spiritual equilibrium and his God-given potentialities.

We also know from scripture that hands represent wealth or the "work of our hands." *"And let the [gracious] favor of the Lord our God be on us; confirm for us the work of our hands—yes, confirm the work of our hands"* (Ps. 90:17). Feet in scripture represent our God-given destiny. *"The steps of a [good and righteous] man are directed and established by the Lord, and He delights in his way [and blesses his path]"* (Ps. 37:23). So when the Bible says the Lord will direct our paths, He is referencing the steps of destiny we are supposed to take during our earthly pilgrimage.

Consequently, when Jesus' hands and feet were pierced, He destroyed the spirit of unproductiveness (failed projects) and the spirit behind aborted destinies. Some of you who are reading this book have tried unsuccessfully to launch a business or build a house. Some of you are tired of watching people around you walk in their destiny while yours remains stubbornly elusive. I have good news for you—Jesus paid the price through His blood for you to succeed at wealth creation and walk in your God-given destiny. *One of the dangerous prayers in this book deals with uprooting the altar of unproductiveness or abortion.*

7. Side Pierced by the Spear

> *But one of the soldiers pierced His side with a spear, and immediately blood and water came [flowing] out* (John 19:34).

The seventh time Jesus Christ shed His blood was when they pierced His side with a spear. The Bible says that blood and water came out after the Roman soldier used a spear to pierce His side. So what does this symbolize? Jesus' spear-pierced side represents a broken heart or a heart in deep mourning. This is a heart saturated with grief. Some of you who are reading this book went through a very traumatic event, such as a divorce, the sudden death of your child or loved one, or you were sexually molested and one of these things broke your heart. You may be a person who walks through every day of your life oriented with unending grief. I have good news for you—Jesus paid the price for you to be set free from the spirit of a broken heart. Jesus will give you the oil of joy for the spirit of mourning. *One of the dangerous prayers in this book deals with uprooting the altar of a broken heart or mourning.*

The Blood of Jesus Cleanses Your Bloodline

> *Son of man, cause Jerusalem to know, understand, and realize her [idolatrous] abominations [that they] are disgusting, detestable, and shamefully vile. And say, Thus says the Lord*

God to Jerusalem [representing Israel]: Your [spiritual] ori-
gin and your birth are thoroughly Canaanitish; your [spir-
itual] father was an Amorite and your [spiritual] mother a
Hittite. And as for your birth, on the day you were born your
navel cord was not cut, nor were you washed with water to
cleanse you, nor rubbed with salt or swaddled with bands at
all (Ezekiel 16:2-4 AMPC).

The first time I appeared on the *It's Supernatural!* TV show with my dear friend Sid Roth was in August of 2013. I had just written a self-published book called *Jumping the Line: Breaking Generational Curses* that taught people a new way of breaking generational curses permanently, through a powerful prophetic act known as "jumping the line." Literally hundreds of thousands of people around the world have gone through this life-changing prophetic act. Mighty miracles of deliverance from generational iniquity have transpired, to the glory of God!

When I was writing this book, the Lord opened me up to the mystery of the *spiritual umbilical cord.* In the sixteenth chapter of Ezekiel, God bemoans the rampant idolatry of the people of Jerusalem. Then the Lord goes a step further and gives a spiritual diagnosis to the ills of Jerusalem to explain the rampant idolatry among His people in Jerusalem. God says, *"Your [spiritual] origin and your birth are thoroughly Canaanitish; your [spiritual] father was an Amorite and your [spiritual] mother a Hittite."* God connects the people's spiritual origins to the genetic tendency of the people to move in the direction of idolatry and building evil altars. Even though they were God's chosen people through the Abrahamic covenant, they were genetically connected to the idolatrous bloodlines of the Amorites and Hittites. Any student of the Bible knows that the Amorites and Hittites were custodians of idols and evil altars. So Jerusalem's genetic tendency to move in the direction of worshiping idols and erecting evil altars to these demon-gods was woven into their DNA. *Thankfully, the blood of Jesus can cleanse and rescue us from the legal claims of idols and evil altars that were planted in our bloodlines long before we were born.* Most importantly, we can prosecute these idols and evil altars in the Courts of Heaven. According to the book of Romans, the blood of Jesus can time travel into our past through our bloodline and cleanse us thoroughly.

> *Whom God set forth as a propitiation by His blood, through faith, to demonstrate His righteousness, because in His forbearance God had **passed over the sins that were previously committed*** (Romans 3:25 NKJV).

In Your Blood, Live!

> *And when I passed by you and saw you rolling about in your blood, I said to you in your blood, Live! Yes, I said to you still in your natal blood, Live!* (Ezekiel 16:6 AMPC)

As the Lord continued to unravel the mystery of the spiritual umbilical cord, He showed me something that I had never seen before. He dropped the revelatory bombshell when He drew my attention to this verse: *"And as for your birth, on the day you were born your navel* [umbilical] *cord was not cut, nor were you washed with water to cleanse you, nor rubbed with salt or swaddled with bands at all"* (Ezek. 16:4 AMPC). When I saw this verse, a flash of revelation went through my spirit! I found myself in disbelief saying to myself, "No way! How can any midwife deliver a baby without cutting the umbilical cord that connects the baby to its mother? Even uneducated midwives in primitive cultures know this basic fact!" Then the Holy Spirit said to me, "Francis, it's true that all midwives cut the umbilical cord when a child is born. *But who cuts the spiritual umbilical cord that connects you spiritually to all the spiritual tendencies, idiosyncrasies, and iniquities of your ancestral bloodline?"*

Suddenly the light bulb of revelation exploded inside me. Then the Holy Spirit fixed my eyes on the sixth verse in the passage and sealed the essence of the revelation. *"And when I passed by you and saw you rolling about in your blood, I said to you in your blood, Live! Yes, I said to you still in your natal blood, Live!"* The Lord showed me that if our spiritual umbilical cord to our natural ancestors is not supernaturally cut, we will continue to struggle with the same tendencies, idols, and evil altars that ruled over our genetic progenitors. In my book *Jumping the Line: Breaking Generational Curses*, I had focused my attention on being free from these genetic tendencies. However, I never saw at the time that the same passage of scripture contains the divine remedy to prosecuting idols and evil altars that have controlled and oppressed many people through their ancestral bloodlines. Thankfully, in this book we move a step further, glory to God!

Life Application Section

Memory Verse

> *And being in agony [deeply distressed and anguished; almost to the point of death], He prayed more intently; and His sweat became like drops of blood, falling down on the ground* (Luke 22:44).

Reflections

1. Name seven ways Jesus shed His blood.

    _____

    _____

    _____

    _____

2. Can the blood of Jesus cleanse your ancestral bloodline?

    _____

    _____

    _____

    _____

Chapter Six

Before You Enter the Courtroom

We are almost there! We are getting ready to delve into the second half of this precious book, which is a section I affectionately call *the book of dangerous prayers*. I have prepared some very powerful prayers for uprooting evil altars in your life and bloodline that are working against you in the realm of the spirit. These prayers of activation are music to your ears but *dangerous battle cries* to satan and his demonic minions because the prayers will destroy the works of the devil in your life and family. However, coming before the Courts of Heaven requires that we understand the basic spiritual protocols of presenting our cases before the Courts of Heaven.

Because the protocol of presenting cases before the Courts of Heaven is standardized, I have taken the liberty of quoting this section verbatim from my book *Issuing Divine Restraining Orders from the Courts of Heaven*, published by Destiny Image. If you haven't read this book, please get it right away! I recorded a life-changing television show on Sid Roth's *It's Supernatural!* on the subject of issuing divine restraining orders that I encourage you to watch on my YouTube channel. This book and the one you are now holding in your hands are two lethal power twins against the work of the devil.

Get Off the Battlefield

As Robert Henderson shares in his book, *Operating in the Courts of Heaven*:

The first thing we must do to step into the courts of heaven is to get off the battlefield. We have to recognize the need for legal precedents to be set before we run to the battle. We are in a conflict, but it is a legal one. Remember that Jesus never pictures prayer in the battlefield context. He did put prayer however in a courtroom or judicial setting in Luke 18:1-8.

Stand On Jesus' Finished Work

After this, Jesus, knowing that all things were now accomplished, that the Scripture might be fulfilled, said, "I thirst!" Now a vessel full of sour wine was sitting there; and they filled a sponge with sour wine, put it on hyssop, and put it to His mouth. So when Jesus had received the sour wine, He said, "It is finished!" And bowing His head, He gave up His spirit (John 19:28-30 NKJV).

The second thing we must do is realize that approaching the Courts of Heaven must be based upon the finished work of Christ on the cross. Without this substitutionary work of our Savior, none of us qualify to approach the courts of a Holy God.

Repent

The third thing we must do before approaching the Courts of Heaven is realize that we need to ask the Holy Spirit to search our hearts and see if there is any unconfessed sin in our life. It is very interesting to me that repentance is at the heart of entering the Kingdom. The introduction of the gospel of the Kingdom by both John the Baptist and Jesus was directly connected to the act of repenting.

> *From that time Jesus began to preach and to say, "Repent, for the kingdom of heaven is at hand"* (Matthew 4:17 NKJV).

To "repent" means to *change your mind and reverse course*. Repentance resets your relationship with God and gives you a favorable standing in the Courts of Heaven. So it's quite sad when you hear some proponents of the "grace message" telling Christians they only need to repent once. As if bornagain believers are incapable of sinning against God in this body of flesh.

Ask for the Court to Be Seated

> *A fiery stream issued and came forth from before Him. A thousand thousands ministered to Him; ten thousand times ten thousand stood before Him. The court was seated, and the books were opened* (Daniel 7:10 NKJV).

The fourth thing we must do before approaching the Courts of Heaven is ask that the Courts of Heaven be seated to hear our case. We make this request in and through the mighty name of Jesus Christ our Savior and Lord. It's impossible to get a judicial ruling from any court of law if the court is not yet seated. This is why no courtroom battle ever proceeds until the judge has been seated. Once the court is seated we can then ask for the books of our destiny to be opened. At this juncture we can also ask the Court of Heaven to compel satan to also open his books of accusations against us, so they can be read aloud in court!

Present Your Case with Boldness

Let us therefore come boldly to the throne of grace, that we may obtain mercy and find grace to help in time of need (Hebrews 4:16 NKJV).

Boldness is an important spiritual ingredient for approaching the Throne of Grace. It demonstrates our confidence in the finished work of Christ and the goodness of God. When we approach the Courts of Heaven it's important that we do so in a spirit of boldness and not fear. Fear actually works against us and gives the devil legal footing against us in the Courts of Heaven. This is why the Bible says a person who fears in not perfected in the love of God (see 1 John 4:18).

Wait for the Spirit's Witness

The Spirit Himself bears witness with our spirit that we are children of God (Romans 8:16 NKJV).

One of the most important things we can do while we are presenting our case in the Courts of Heaven is wait for the witness of the Holy Spirit before we leave the courtroom. As I stated earlier, the Holy Spirit is the highest officer of the Courts of Heaven operating on earth today. He'll you give a witness in your spirit when the righteous verdict or divine restraining order you're seeking has been granted. If it has not been granted ask the Holy Spirit, "Why?" He's faithful to answer you promptly, because all of Heaven wants to answer your prayers.

Receive the Court's Verdict by Faith

When Jesus had raised Himself up and saw no one but the woman, He said to her, "Woman, where are those accusers of yours? Has no one condemned you?" She said, "No one, Lord." And Jesus said to her, "Neither do I condemn you; go and sin no more" (John 8:10-11 NKJV).

No legal case inside any courtroom is ever considered complete until a final verdict has been rendered. If a verdict has not been rendered, it may mean that the prosecutor has more evidence against the accused that the courts must also consider or the defense attorneys have witness testimony or evidence on behalf of their client that they want the courts to consider. This is why it's important for you to be persistent until the Courts of Heaven have rendered a righteous verdict on your behalf. The devil can only resist the Courts of Heaven from rendering a righteous verdict on your behalf because he still has legal grounds to do so. Ask the Holy Spirit to show you what is in satan's evidence dockets so you can render it useless. When your righteous verdict is rendered, you must *receive it by faith*. This is because everything in the Kingdom of God is received by faith. You will not get a physical courier with a physical letter stating your righteous verdict. But believe me, a verdict rendered by the Courts of Heaven is more real and consequential than any verdict rendered by a natural court of law.

Reinforce Your Righteous Verdict Daily Through Thanksgiving

In everything give thanks; for this is the will of God in Christ Jesus for you (1 Thessalonians 5:18 NKJV).

One of the most powerful weapons in the Kingdom of God is *thanksgiving*. Thanksgiving places us in an attitude of continual praise over what the Lord has already done for us. Thanksgiving is so powerful that God has made it His direct will for all of His children. Thanksgiving feeds your spirit with hopeful anticipation. Thanksgiving feeds the spirit of expectancy inside of you. Miracles only happen in spiritual atmospheres charged with divine expectancy. Once the Holy Spirit gives you the "witness" that the *divine restraining order* you requested has been granted, it's important that you maintain an attitude of thanksgiving in the aftermath.

It's Time to Jump the Line!

> *So the people shouted [the battle cry], and the priests blew the trumpets. When the people heard the sound of the trumpet, they raised a great shout and the wall [of Jericho] fell down, so that the sons of Israel went up into the city, every man straight ahead [climbing over the rubble], and they overthrew the city* (Joshua 6:20).

The Bible is full of prophetic acts that point to higher truths or realities in the realm of the spirit, such as the children of Israel marching seven times around the walls of Jericho. These walls were impregnable walls, several meters thick. How could people walk around the walled city and then give a shout and the impregnable walls began to collapse into rubble? Unless their marching around the city and shout of praise were connected to some very powerful hidden supernatural power source.

Since the Lord gave me the prophetic act of having people jump over a line (representing their corrupted ancestral bloodlines), thousands have been gloriously set free from years of generational bondage. I want you to stand up right now and find a rope, electric cable, or red ribbon (preferably) and place it on the floor in front of your feet. Then I want you to pray aloud the following prayer of activation, and when you finish the prayer *jump over the line* in front of you with a shout of praise to the Lord. After you jump the line, spend some quality time praising and worshiping God.

Before You Jump!

1. Do not cross over the line in the opposite direction after you jump—please pick it up from the floor. You don't want to reverse the prophetic act.

2. You will need to know your father's surname and your mother's maiden name before you jump the bloodline. You will use these two names to renounce iniquities attached to your bloodline.

3. Do not stay silent after you jump the line; give God your highest praise.

4. Make sure that you mix this prophetic act with faith in the finished work of Jesus or it profits you nothing!

Prayer of Activation

Pray this loudly before you jump the bloodline:

> Heavenly Father, I come before Your heavenly supreme court in Jesus' name to receive Your righteous judgment over my genetic and bloodline inheritance. Righteous Judge, I am trusting You to cut off the spiritual umbilical

cord that connects me to the corrupted bloodlines of my natural ancestors, in Jesus' name.

Heavenly Father, I willingly and joyfully **denounce** the [insert your father's last name here]'s **bloodline**!

Heavenly Father, I willingly and joyfully **denounce** the [insert your mother's maiden name here]'s **bloodline**!

I denounce the corrupted bloodlines that my father's and mother's names represent. I renounce all the demonic technologies and iniquities that are attached to these names all the way back to the first Adam, in Jesus' name I pray. I decree that my ancestral bloodlines can no longer influence my life negatively. I give up my father's and mother's ancestral bloodlines in order to possess Yeshua's holy and flawless prophetic bloodline and lineage. I decree and declare that Jesus' genetic inheritance is now my inheritance.

Heavenly Father, as I prepare to jump over the prophetic bloodline, I denounce all illegal trades that I and my forefathers have ever made on satan's trading floors in the second heaven that have given satan the legal grounds in the Courts of Heaven to bind me and afflict me through evil altars. I repent in Jesus' name for all transgressions against the Lord that my ancestors and I ever created on satan's trading floors. Heavenly Father, as I prepare to jump over the prophetic bloodline, I release my faith for the healing of my body and all genetic anomalies, in Yeshua's name I pray.

Heavenly Father, I also beseech You to deliver me permanently from all generational curses in my bloodline by superimposing Jesus' flawless bloodline over me. Thank You for healing me from any and all genetic deficiencies, in the name of Jesus Christ. I also decree that when I jump over the prophetic bloodline I will be jumping directly into the glory realm of God where all miracles reside, in Yeshua's name I pray.

Now Jump!

You did it! You are *now ready* to go through *The Book of Dangerous Prayers that Destroy Evil Altars!*

Life Application Section

Memory Verse

> *When Jesus had raised Himself up and saw no one but the woman, He said to her, "Woman, where are those accusers of yours? Has no one condemned you?" She said, "No one, Lord." And Jesus said to her, "Neither do I condemn you; go and sin no more"* (John 8:10-11 NKJV).

Reflections

1. Why do we need to get off the battlefield before we enter the Courts of Heaven?

   _____

   _____

   _____

   _____

2. Explain why faith is important to operating in the Courts of Heaven?

   _____

   _____

   _____

   _____

SECTION TWO

Welcome to the Book of
DANGEROUS PRAYERS

Hilkiah the high priest said to Shaphan the scribe, "I have found the Book of the Law in the house (temple) of the Lord." Hilkiah gave the book to Shaphan, and he read it. Shaphan the scribe came to the king and brought back word to him: "Your servants have emptied out the money that was found in the house, and have placed it in the hands of the workmen who have been appointed over the house of the Lord." Then Shaphan the scribe told the king, "Hilkiah the priest has given me a book." And Shaphan read it [aloud] before the king.

—2 Kings 22:8-10

The Book of Dangerous Prayers, which is section two of this book, is the most proactive part of this book. This is where you get to actively participate in your own deliverance. The prayers I have drafted here are truly dangerous to the evil altars satan has been using to fight you and delay your destiny. If you "mix them with faith" they will become very profitable to you and your family!

Chapter Seven

Prayers of Activation:

Applying Dangerous Prayers that Uproot Evil Altars, Now!

I t would be a mistake to close out a book such as this without giving you tools for activating God's miraculous power in your life for the uprooting of satanic evil altars, some of which have been in your bloodline for generations. So this section of the book is going to focus on the different prayers of activation you can use to prosecute and uproot different types of evil altars in the Courts of Heaven. You can use the prayers of activation for yourself or you can have people you are praying for repeat the prayers after you. It's my deepest prayer to God, our heavenly Father, that together we will plunder hell and populate heaven as satan's power is broken off you and others.

Prayer #1

Uprooting the
Altar of Premature Death

The thief comes only in order to steal and kill and destroy. I came that they may have and enjoy life, and have it in abundance [to the full, till it overflows].

—John 10:10

God is to us a God of acts of salvation; and to God the Lord belong escapes from death [setting us free].

—Psalm 68:20

O ne of the greatest gifts God can ever give a person outside of experiencing the saving knowledge of Jesus Christ is the gift of a long life. The Bible is replete with God's promises for a long and healthy life. A long life means that we get more chances in our hourglass to accomplish more things for God's Kingdom, not to mention the number of lost souls we can reach with the good news of the Kingdom if we just had more time. One of my favorite scriptural promises on living a long life was coined by King David.

> I will not die, but live, and declare the works and recount the
> illustrious acts of the Lord (Psalm 118:17).

Satan knows the importance of having a long life, because he knows that purpose is time sensitive according to Ecclesiastes 3:1. Consequently, his favorite strategy is to assign the spirit of premature death against people of destiny. God has used me several times to rescue people who should have died prematurely. Before you pray the activation prayer that follows this paragraph, I want you to read Psalm 118:17 loudly, several times, until faith begins to build in your spirit! You must determine in your spirit before you pray this prayer that you refuse to die before your appointed time. Tell the devil that you will live a long and healthy life, in Jesus' name.

Prayer of Activation

1. Address the Father in Praise and Worship

Heavenly Father, holy is Your name and greatly to be praised. I worship and adore You in Jesus' name. May Your Kingdom manifest in my life as it is in Heaven. Plead my cause, O Lord, with those who strive with me; fight against any entity or person who is contending against me. Heavenly Father, it is written in Psalm 27:6, *"And now my head will be lifted up above my enemies around me, in His tent I will offer sacrifices with shouts of joy; I will sing, yes, I will sing praises to the Lord."* Abba, I enjoin my worship to the heavenly chorus of worship of Your holy angels and the crowd of witnesses, in Jesus' name.

2. Ask for the Court to Be Seated

Heavenly Father, Righteous Judge, I ask that the Courts of Heaven be seated according to Daniel 7:9-10 and that all books related to this case be opened. I ask this in Jesus' mighty name. It is written:

> *I kept looking until thrones were set up, and the Ancient of Days (God) took His seat; His garment was white as snow*

and the hair of His head like pure wool. His throne was flames of fire; its wheels were a burning fire. A river of fire was flowing and coming out from before Him; a thousand thousands were attending Him, and ten thousand times ten thousand were standing before Him; the court was seated, and the books were opened.

Heavenly Father, I am requesting the privilege of standing before the courtroom of the Ancient of Days according to what was revealed to the prophet Daniel, in Jesus' name, I pray. Heavenly Father, I stand in Your royal courtroom because of the blood and finished work of Jesus on the cross. I have come to receive Your righteous judgment over my life against the spirit and altar of *premature death* that satan planted in my generational bloodline. Heavenly Father, I call upon Your holy angels to be witnesses to my lawsuit and righteous prosecution of the evil altar of *premature death*. I decree and declare that this evil altar of *premature death* will not kill me or my family members before our appointed time; neither will it kill the divine relationships I need to achieve my God-given destiny here on earth, in Jesus' name I pray.

3. Surrender Your Rights to Self-Representation to the Lord as Your Advocate

Heavenly Father, Your Word in First John 2:1-2 says, "*My little children, these things I write to you, so that you may not sin. And if anyone sins, we have an Advocate with the Father, Jesus Christ the righteous. And He Himself is the propitiation for our sins, and not for ours only but also for the whole world*" (NKJV). I thank You that Jesus is my faithful Advocate before the Righteous Judge in the Courts of Heaven. Lord Jesus, I surrender my rights to self-representation and summon You as my Advocate to help me plead my case before the Righteous Judge and prosecute the evil of altar of *premature death* that satan planted in my bloodline. I also ask the blessed Holy Spirit, who is the highest officer of the Courts of Heaven here on earth, to make me sensitive to the proceedings of this Court in order to successfully prosecute the evil altar of *premature death* in Jesus' name.

4. Summon the Evil Altar and the Idol That Sits on It to Appear in Court

Heavenly Father, even as I stand in Your royal courtroom I present myself as a living sacrifice, holy and acceptable before You according to Romans 12:1. Heavenly Father, Righteous Judge, I summon the altar of *premature death* in my bloodline and the idol that sits on it to appear in Your royal courtroom to face prosecution in Jesus' name. For it is written in First Corinthians 6:3, *"Do you not know that we [believers] will judge angels? How much more then [as to] matters of this life?"* Heavenly Father, I exercise my God-given authority in Christ Jesus to judge demons and principalities, in Jesus' name I pray. Righteous Judge, it is also written in the Constitution of Your Kingdom in First John 3:8, *"For this purpose the Son of God was manifested, that He might destroy the works of the devil"* (NKJV).

5. Address Satan's Accusations and Agree with the Adversary

Heavenly Father, I know that until the end of the age of sin, satan still has legal access to the Courts of Heaven to level accusations against the children of men; for it is written in the book of Revelation 12:10:

> *Then I heard a loud voice in heaven, saying, "Now the salvation, and the power, and the kingdom (dominion, reign) of our God, and the authority of His Christ have come; for the accuser of our [believing] brothers and sisters has been thrown down [at last], he who accuses them and keeps bringing charges [of sinful behavior] against them before our God day and night."*

Heavenly Father, the Lord Jesus also said in the book of Matthew 5:25:

Come to terms quickly [at the earliest opportunity] with your opponent at law while you are with him on the way [to court], so that your opponent does not hand you over to the judge, and the judge to the guard, and you are thrown into prison.

Heavenly Father, in all humility, while renouncing the spirit of pride, I choose to quickly agree with the legal accusations of my adversary, satan. Righteous Judge, every accusation that satan has filed against me and my bloodline in this Court is true.

6. Repent

Heavenly Father, I repent for my personal transgressions, and for the sins and iniquities of my forefathers that opened the door for the spirit and altar of *premature death* to oppress my life, in Jesus' name I pray. Lord, every sin of my forefathers that the enemy is using as a legal right to build cases against me and to marry me to *premature death,* I ask that the blood of Jesus would just wash them away. I also repent for self-inflicted word curses and all covenants with demons that have existed in my ancestral bloodline. I am asking that every covenant with demonic powers will now be revoked and that their right to claim me and my bloodline would now be dismissed before Your court, in Jesus' name. Thank You, Lord, for revoking these demonic covenants and evil altars in Jesus' mighty name! Heavenly Father, in my heartfelt desire to divorce myself from the spirit and altar of *premature death*, I give back everything and anything that the devil would say came from his kingdom. I only want what the blood of Jesus has secured for me.

7. *Appeal to the Blood of Jesus to Wipe Out All Sin (Satan's Evidence)*

Lord Jesus, thank You for cleansing me by Your blood so satan has no legal footing against me in Your courtroom. It is written in First John 1:9:

> *If we [freely] admit that we have sinned and confess our sins,*
> *He is faithful and just [true to His own nature and promises],*
> *and will forgive our sins and cleanse us continually from all*
> *unrighteousness [our wrongdoing, everything not in confor-*
> *mity with His will and purpose].*

Righteous Judge, I appeal to the blood of Jesus to wipe out all my shortcomings, transgressions, and iniquities, in Jesus' name, I pray. I receive by faith the cleansing power of the blood of Jesus.

8. *Ask the Court to Dismiss All of Satan's Accusations and Charges*

Heavenly Father, based upon Jesus' finished work and my heartfelt repentance, I now move on the Court of Heaven to dismiss all of satan's accusations and charges against me and my bloodline in Jesus' name. For it is written that the accuser of the brethren has been cast down. So, I ask You Father to cast down all of satan's accusations against me, in Jesus' name, I pray.

9. *Ask the Lord to Send Angels to Destroy the Evil Altar and Execute the Lord's Judgment Against It*

Heavenly Father, Righteous Judge, I ask that You send high-ranking angelic officers of the Courts who excel in strength to execute the judgment of Your supreme court and destroy the evil altar of *premature death* and the idol that sits on it that satan planted in my bloodline, in Jesus' name I pray. By the spirit of prophecy, I prophesy the complete destruction of the evil altar of *premature death* in my life, in Jesus' name. For it is written in Psalm 91:11-12, *"For He will command His angels in regard to you, to protect and defend and guard you in all your ways [of obedience and service]. They will lift you up in their hands, so that you do not [even] strike your foot against a stone."* I receive angelic assistance, right now, in Jesus' name.

10. Present Scriptures That Will Be Used in Issuing a Divine Restraining Order

Heavenly Father, I present before Your Supreme Court the following scriptures as my rock-solid evidence against the spirit and altar of *premature death* in my life. It is written:

> *He shall call upon Me, and I will answer him; I will be with him in trouble; I will deliver him and honor him. With long life I will satisfy him, and show him My salvation* (Psalm 91:15-16 NKJV).

> *The thief does not come except to steal, and to kill, and to destroy. I have come that they may have life, and that they may have it more abundantly* (John 10:10 NKJV).

> *I shall not die but live, and declare the works and recount the illustrious acts of the Lord* (Psalm 118:17 AMPC).

Righteous Judge, based upon the aforementioned scriptures, it is clear that the spirit and altar of *premature death*, if allowed to succeed, would cause great injury to my life, destiny, and also inflict irreparable damage to the purposes of God. I ask that that every legal right the spirit and altar of *premature death* is holding be revoked in Jesus' glorious name. Righteous Judge, based upon the aforementioned scriptures, it is clear that I qualify for a divine restraining order against the altar of *premature death* and the idol that sits on it, in Jesus' name.

11. Ask the Court to Issue a Divine Restraining Order and Receive the Divine Restraining Order by Faith

Heavenly Father, Righteous Judge, I now ask that a divine restraining order and a permanent injunction against the spirit and altar of *premature death* in my life would now be issued by the authority of Your Supreme Court, in Jesus' name. Heavenly Father, I decree and declare that any and all forms of *premature death* plans the devil has issued or is orchestrating against my life are now cancelled in Jesus' glorious name. Heavenly Father, I receive this divine restraining order and permanent injunction by faith, in Jesus' name. For it is written in the Constitution of Your Kingdom in Hebrews 11:6, *"But without faith it is impossible to [walk with God and] please Him, for whoever comes [near] to God must [necessarily] believe that God exists and that He rewards those who [earnestly and diligently] seek Him."* I believe and declare by faith that the spirit and altar of *premature death* in my life has been judged, in Jesus' name!

12. Ask the Lord to Seal Your Righteous Verdict and Court Proceedings in the Blood of Jesus

Heavenly Father, Righteous Judge, I now ask You to seal my righteous verdict against the spirit and altar of *premature death* in the precious blood of Jesus. May You also cover with the blood of Jesus all my legal proceedings in this Court in Jesus' name. I decree and declare that my righteous verdict of release and breakthrough from the evil altar of *premature death* is now secured in the documents of the Courts of Heaven. For it is written in John's Gospel, chapter 8:36, *"So if the Son makes you free, then you are unquestionably free."* I decree and declare that I am free of the evil altar of *premature death* in Jesus' name, amen!

Prayer #2

Uprooting the Altar of Stagnation

The Lord our God spoke to us at Horeb, saying, "You have stayed long enough on this mountain. Turn and resume your journey, and go to the hill country of the Amorites, and to all their neighbors in the Arabah, in the hill country and in the lowland (the Shephelah), in the Negev (South country) and on the coast of the [Mediterranean] Sea, the land of the Canaanites, and Lebanon, as far as the great river, the river Euphrates. Look, I have set the land before you; go in and take possession of the land which the Lord swore (solemnly promised) to your fathers, to Abraham, to Isaac, and to Jacob, to give to them and to their descendants after them."

—Deuteronomy 1:6-8

God is a God of movement! Everywhere we see God in the Bible, He is moving and never static. It's no wonder when any living thing starts to die, its mobility is one of the first things to go. Most importantly, as believers we are designed to flow and grow from glory to glory according to Second Corinthians 3:18:

> And we all, with unveiled face, continually seeing as in a mirror the glory of the Lord, are progressively being transformed into His image from [one degree of] glory to [even more] glory, which comes from the Lord, [who is] the Spirit.

In Deuteronomy 1:6-8, God rebuked the people of Israel for wasting their time going around the same mountain. Does this ring a bell with you or does it remind you of someone you know who has been stuck at the same place for the longest time? Satan knows the importance of movement in a person's life that leads to progress, success, and a better life, especially when you have a calling from God to reach the masses. Unfortunately, I have met too many of God's people who love Jesus but are desperately stuck. Everything is stagnant in their life. They just can't seem to get ahead. The truth of the matter is that they are victims of a vicious evil altar known as the *altar of stagnation*. Thankfully, this evil altar can be destroyed in the Courts of Heaven!

Prayer of Activation

1. Address the Father in Praise and Worship

Heavenly Father, holy is Your name and greatly to be praised. I worship and adore You in Jesus' name. May Your Kingdom manifest in my life as it is in Heaven. Plead my cause, O Lord, with those who strive with me; fight against any entity or person who is contending against me. Heavenly Father, it is written in Psalm 27:6, *"And now my head will be lifted up above my enemies around me, in His tent I will offer sacrifices with shouts of joy; I will sing, yes, I will sing praises to the Lord."* Abba, I enjoin my worship to the heavenly chorus of worship of Your holy angels and the crowd of witnesses, in Jesus' name.

2. Ask for the Court to Be Seated

Heavenly Father, Righteous Judge, I ask that the Courts of Heaven be seated according to Daniel 7:9-10. I ask this in Jesus' mighty name. It is written:

I kept looking until thrones were set up, and the Ancient of Days (God) took His seat; His garment was white as snow and the hair of His head like pure wool. His throne was flames of fire; its wheels were a burning fire. A river of fire was flowing and coming out from before Him; a thousand thousands were attending Him, and ten thousand times ten thousand were standing before Him; the court was seated, and the books were opened.

Heavenly Father, I am requesting the privilege of standing before the courtroom of the Ancient of Days according to what was revealed to the prophet Daniel, in Jesus' name, I pray. Heavenly Father, I stand in Your royal courtroom because of the blood and finished work of Jesus on the cross. I have come to receive Your righteous judgment over my life against the spirit and altar of *stagnation* that satan planted in my generational bloodline. Heavenly Father, I call upon Your holy angels to be witnesses to my lawsuit and righteous prosecution of the evil altar of *stagnation*. I decree and declare that this evil altar of *stagnation* will no longer arrest my progress or that of my family members; neither will it hinder my ability to excel in life and business, in Jesus' name I pray.

3. Surrender Your Rights to Self-Representation to the Lord as Your Advocate

Heavenly Father, Your Word in First John 2:1-2 says, "*My little children, these things I write to you, so that you may not sin. And if anyone sins, we have an Advocate with the Father, Jesus Christ the righteous. And He Himself is the propitiation for our sins, and not for ours only but also for the whole world*" (NKJV). I thank You that Jesus is my faithful Advocate before the Righteous Judge in the Courts of Heaven. Lord Jesus, I surrender my rights to self-representation and summon You as my Advocate to help me plead my case before the Righteous Judge and prosecute the evil of altar of *stagnation* that satan planted in my bloodline to cause arrested development. I also ask the blessed Holy Spirit, who is the highest officer of the Courts of Heaven here on earth, to make me sensitive to the proceedings of this Court in order to successfully prosecute the evil altar of *stagnation* in Jesus' name.

4. Summon the Evil Altar and the Idol That Sits on It to Appear in Court

Heavenly Father, even as I stand in Your royal courtroom I present myself as a living sacrifice, holy and acceptable before You according to Romans 12:1. Heavenly Father, Righteous Judge, I summon the altar of *stagnation* in my bloodline and the idol that sits on it to appear in Your royal courtroom to face prosecution in Jesus' name. For it is written in First Corinthians 6:3, *"Do you not know that we [believers] will judge angels? How much more then [as to] matters of this life?"* Heavenly Father, I exercise my God-given authority in Christ Jesus to judge demons and principalities, in Jesus' name I pray. Righteous Judge, it is also written in the Constitution of Your Kingdom in First John 3:8, *"For this purpose the Son of God was manifested, that He might destroy the works of the devil"* (NKJV).

5. Address Satan's Accusations and Agree with the Adversary

Heavenly Father, I know that until the end of the age of sin, satan still has legal access to the Courts of Heaven to level accusations against the children of men; for it is written in the book of Revelation 12:10:

> *Then I heard a loud voice in heaven, saying, "Now the salvation, and the power, and the kingdom (dominion, reign) of our God, and the authority of His Christ have come; for the accuser of our [believing] brothers and sisters has been thrown down [at last], he who accuses them and keeps bringing charges [of sinful behavior] against them before our God day and night."*

Heavenly Father, the Lord Jesus also said in the book of Matthew 5:25:

> *Come to terms quickly [at the earliest opportunity] with your*
> *opponent at law while you are with him on the way [to court],*
> *so that your opponent does not hand you over to the judge, and*
> *the judge to the guard, and you are thrown into prison.*

Heavenly Father, in all humility, while renouncing the spirit of pride, I choose to quickly agree with the legal accusations of my adversary, satan. Righteous Judge, every accusation that satan has filed against me and my bloodline in this Court is true.

6. Repent

Heavenly Father, I repent for my personal transgressions, and for the sins and iniquities of my forefathers that opened the door for the spirit and altar of *stagnation* to oppress my life, in Jesus' name I pray. Lord, every sin of my forefathers that the enemy is using as a legal right to build cases against me and to deny me my destiny, I ask that the blood of Jesus would just wash them away. I also repent for self-inflicted word curses and all covenants with demons that have existed in my ancestral bloodline. I am asking that every covenant with demonic powers will now be revoked and that their right to claim me and my bloodline would now be dismissed before Your court, in Jesus' name. Thank You, Lord, for revoking these demonic covenants and evil altars in Jesus' mighty name! Heavenly Father, in my heartfelt desire to divorce myself from the spirit and altar of *stagnation*, I give back everything and anything that the devil would say came from his kingdom. I only want what the blood of Jesus has secured for me.

7. *Appeal to the Blood of Jesus to Wipe Out All Sin (Satan's Evidence)*

Lord Jesus, thank You for cleansing me by Your blood so satan has no legal footing against me in Your courtroom. It is written in First John 1:9:

> *If we [freely] admit that we have sinned and confess our sins, He is faithful and just [true to His own nature and promises], and will forgive our sins and cleanse us continually from all unrighteousness [our wrongdoing, everything not in conformity with His will and purpose].*

Righteous Judge, I appeal to the blood of Jesus to wipe out all my shortcomings, transgressions, and iniquities, in Jesus' name, I pray. I receive by faith the cleansing power of the blood of Jesus.

8. *Ask the Court to Dismiss All of Satan's Accusations and Charges*

Heavenly Father, based upon Jesus' finished work and my heartfelt repentance, I now move on the Court of Heaven to dismiss all of satan's accusations and charges against me and my bloodline in Jesus' name. For it is written that the accuser of the brethren has been cast down. So, I ask You Father to cast down all of satan's accusations against me, in Jesus' name, I pray.

9. *Ask the Lord to Send Angels to Destroy the Evil Altar and Execute the Lord's Judgment Against It*

Heavenly Father, Righteous Judge, I ask that You send high-ranking angelic officers of the Courts who excel in strength to execute the judgment of Your supreme court and destroy the evil altar of *stagnation* and the idol that sits on it that satan planted in my bloodline, in Jesus' name I pray. By the spirit of prophecy, I prophesy the complete destruction of the evil altar of *stagnation* in my life, in Jesus' name. For it is written in Psalm 91:11-12, *"For He will command His angels in regard to you, to protect and defend and guard you in all your ways [of obedience and service]. They will lift you up in their hands, so that you do not [even] strike your foot against a stone."* I receive angelic assistance, right now, in Jesus' name.

10. Present Scriptures That Will Be Used in Issuing a Divine Restraining Order

Heavenly Father, I present before Your Supreme Court the following scriptures as my rock-solid evidence against the spirit and altar of *stagnation* in my life. It is written:

> *The righteous will flourish like the date palm [long-lived, upright and useful]; they will grow like a cedar in Lebanon [majestic and stable]* (Psalm 92:12).

> *And he will be like a tree firmly planted [and fed] by streams of water, which yields its fruit in its season; its leaf does not wither; and in whatever he does, he prospers [and comes to maturity]* (Psalm 1:3).

Righteous Judge, based upon the aforementioned scriptures, it is clear that the spirit and altar of *stagnation*, if allowed to succeed, would cause great injury to my life, destiny, and also inflict irreparable damage to the purposes of God. I ask that that every legal right the spirit and altar of *stagnation* is holding be revoked in Jesus' glorious name. Righteous Judge, based upon the aforementioned scriptures, it is clear that I qualify for a divine restraining order against the altar of *stagnation* and the idol that sits on it, in Jesus' name.

11. Ask the Court to Issue a Divine Restraining Order and Receive the Divine Restraining Order by Faith

Heavenly Father, Righteous Judge, I now ask that a divine restraining order and a permanent injunction against the spirit and altar of *stagnation* in my life would now be issued by the authority of Your Supreme Court, in Jesus' name. Heavenly Father, I decree and declare that any and all forms of spiritual or financial *stagnation* the devil has issued or is orchestrating against my life are now cancelled in Jesus' glorious name. Heavenly Father, I receive this divine restraining order and permanent injunction by faith, in Jesus' name. For it is written in the Constitution of Your Kingdom in Hebrews 11:6, *"But without faith it is impossible to [walk with God and] please Him, for whoever comes [near] to God must [necessarily] believe that God exists and that He rewards those who [earnestly and diligently] seek Him."* I believe and declare by faith that the spirit and altar of *stagnation* in my life has been judged, in Jesus' name!

12. Ask the Lord to Seal Your Righteous Verdict and Court Proceedings in the Blood of Jesus

Heavenly Father, Righteous Judge, I now ask You to seal my righteous verdict against the spirit and altar of *stagnation* in the precious blood of Jesus. May You also cover with the blood of Jesus all my legal proceedings in this Court in Jesus' name. I decree and declare that my righteous verdict of release and breakthrough from the evil altar of *stagnation* is now secured in the documents of the Courts of Heaven. For it is written in John's Gospel, chapter 8:36, *"So if the Son makes you free, then you are unquestionably free."* I decree and declare that I am free of the evil altar of *stagnation* in Jesus' name.

Prayer #3

Uprooting the Altar of Frustration

Let us not grow weary or become discouraged in doing good, for at the proper time we will reap, if we do not give in.

—**Galatians 6:9**

Have you ever been frustrated? It's not a very good feeling, is it? Frustration robs you of your peace of mind, while it simultaneously tries to smother you with a cloak of hopelessness. Frustration can also poison good and divine relationships that God assigned to your life. Dictionary.com rightfully defines *frustration* as "a feeling of dissatisfaction, often accompanied by anxiety or depression, resulting from unfulfilled needs or unresolved problems." So many well-meaning Christians are haunted by unending frustration—it seems like everything they touch gets frustrated by the enemy. I have seen them shed tears in front of me and throw up their arms as they resign themselves to a life of failure and mediocrity. I have never once believed this was God's lot for anyone this side of heaven. After God gave me revelation on the battle of altars, I saw repetitive frustration in some people's lives changed. I now know that most people whose efforts are frustrated by unseen forces are battling an evil altar of *frustration* that is speaking against them in the spiritual realm. I wrote this prayer for you!

Prayer of Activation

1. Address the Father in Praise and Worship

Heavenly Father, holy is Your name and greatly to be praised. I worship and adore You in Jesus' name. May Your Kingdom manifest in my life as it is in Heaven. Plead my cause, O Lord, with those who strive with me; fight against any entity or person who is contending against me. Heavenly Father, it is written in Psalm 27:6, *"And now my head will be lifted up above my enemies around me, in His tent I will offer sacrifices with shouts of joy; I will sing, yes, I will sing praises to the Lord."* Abba, I enjoin my worship to the heavenly chorus of worship of Your holy angels and the crowd of witnesses, in Jesus' name.

2. Ask for the Court to Be Seated

Heavenly Father, Righteous Judge, I ask that the Courts of Heaven be seated according to Daniel 7:9-10. I ask this in Jesus' mighty name. It is written:

> *I kept looking until thrones were set up, and the Ancient of Days (God) took His seat; His garment was white as snow and the hair of His head like pure wool. His throne was flames of fire; its wheels were a burning fire. A river of fire was flowing and coming out from before Him; a thousand thousands were attending Him, and ten thousand times ten thousand were standing before Him; the court was seated, and the books were opened.*

Heavenly Father, I am requesting the privilege of standing before the courtroom of the Ancient of Days according to what was revealed to the prophet Daniel, in Jesus' name, I pray. Heavenly Father, I stand in Your royal

courtroom because of the blood and finished work of Jesus on the cross. I have come to receive Your righteous judgment over my life against the spirit and altar of *frustration* that satan planted in my generational bloodline. Heavenly Father, I call upon Your holy angels to be witnesses to my lawsuit and righteous prosecution of the evil altar of *frustration*. I decree and declare that this evil altar of *frustration* will not frustrate the grace of God upon my life. Neither will it frustrate important divine relationships in my life; neither will it frustrate my career or business ventures, in Jesus' name I pray.

3. Surrender Your Rights to Self-Representation to the Lord as Your Advocate

Heavenly Father, Your Word in First John 2:1-2 says, *"My little children, these things I write to you, so that you may not sin. And if anyone sins, we have an Advocate with the Father, Jesus Christ the righteous. And He Himself is the propitiation for our sins, and not for ours only but also for the whole world."* I thank you that Jesus is my faithful Advocate before the Righteous Judge in the Courts of Heaven. Lord Jesus, I surrender my rights to self-represen-tation and summon You as my Advocate to help me plead my case before the Righteous Judge and prosecute the evil of altar of frustration that satan planted in my bloodline. I also ask the blessed Holy Spirit, who is the highest officer of the Courts of Heaven here on earth, to make me sensitive to the proceedings of this Court in order to successfully prosecute the evil altar of *frustration* in Jesus' name.

4. Summon the Evil Altar and the Idol That Sits on It to Appear in Court

Heavenly Father, even as I stand in Your royal courtroom I present myself as a living sacrifice, holy and acceptable before You according to Romans 12:1. Heavenly Father, Righteous Judge, I summon the altar of *frustration* in my bloodline and the idol that sits on it to appear in Your royal courtroom

to face prosecution in Jesus' name. For it is written in First Corinthians 6:3, *"Do you not know that we [believers] will judge angels? How much more then [as to] matters of this life?"* Heavenly Father, I exercise my God-given authority in Christ Jesus to judge demons and principalities, in Jesus' name I pray. Righteous Judge, it is also written in the Constitution of Your Kingdom in First John 3:8, *"For this purpose the Son of God was manifested, that He might destroy the works of the devil"* (NKJV).

5. Address Satan's Accusations and Agree with the Adversary

Heavenly Father, I know that until the end of the age of sin, satan still has legal access to the Courts of Heaven to level accusations against the children of men; for it is written in the book of Revelation 12:10:

> *Then I heard a loud voice in heaven, saying, "Now the salvation, and the power, and the kingdom (dominion, reign) of our God, and the authority of His Christ have come; for the accuser of our [believing] brothers and sisters has been thrown down [at last], he who accuses them and keeps bringing charges [of sinful behavior] against them before our God day and night."*

Heavenly Father, the Lord Jesus also said in the book of Matthew 5:25:

> *Come to terms quickly [at the earliest opportunity] with your opponent at law while you are with him on the way [to court], so that your opponent does not hand you over to the judge, and the judge to the guard, and you are thrown into prison.*

Heavenly Father, in all humility, while renouncing the spirit of pride, I choose to quickly agree with the legal accusations of my adversary, satan. Righteous Judge, every accusation that satan has filed against me and my bloodline in this Court is true.

6. Repent

Heavenly Father, I repent for my personal transgressions, and for the sins and iniquities of my forefathers that opened the door for the spirit and altar of *frustration* to oppress my life, in Jesus' name I pray. Lord, every sin of my forefathers that the enemy is using as a legal right to build cases against me and to deny me my destiny, I ask that the blood of Jesus would just wash them away. I also repent for self-inflicted word curses and all covenants with demons that have existed in my ancestral bloodline. I am asking that every covenant with demonic powers will now be revoked and that their right to claim me and my bloodline would now be dismissed before Your court, in Jesus' name. Thank You, Lord, for revoking these demonic covenants and evil altars in Jesus' mighty name! Heavenly Father, in my heartfelt desire to divorce myself from the spirit and altar of *frustration*, I give back everything and anything that the devil would say came from his kingdom. I only want what the blood of Jesus has secured for me.

7. Appeal to the Blood of Jesus to Wipe Out All Sin (Satan's Evidence)

Lord Jesus, thank You for cleansing me by Your blood so satan has no legal footing against me in Your courtroom. It is written in First John 1:9:

> If we [freely] admit that we have sinned and confess our sins,
> He is faithful and just [true to His own nature and promises],
> and will forgive our sins and cleanse us continually from all
> unrighteousness [our wrongdoing, everything not in confor-
> mity with His will and purpose].

Righteous Judge, I appeal to the blood of Jesus to wipe out all my short-comings, transgressions, and iniquities, in Jesus' name, I pray. I receive by faith the cleansing power of the blood of Jesus.

8. *Ask the Court to Dismiss All of Satan's Accusations and Charges*

Heavenly Father, based upon Jesus' finished work and my heartfelt repentance, I now move on the Court of Heaven to dismiss all of satan's accusations and charges against me and my bloodline in Jesus' name. For it is written that the accuser of the brethren has been cast down. So, I ask You Father to cast down all of satan's accusations against me, in Jesus' name, I pray.

9. *Ask the Lord to Send Angels to Destroy the Evil Altar and Execute the Lord's Judgment Against It*

Heavenly Father, Righteous Judge, I ask that You send high-ranking angelic officers of the Courts who excel in strength to execute the judgment of Your supreme court and destroy the evil altar of *frustration* and the idol that sits on it that satan planted in my bloodline, in Jesus' name I pray. By the spirit of prophecy, I prophesy the complete destruction of the evil altar of *frustration* in my life, in Jesus' name. For it is written in Psalm 91:11-12, *"For He will command His angels in regard to you, to protect and defend and guard you in all your ways [of obedience and service]. They will lift you up in their hands, so that you do not [even] strike your foot against a stone."* I receive angelic assistance, right now, in Jesus' name.

10. *Present Scriptures That Will Be Used in Issuing a Divine Restraining Order*

Heavenly Father, I present before Your Supreme Court the following scriptures as my rock-solid evidence against the spirit and altar of *frustration* in my life. It is written:

> *I do not frustrate the grace of God: for if righteousness come by the law, then Christ is dead in vain* (Galatians 2:21 KJV).

"No weapon that is formed against you will succeed; and every tongue that rises against you in judgment you will condemn. This [peace, righteousness, security, and triumph over opposition] is the heritage of the servants of the Lord, and this is their vindication from Me," says the Lord (Isaiah 54:17).

Righteous Judge, based upon the aforementioned scriptures, it is clear that the spirit and altar of *frustration*, if allowed to succeed, would cause great injury to my life, destiny, and also inflict irreparable damage to the purposes of God. I ask that that every legal right the spirit and altar of *frustration* is holding be revoked in Jesus' glorious name. Righteous Judge, based upon the aforementioned scriptures, it is clear that I qualify for a divine restraining order against the altar of *frustration* and the idol that sits on it, in Jesus' name.

11. Ask the Court to Issue a Divine Restraining Order and Receive the Divine Restraining Order by Faith

Heavenly Father, Righteous Judge, I now ask that a divine restraining order and a permanent injunction against the spirit and altar of *frustration* in my life would now be issued by the authority of Your Supreme Court, in Jesus' name. Heavenly Father, I decree and declare that any and all forms of *frustration* plans the devil has issued or is orchestrating against my life are now cancelled in Jesus' glorious name. Heavenly Father, I receive this divine restraining order and permanent injunction by faith, in Jesus' name. For it is written in the Constitution of Your Kingdom in Hebrews 11:6, *"But without faith it is impossible to [walk with God and] please Him, for whoever comes [near] to God must [necessarily] believe that God exists and that He rewards those who [earnestly and diligently] seek Him."* I believe and declare by faith that the spirit and altar of *frustration* in my life has been judged, in Jesus' name!

12. Ask the Lord to Seal Your Righteous Verdict and Court Proceedings in the Blood of Jesus

Heavenly Father, Righteous Judge, I now ask You to seal my righteous verdict against the spirit and altar of *frustration* in the precious blood of Jesus. May You also cover with the blood of Jesus all my legal proceedings in this Court in Jesus' name. I decree and declare that my righteous verdict of release and breakthrough from the evil altar of *frustration* is now secured in the documents of the Courts of Heaven. For it is written in John's Gospel, chapter 8:36, *"So if the Son makes you free, then you are unquestionably free."* I decree and declare that I am free of the evil altar of *stagnation* in Jesus' name, amen!

Prayer #4

Uprooting the Altar of Depression

Why are you in despair, O my soul? And why are you restless and disturbed within me? Hope in God and wait expectantly for Him, for I shall again praise Him, the help of my [sad] countenance and my God.

—Psalm 43:5

I attend a very vibrant church in Georgia. A while back one of our members killed himself inside his car in his garage, due to the depression he battled continuously. He finally decided his family was better off with him dead than alive—so he committed suicide! How tragic! A few years ago, my ministry received a $600 seed from a woman in Florida whom I had never met. Her seed came with a message in which she was thanking me profusely for my book *Breaking Generational Curses under the Order of Melchizedek*. Spiritual curiosity got the best of me, so I decided to call. The story she told me both broke my heart and filled me with hope at the same time. She told me that when she was in Kansas City visiting Mike Bickle's church, one of her friends gave her a copy of my book and told her how to "jump the bloodline" in order to break generational curses. She did it and her life changed drastically. Then she took it to a friend whose family struggled with bipolar disorder.

She told me that her friend's young sister had committed suicide with a gun because she was tired of living with bipolar disorder, with all its depressive mood swings. Her friend's sister's suicide triggered the bipolar disorder in the remaining sister who blamed herself for not stopping her sister's tragic death. *However,* after this woman led her friend in the prophetic act of jumping the bloodline to break curses, her friend got completely delivered from bipolar disorder and came off all the meds. The moral of this story is that there are many contributing factors as to why some battle with chronic depression. Chief among them is the presence of an evil altar of depression in their bloodline that has never been arrested in the Courts of Heaven. The following prayer is for everyone battling the evil altar of depression.

Prayer of Activation

1. Address the Father in Praise and Worship

Heavenly Father, holy is Your name and greatly to be praised. I worship and adore You in Jesus' name. May Your Kingdom manifest in my life as it is in Heaven. Plead my cause, O Lord, with those who strive with me; fight against any entity or person who is contending against me. Heavenly Father, it is written in Psalm 27:6, *"And now my head will be lifted up above my enemies around me, in His tent I will offer sacrifices with shouts of joy; I will sing, yes, I will sing praises to the Lord."* Abba, I enjoin my worship to the heavenly chorus of worship of Your holy angels and the crowd of witnesses, in Jesus' name.

2. Ask for the Court to Be Seated

Heavenly Father, Righteous Judge, I ask that the Courts of Heaven be seated according to Daniel 7:9-10. I ask this in Jesus' mighty name. It is written:

> *I kept looking until thrones were set up, and the Ancient of Days (God) took His seat; His garment was white as snow*

and the hair of His head like pure wool. His throne was flames of fire; its wheels were a burning fire. A river of fire was flowing and coming out from before Him; a thousand thousands were attending Him, and ten thousand times ten thousand were standing before Him; the court was seated, and the books were opened.

Heavenly Father, I am requesting the privilege of standing before the courtroom of the Ancient of Days according to what was revealed to the prophet Daniel, in Jesus' name, I pray. Heavenly Father, I stand in Your royal courtroom because of the blood and finished work of Jesus on the cross. I have come to receive Your righteous judgment over my life against the spirit and altar of *depression* that satan planted in my generational bloodline. Heavenly Father, I call upon Your holy angels to be witnesses to my lawsuit and righteous prosecution of the evil altar of *depression*. I decree and declare that this evil altar of *depression* will not cause my soul to be downcast; neither will it kill the joy of the Lord, which is my strength, in Jesus' name I pray.

3. Surrender Your Rights to Self-Representation to the Lord as Your Advocate

Heavenly Father, Your Word in First John 2:1-2 says, "*My little children, these things I write to you, so that you may not sin. And if anyone sins, we have an Advocate with the Father, Jesus Christ the righteous. And He Himself is the propitiation for our sins, and not for ours only but also for the whole world*" (NKJV). I thank You that Jesus is my faithful Advocate before the Righteous Judge in the Courts of Heaven. Lord Jesus, I surrender my rights to self-representation and summon You as my Advocate to help me plead my case before the Righteous Judge and prosecute the evil of altar of *depression* that satan planted in my bloodline. I also ask the blessed Holy Spirit, who is the highest officer of the Courts of Heaven here on earth, to make me sensitive to the proceedings of this Court in order to successfully prosecute the evil altar of *depression* in Jesus' name.

4. Summon the Evil Altar and the Idol That Sits on It to Appear in Court

Heavenly Father, even as I stand in Your royal courtroom I present myself as a living sacrifice, holy and acceptable before You according to Romans 12:1. Heavenly Father, Righteous Judge, I summon the altar of *depression* in my bloodline and the idol that sits on it to appear in Your royal courtroom to face prosecution in Jesus' name. For it is written in First Corinthians 6:3, *"Do you not know that we [believers] will judge angels? How much more then [as to] matters of this life?"* Heavenly Father, I exercise my God-given authority in Christ Jesus to judge demons and principalities, in Jesus' name I pray. Righteous Judge, it is also written in the Constitution of Your Kingdom in First John 3:8, *"For this purpose the Son of God was manifested, that He might destroy the works of the devil"* (NKJV).

5. Address Satan's Accusations and Agree with the Adversary

Heavenly Father, I know that until the end of the age of sin, satan still has legal access to the Courts of Heaven to level accusations against the children of men; for it is written in the book of Revelation 12:10:

> *Then I heard a loud voice in heaven, saying, "Now the salvation, and the power, and the kingdom (dominion, reign) of our God, and the authority of His Christ have come; for the accuser of our [believing] brothers and sisters has been thrown down [at last], he who accuses them and keeps bringing charges [of sinful behavior] against them before our God day and night."*

Heavenly Father, the Lord Jesus also said in the book of Matthew 5:25:

*Come to terms quickly [at the earliest opportunity] with your
opponent at law while you are with him on the way [to court],
so that your opponent does not hand you over to the judge, and
the judge to the guard, and you are thrown into prison.*

Heavenly Father, in all humility, while renouncing the spirit of pride,
I choose to quickly agree with the legal accusations of my adversary, satan.
Righteous Judge, every accusation that satan has filed against me and my
bloodline in this Court is true.

6. Repent

Heavenly Father, I repent for my personal transgressions, and for the
sins and iniquities of my forefathers that opened the door for the spirit
and altar of *depression* to oppress my life, in Jesus' name I pray. Lord, every
sin of my forefathers that the enemy is using as a legal right to build cases
against me and to deny me my destiny, I ask that the blood of Jesus would
just wash them away. I repent for focusing on my imperfections instead of
Jesus's finished work. I also repent for self-inflicted word curses and all covenants with demons of *depression* that have existed in my ancestral bloodline. I am asking that every covenant with demonic powers will now be
revoked and that their right to claim me and my bloodline would now be
dismissed before Your court, in Jesus' name. Thank You, Lord, for revoking these demonic covenants and evil altars of *depression* in Jesus' mighty
name! Heavenly Father, in my heartfelt desire to divorce myself from the
spirit and altar of *depression*, I give back everything and anything that the
devil would say came from his kingdom. I only want what the blood of
Jesus has secured for me.

7. *Appeal to the Blood of Jesus to Wipe Out All Sin (Satan's Evidence)*

Lord Jesus, thank You for cleansing me by Your blood so satan has no legal footing against me in Your courtroom. It is written in First John 1:9:

> *If we [freely] admit that we have sinned and confess our sins, He is faithful and just [true to His own nature and promises], and will forgive our sins and cleanse us continually from all unrighteousness [our wrongdoing, everything not in conformity with His will and purpose].*

Righteous Judge, I appeal to the blood of Jesus to wipe out all my shortcomings, transgressions, and iniquities, in Jesus' name, I pray. I receive by faith the cleansing power of the blood of Jesus.

8. *Ask the Court to Dismiss All of Satan's Accusations and Charges*

Heavenly Father, based upon Jesus' finished work and my heartfelt repentance, I now move on the Court of Heaven to dismiss all of satan's accusations and charges against me and my bloodline in Jesus' name. For it is written that the accuser of the brethren has been cast down. So, I ask You Father to cast down all of satan's accusations against me, in Jesus' name, I pray.

9. *Ask the Lord to Send Angels to Destroy the Evil Altar and Execute the Lord's Judgment Against It*

Heavenly Father, Righteous Judge, I ask that You send high-ranking angelic officers of the Courts who excel in strength to execute the judgment of Your supreme court and destroy the evil altar of *depression* and the idol that sits on it that satan planted in my bloodline, in Jesus' name I pray. By the spirit of prophecy, I prophesy the complete destruction of the evil altar of *depression* in my life, in Jesus' name. For it is written in Psalm 91:11-12, *"For He will command His angels in regard to you, to protect and defend and guard you in all your ways [of obedience and service]. They will lift you up in their hands, so that you do not [even] strike your foot against a stone."* I receive angelic assistance, right now, in Jesus' name.

10. Present Scriptures That Will Be Used in Issuing a Divine Restraining Order

Heavenly Father, I present before Your Supreme Court the following scriptures as my rock-solid evidence against the spirit and altar of depression in my life. It is written:

> *Then Ezra said to them, "Go [your way], eat the rich festival food, drink the sweet drink, and send portions to him for whom nothing is prepared; for this day is holy to our Lord. And do not be worried, for the joy of the Lord is your strength and your stronghold"* (Nehemiah 8:10).
>
> *A heart full of joy and goodness makes a cheerful face, but when a heart is full of sadness the spirit is crushed* (Proverbs 15:13).

Righteous Judge, based upon the aforementioned scriptures, it is clear that the spirit and altar of *depression*, if allowed to succeed, would cause great injury to my life, destiny, and also inflict irreparable damage to the purposes of God. I ask that that every legal right the spirit and altar of *depression* is holding be revoked in Jesus' glorious name. Righteous Judge, based upon the aforementioned scriptures, it is clear that I qualify for a divine restraining order against the altar of *depression* and the idol that sits on it, in Jesus' name.

11. Ask the Court to Issue a Divine Restraining Order and Receive the Divine Restraining Order by Faith

Heavenly Father, Righteous Judge, I now ask that a divine restraining order and a permanent injunction against the spirit and altar of *depression* in my life would now be issued by the authority of Your Supreme Court, in Jesus' name. Heavenly Father, I decree and declare that any and all forms of *depression* plans the devil has issued or is orchestrating against my life are now cancelled in Jesus' glorious name. Heavenly Father, I receive this divine restraining order and permanent injunction by faith, in Jesus' name. For it is written in the Constitution of Your Kingdom in Hebrews 11:6, *"But without faith it is impossible to [walk with God and] please Him, for whoever comes [near] to God must [necessarily] believe that God exists and that He rewards those who [earnestly and diligently] seek Him."* I believe and declare by faith that the spirit and altar of *depression* in my life has been judged, in Jesus' name!

12. Ask the Lord to Seal Your Righteous Verdict and Court Proceedings in the Blood of Jesus

Heavenly Father, Righteous Judge, I now ask You to seal my righteous verdict against the spirit and altar of *depression* in the precious blood of Jesus. May You also cover with the blood of Jesus all my legal proceedings in this Court in Jesus' name. I decree and declare that my righteous verdict of release and breakthrough from the evil altar of *depression* is now secured in the documents of the Courts of Heaven. For it is written in John's Gospel, chapter 8:36, *"So if the Son makes you free, then you are unquestionably free."* I decree and declare that I am free of the evil altar of *depression* in Jesus' name, amen!

Prayer #5

Uprooting the Altar of Sexual Perversion

Therefore God gave them over in the lusts of their own hearts to [sexual] impurity, so that their bodies would be dishonored among them [abandoning them to the degrading power of sin], because [by choice] they exchanged the truth of God for a lie, and worshiped and served the creature rather than the Creator, who is blessed forever! Amen.

—Romans 1:24-25

I did not live in the ancient city of Rome during the peak of the Roman Empire, so I cannot authoritatively speak to the level of sexual perversion in that city, even though historians say sex and prostitution were rampant in ancient Rome. However, I know this—today's culture is hyper-sexualized. Even simple commercials about cars, cosmetics, and food has a sexual connation attached to it. We are also living at a time in history when the ancient and sacred boundaries between male and female genders are collapsing under the weight of a global transgender movement determined to push the boundaries of sex and sexuality. To say that sexual perversion is rampant in this day and age is quite an understatement. Many Christian marriages are collapsing under the weight of extramarital affairs and addiction to pornography. Nevertheless, many of you reading this book want to a live a life of holiness before the Lord. If you discover that are you are struggling to stay sexually pure, it may be due to an evil altar of *sexual perversion* that satan planted in your bloodline. This powerful prayer of activation is for you. You can be delivered from being an attendant to the altar of sexual addiction.

Prayer of Activation

1. Address the Father in Praise and Worship

Heavenly Father, holy is Your name and greatly to be praised. I worship and adore You in Jesus' name. May Your Kingdom manifest in my life as it is in Heaven. Plead my cause, O Lord, with those who strive with me; fight against any entity or person who is contending against me. Heavenly Father, it is written in Psalm 27:6, *"And now my head will be lifted up above my enemies around me, in His tent I will offer sacrifices with shouts of joy; I will sing, yes, I will sing praises to the Lord."* Abba, I enjoin my worship to the heavenly chorus of worship of Your holy angels and the crowd of witnesses, in Jesus' name.

2. Ask for the Court to Be Seated

Heavenly Father, Righteous Judge, I ask that the Courts of Heaven be seated according to Daniel 7:9-10. I ask this in Jesus' mighty name. It is written:

> *I kept looking until thrones were set up, and the Ancient of Days (God) took His seat; His garment was white as snow and the hair of His head like pure wool. His throne was flames of fire; its wheels were a burning fire. A river of fire was flowing and coming out from before Him; a thousand thousands were attending Him, and ten thousand times ten thousand were standing before Him; the court was seated, and the books were opened.*

Heavenly Father, I am requesting the privilege of standing before the courtroom of the Ancient of Days according to what was revealed to the prophet Daniel, in Jesus' name, I pray. Heavenly Father, I stand in Your royal courtroom because of the blood and finished work of Jesus on the cross. I have come to receive Your righteous judgment over my life against the spirit and altar of *sexual perversion* that satan planted in my soul, DNA and generational bloodline. Heavenly Father, I call upon Your holy angels to be witnesses to my lawsuit and righteous prosecution of the evil altar of *sexual perversion*. I decree and declare that this evil altar of *sexual perversion* will not transform me into a sex addict or pervert a healthy view of the opposite sex, in Jesus' name I pray.

3. Surrender Your Rights to Self-Representation to the Lord as Your Advocate

Heavenly Father, Your Word in First John 2:1-2 says, "*My little children, these things I write to you, so that you may not sin. And if anyone sins, we have an Advocate with the Father, Jesus Christ the righteous. And He Himself is the propitiation for our sins, and not for ours only but also for the whole world*" (NKJV). I thank You that Jesus is my faithful Advocate before the Righteous Judge in the Courts of Heaven. Lord Jesus, I surrender my rights to self-representation and summon You as my Advocate to help me plead my case before the Righteous Judge and prosecute the evil of altar of *sexual perversion* that satan planted in my bloodline. I also ask the blessed Holy Spirit, who is the highest officer of the Courts of Heaven here on earth, to make me sensitive to the proceedings of this Court in order to successfully prosecute the evil altar of *sexual perversion* in Jesus' name.

4. *Summon the Evil Altar and the Idol That Sits on It to Appear in Court*

Heavenly Father, even as I stand in Your royal courtroom I present myself as a living sacrifice, holy and acceptable before You according to Romans 12:1. Heavenly Father, Righteous Judge, I summon the altar of *sexual perversion* in my bloodline and the idol that sits on it to appear in Your royal courtroom to face prosecution in Jesus' name. For it is written in First Corinthians 6:3, *"Do you not know that we [believers] will judge angels? How much more then [as to] matters of this life?"* Heavenly Father, I exercise my God-given authority in Christ Jesus to judge demons and principalities, in Jesus' name I pray. Righteous Judge, it is also written in the Constitution of Your Kingdom in First John 3:8, *"For this purpose the Son of God was manifested, that He might destroy the works of the devil"* (NKJV).

5. *Address Satan's Accusations and Agree with the Adversary*

Heavenly Father, I know that until the end of the age of sin, satan still has legal access to the Courts of Heaven to level accusations against the children of men; for it is written in the book of Revelation 12:10:

> *Then I heard a loud voice in heaven, saying, "Now the salvation, and the power, and the kingdom (dominion, reign) of our God, and the authority of His Christ have come; for the accuser of our [believing] brothers and sisters has been thrown down [at last], he who accuses them and keeps bringing charges [of sinful behavior] against them before our God day and night."*

Heavenly Father, the Lord Jesus also said in the book of Matthew 5:25:

> *Come to terms quickly [at the earliest opportunity] with your opponent at law while you are with him on the way [to court],*

so that your opponent does not hand you over to the judge, and the judge to the guard, and you are thrown into prison.

Heavenly Father, in all humility, while renouncing the spirit of pride, I choose to quickly agree with the legal accusations of my adversary, satan. Righteous Judge, every accusation that satan has filed against me and my bloodline in this Court is true.

6. Repent

Heavenly Father, I repent for my personal transgressions, and for the sins and iniquities of my forefathers that opened the door for the spirit and altar of *sexual perversion* to oppress my life, in Jesus' name I pray. Lord, every sin of my forefathers that the enemy is using as a legal right to build cases against me and to bind me to *sexual perversion*, I ask that the blood of Jesus would just wash them away. I also repent for self-inflicted word curses and all covenants with demons of *sexual perversion* that have existed in my ancestral bloodline. I am asking that every covenant with demonic powers will now be revoked and that their right to claim me and my bloodline would now be dismissed before Your court, in Jesus' name. Thank You, Lord, for revoking these demonic covenants and evil altars of *sexual perversion* in Jesus' mighty name! Heavenly Father, in my heartfelt desire to divorce myself from the spirit and altar of *sexual perversion*, I give back everything and anything that the devil would say came from his kingdom. I only want what the blood of Jesus has secured for me.

7. Appeal to the Blood of Jesus to Wipe Out All Sin (Satan's Evidence)

Lord Jesus, thank You for cleansing me by Your blood so satan has no legal footing against me in Your courtroom. It is written in First John 1:9:

If we [freely] admit that we have sinned and confess our sins, He is faithful and just [true to His own nature and promises], and will forgive our sins and cleanse us continually from all unrighteousness [our wrongdoing, everything not in confor-mity with His will and purpose].

Righteous Judge, I appeal to the blood of Jesus to wipe out all my short-comings, transgressions, and iniquities, in Jesus' name, I pray. I receive by faith the cleansing power of the blood of Jesus.

8. Ask the Court to Dismiss All of Satan's Accusations and Charges

Heavenly Father, based upon Jesus' finished work and my heartfelt repentance, I now move on the Court of Heaven to dismiss all of satan's accusations and charges against me and my bloodline in Jesus' name. For it is written that the accuser of the brethren has been cast down. So, I ask You Father to cast down all of satan's accusations against me, in Jesus' name, I pray.

9. Ask the Lord to Send Angels to Destroy the Evil Altar and Execute the Lord's Judgment Against It

Heavenly Father, Righteous Judge, I ask that You send high-ranking angelic officers of the Courts who excel in strength to execute the judgment of Your supreme court and destroy the evil altar of *sexual perversion* and the idol that sits on it that satan planted in my bloodline, in Jesus' name I pray. By the spirit of prophecy, I prophesy the complete destruction of the evil altar of *sexual perversion* in my life, in Jesus' name. For it is written in Psalm 91:11-12, *"For He will command His angels in regard to you, to protect and defend and guard you in all your ways [of obedience and service]. They will lift you up in their hands, so that you do not [even] strike your foot against a stone."* I receive angelic assistance, right now, in Jesus' name.

10. Present Scriptures That Will Be Used in Issuing a Divine Restraining Order

Heavenly Father, I present before Your Supreme Court the following scriptures as my rock-solid evidence against the spirit and altar of *sexual perversion* in my life. It is written:

> *For God has not called us to impurity, but to holiness [to be dedicated, and set apart by behavior that pleases Him, whether in public or in private]* (1 Thessalonians 4:7).
>
> *Continually pursue peace with everyone, and the sanctification without which no one will [ever] see the Lord* (Hebrews 12:14).

Righteous Judge, based upon the aforementioned scriptures, it is clear that the spirit and altar of *sexual perversion*, if allowed to succeed, would cause great injury to my life, destiny, and also inflict irreparable damage to the purposes of God. I ask that that every legal right the spirit and altar of *sexual perversion* is holding be revoked in Jesus' glorious name. Righteous Judge, based upon the aforementioned scriptures, it is clear that I qualify for a divine restraining order against the altar of *sexual perversion* and the idol that sits on it, in Jesus' name.

11. Ask the Court to Issue a Divine Restraining Order and Receive the Divine Restraining Order by Faith

Heavenly Father, Righteous Judge, I now ask that a divine restraining order and a permanent injunction against the spirit and altar of *sexual perversion* in my life would now be issued by the authority of Your Supreme Court, in Jesus' name. Heavenly Father, I decree and declare that any and all forms of *sexual perversion* plans the devil has issued or is orchestrating against my life are now cancelled in Jesus' glorious name. Heavenly Father,

I receive this divine restraining order and permanent injunction by faith, in Jesus' name. For it is written in the Constitution of Your Kingdom in Hebrews 11:6, *"But without faith it is impossible to [walk with God and] please Him, for whoever comes [near] to God must [necessarily] believe that God exists and that He rewards those who [earnestly and diligently] seek Him."* I believe and declare by faith that the spirit and altar of *sexual perversion* in my life has been judged, in Jesus' name!

12. Ask the Lord to Seal Your Righteous Verdict and Court Proceedings in the Blood of Jesus

Heavenly Father, Righteous Judge, I now ask You to seal my righteous verdict against the spirit and altar of *sexual perversion* in the precious blood of Jesus. May You also cover with the blood of Jesus all my legal proceedings in this Court in Jesus' name. I decree and declare that my righteous verdict of release and breakthrough from the evil altar of *sexual perversion* is now secured in the documents of the Courts of Heaven. For it is written in John's Gospel, chapter 8:36, *"So if the Son makes you free, then you are unquestionably free."* I decree and declare that I am free of the evil altar of *sexual perversion* in Jesus' name, amen!

Prayer #6

Uprooting the Altar of Poverty

The rich man's wealth is his fortress; the ruin of the poor is their poverty.

—Proverbs 10:15

My apostolic travels in my service to the cause of Christ have taken me, so far, to four continents of the world. I have yet to visit a country or a people who enjoy living in abject poverty. It goes without saying that no one enjoys poverty. This proves that the systemic poverty we see around the world is demonically engineered on so many levels. Proverbs 10:15 declares unequivocally that the ruin of the poor is their poverty! I have seen young girls throw themselves in the arms of men old enough to be their grandfathers in order to escape the clutches of poverty. While they are many reasons people are poor, one of the main culprits is the presence of evil altars of poverty in so many people's bloodlines. The good news is that Jesus became poor so that we through His poverty might be made rich. On the cross, Jesus paid the ultimate price to redeem us from the curse of the law, which included systemic poverty. Because of Jesus' finished work on the cross, we have the legal right to enter the Courts of Heaven to prosecute and overthrow all altars of poverty. This powerful prayer of activation is for you!

Prayer of Activation

1. Address the Father in Praise and Worship

Heavenly Father, holy is Your name and greatly to be praised. I worship and adore You in Jesus' name. May Your Kingdom manifest in my life as it is in Heaven. Plead my cause, O Lord, with those who strive with me; fight against any entity or person who is contending against me. Heavenly Father, it is written in Psalm 27:6, *"And now my head will be lifted up above my enemies around me, in His tent I will offer sacrifices with shouts of joy; I will sing, yes, I will sing praises to the Lord."* Abba, I enjoin my worship to the heavenly chorus of worship of Your holy angels and the crowd of witnesses, in Jesus' name.

2. Ask for the Court to Be Seated

Heavenly Father, Righteous Judge, I ask that the Courts of Heaven be seated according to Daniel 7:9-10. I ask this in Jesus' mighty name. It is written:

> *I kept looking until thrones were set up, and the Ancient of Days (God) took His seat; His garment was white as snow and the hair of His head like pure wool. His throne was flames of fire; its wheels were a burning fire. A river of fire was flowing and coming out from before Him; a thousand thousands were attending Him, and ten thousand times ten thousand were standing before Him; the court was seated, and the books were opened.*

Heavenly Father, I am requesting the privilege of standing before the courtroom of the Ancient of Days according to what was revealed to the prophet Daniel, in Jesus' name, I pray. Heavenly Father, I stand in Your royal

courtroom because of the blood and finished work of Jesus on the cross. I have come to receive Your righteous judgment over my life against the spirit and altar of *poverty* that satan planted in my generational bloodline. Heavenly Father, I call upon Your holy angels to be witnesses to my lawsuit and righteous prosecution of the evil altar of *poverty*. I decree and declare that this evil altar of *poverty* will not starve my God-given dreams or stop God-ordained destiny helpers from sowing finances into my life, in Jesus' name I pray.

3. Surrender Your Rights to Self-Representation to the Lord as Your Advocate

Heavenly Father, Your Word in First John 2:1-2 says, "*My little children, these things I write to you, so that you may not sin. And if anyone sins, we have an Advocate with the Father, Jesus Christ the righteous. And He Himself is the propitiation for our sins, and not for ours only but also for the whole world*" (NKJV). I thank You that Jesus is my faithful Advocate before the Righteous Judge in the Courts of Heaven. Lord Jesus, I surrender my rights to self-representation and summon You as my Advocate to help me plead my case before the Righteous Judge and prosecute the evil of altar of *poverty* that satan planted in my bloodline. I also ask the blessed Holy Spirit, who is the highest officer of the Courts of Heaven here on earth, to make me sensitive to the proceedings of this Court in order to successfully prosecute the evil altar of *poverty* in Jesus' name.

4. Summon the Evil Altar and the Idol That Sits on It to Appear in Court

Heavenly Father, even as I stand in Your royal courtroom I present myself as a living sacrifice, holy and acceptable before You according to Romans 12:1. Heavenly Father, Righteous Judge, I summon the altar of *poverty* in my bloodline and the idol that sits on it to appear in Your royal courtroom

to face prosecution in Jesus' name. For it is written in First Corinthians 6:3, *"Do you not know that we [believers] will judge angels? How much more then [as to] matters of this life?"* Heavenly Father, I exercise my God-given authority in Christ Jesus to judge demons and principalities, in Jesus' name I pray. Righteous Judge, it is also written in the Constitution of Your Kingdom in First John 3:8, *"For this purpose the Son of God was manifested, that He might destroy the works of the devil"* (NKJV).

5. Address Satan's Accusations and Agree with the Adversary

Heavenly Father, I know that until the end of the age of sin, satan still has legal access to the Courts of Heaven to level accusations against the children of men; for it is written in the book of Revelation 12:10:

> *Then I heard a loud voice in heaven, saying, "Now the salvation, and the power, and the kingdom (dominion, reign) of our God, and the authority of His Christ have come; for the accuser of our [believing] brothers and sisters has been thrown down [at last], he who accuses them and keeps bringing charges [of sinful behavior] against them before our God day and night."*

Heavenly Father, the Lord Jesus also said in the book of Matthew 5:25:

> *Come to terms quickly [at the earliest opportunity] with your opponent at law while you are with him on the way [to court], so that your opponent does not hand you over to the judge, and the judge to the guard, and you are thrown into prison.*

Heavenly Father, in all humility, while renouncing the spirit of pride, I choose to quickly agree with the legal accusations of my adversary, satan. Righteous Judge, every accusation that satan has filed against me and my bloodline in this Court is true.

6. Repent

Heavenly Father, I repent for my personal transgressions, and for the sins and iniquities of my forefathers that opened the door for the spirit and altar of *poverty* to oppress my life, in Jesus' name I pray. Lord, every sin of my forefathers that the enemy is using as a legal right to build cases against me and to deny me my destiny, I ask that the blood of Jesus would just wash them away. I repent for stinginess and anything that I have in common with the spirit of *poverty*. I also repent for self-inflicted word curses and all covenants with demons that have existed in my ancestral bloodline, especially covenants with the spirit of *poverty*. I am asking that every covenant with demonic powers will now be revoked and that their right to claim me and my bloodline would now be dismissed before Your court, in Jesus' name. Thank You, Lord, for revoking these demonic covenants and evil altars in Jesus' mighty name! Heavenly Father, in my heartfelt desire to divorce myself from the spirit and altar of *poverty*, I give back everything and anything that the devil would say came from his kingdom. I only want what the blood of Jesus has secured for me.

7. Appeal to the Blood of Jesus to Wipe Out All Sin (Satan's Evidence)

Lord Jesus, thank You for cleansing me by Your blood so satan has no legal footing against me in Your courtroom. It is written in First John 1:9:

> If we [freely] admit that we have sinned and confess our sins,
> He is faithful and just [true to His own nature and promises],
> and will forgive our sins and cleanse us continually from all
> unrighteousness [our wrongdoing, everything not in confor-
> mity with His will and purpose].

Righteous Judge, I appeal to the blood of Jesus to wipe out all my short-comings, transgressions, and iniquities, in Jesus' name, I pray. I receive by faith the cleansing power of the blood of Jesus.

8. *Ask the Court to Dismiss All of Satan's Accusations and Charges*

Heavenly Father, based upon Jesus' finished work and my heartfelt repentance, I now move on the Court of Heaven to dismiss all of satan's accusations and charges against me and my bloodline in Jesus' name. For it is written that the accuser of the brethren has been cast down. So, I ask You Father to cast down all of satan's accusations against me, in Jesus' name, I pray.

9. *Ask the Lord to Send Angels to Destroy the Evil Altar and Execute the Lord's Judgment Against It*

Heavenly Father, Righteous Judge, I ask that You send high-ranking angelic officers of the Courts who excel in strength to execute the judgment of Your supreme court and destroy the evil altar of *poverty* and the idol that sits on it that satan planted in my bloodline, in Jesus' name I pray. By the spirit of prophecy, I prophesy the complete destruction of the evil altar of *poverty* in my life, in Jesus' name. For it is written in Psalm 91:11-12, *"For He will command His angels in regard to you, to protect and defend and guard you in all your ways [of obedience and service]. They will lift you up in their hands, so that you do not [even] strike your foot against a stone."* I receive angelic assistance, right now, in Jesus' name.

10. Present Scriptures That Will Be Used in Issuing a Divine Restraining Order

Heavenly Father, I present before Your Supreme Court the following scriptures as my rock-solid evidence against the spirit and altar of *poverty* in my life. It is written:

> *For you are recognizing [more clearly] the grace of our Lord Jesus Christ [His astonishing kindness, His generosity, His gracious favor], that though He was rich, yet for your sake He became poor, so that by His poverty you might become rich (abundantly blessed)* (2 Corinthians 8:9).

> *Let them shout for joy and rejoice, who favor my vindication and want what is right for me; let them say continually, "Let the Lord be magnified, who delights and takes pleasure in the prosperity of His servant"* (Psalm 35:27).

Righteous Judge, based upon the aforementioned scriptures, it is clear that the spirit and altar of *poverty*, if allowed to succeed, would cause great injury to my life, destiny, and also inflict irreparable damage to the purposes of God. I ask that that every legal right the spirit and altar of *poverty* is holding be revoked in Jesus' glorious name. Righteous Judge, based upon the aforementioned scriptures, it is clear that I qualify for a divine restraining order against the altar of *poverty* and the idol that sits on it, in Jesus' name.

11. Ask the Court to Issue a Divine Restraining Order and Receive the Divine Restraining Order by Faith

Heavenly Father, Righteous Judge, I now ask that a divine restraining order and a permanent injunction against the spirit and altar of *poverty* in my life would now be issued by the authority of Your Supreme Court, in Jesus' name. Heavenly Father, I decree and declare that any and all forms of *poverty* the devil is orchestrating against my life is now cancelled in Jesus' glorious name. Heavenly Father, I receive this divine restraining order and permanent injunction by faith, in Jesus' name. For it is written in the Constitution of Your Kingdom in Hebrews 11:6, *"But without faith it is impossible to [walk with God and] please Him, for whoever comes [near] to God must [necessarily] believe that God exists and that He rewards those who [earnestly and diligently] seek Him."* I believe and declare by faith that the spirit and altar of *poverty* in my life has been judged, in Jesus' name!

12. Ask the Lord to Seal Your Righteous Verdict and Court Proceedings in the Blood of Jesus

Heavenly Father, Righteous Judge, I now ask You to seal my righteous verdict against the spirit and altar of *poverty* in the precious blood of Jesus. May You also cover with the blood of Jesus all my legal proceedings in this Court in Jesus' name. I decree and declare that my righteous verdict of release and breakthrough from the evil altar of *poverty* is now secured in the documents of the Courts of Heaven. For it is written in John's Gospel, chapter 8:36, *"So if the Son makes you free, then you are unquestionably free."* I decree and declare that I am free of the evil altar of *poverty* in Jesus' name, amen!

Prayer #7

Uprooting the Altar of Witchcraft

He made his sons pass through the fire [as an offering to his gods] in the Valley of Ben-hinnom; and he practiced witchcraft, used divination, and practiced sorcery, and dealt with mediums and spiritists. He did much evil in the sight of the Lord, provoking Him to anger.

—2 Chronicles 33:6

Perhaps of all the ancient evil vices there is no occultic craft that is as widely known as witchcraft. Unfortunately, witchcraft is a force to reckon with in any country of the world. In the United States of America in the month of October the entire country pays homage to the altar of witchcraft in the form of Halloween. I am convinced that many of the race riots we are now seeing on the streets of America are the chickens coming home to roost in a nation that celebrates witchcraft alongside the Bible. Coming out of Africa where witchcraft is practiced at a very high level, we lived under the fear of this oppressive force. Before I gave my life to Christ, I was attacked viciously by witches during my sleep. I would wake up feeling like I had just survived the Second World War or a strenuous marathon. In those days I dreaded going to sleep and hated the night. Thankfully, after I came to Christ, God gave me dominion over this spirit and people who operate under it. I have seen high-ranking witches give their life to Christ through my ministry.

Nevertheless, witchcraft is not limited to witches and wizards flying on mystical brooms in Harry Potter. Witchcraft can also manifest itself as a spirit of stubbornness toward the things of God or obeying the truth. First Samuel 15:23 (NKJV) says, *"For rebellion is as the sin of witchcraft,"* and Galatians 3:1 (NKJV) says, *"O foolish Galatians! Who has bewitched you that you should not obey the truth?"* From these two passages of Scripture it is clear that God hates these other forms of witchcraft as much He hates the occultic practices such as sorcery, incantations, casting spells, necromancy, star-gazing, astrology, fortune-telling, and so forth. The powerful prayer of activation below is meant to destroy the evil altars of witchcraft of any kind in your bloodline.

Prayer of Activation

1. *Address the Father in Praise and Worship*

Heavenly Father, holy is Your name and greatly to be praised. I worship and adore You in Jesus' name. May Your Kingdom manifest in my life as it is in Heaven. Plead my cause, O Lord, with those who strive with me; fight against any entity or person who is contending against me. Heavenly Father, it is written in Psalm 27:6, *"And now my head will be lifted up above my enemies around me, in His tent I will offer sacrifices with shouts of joy; I will sing, yes, I will sing praises to the Lord."* Abba, I enjoin my worship to the heavenly chorus of worship of Your holy angels and the crowd of witnesses, in Jesus' name.

2. *Ask for the Court to Be Seated*

Heavenly Father, Righteous Judge, I ask that the Courts of Heaven be seated according to Daniel 7:9-10. I ask this in Jesus' mighty name. It is written:

I kept looking until thrones were set up, and the Ancient of Days (God) took His seat; His garment was white as snow and the hair of His head like pure wool. His throne was flames of fire; its wheels were a burning fire. A river of fire was flowing and coming out from before Him; a thousand thousands were attending Him, and ten thousand times ten thousand were standing before Him; the court was seated, and the books were opened.

Heavenly Father, I am requesting the privilege of standing before the courtroom of the Ancient of Days according to what was revealed to the prophet Daniel, in Jesus' name, I pray. Heavenly Father, I stand in Your royal courtroom because of the blood and finished work of Jesus on the cross. I have come to receive Your righteous judgment over my life against the spirit and altar of *witchcraft* that satan planted in my generational bloodline. Heavenly Father, I call upon Your holy angels to be witnesses to my lawsuit and righteous prosecution of the evil altar of *witchcraft*. I decree and declare that this evil altar of *witchcraft* will not destroy me or my family members or stop us from pursuing our God-given destiny here on earth, in Jesus' name I pray.

3. Surrender Your Rights to Self-Representation to the Lord as Your Advocate

Heavenly Father, Your Word in First John 2:1-2 says, *"My little children, these things I write to you, so that you may not sin. And if anyone sins, we have an Advocate with the Father, Jesus Christ the righteous. And He Himself is the propitiation for our sins, and not for ours only but also for the whole world"* (NKJV). I thank You that Jesus is my faithful Advocate before the Righteous Judge in the Courts of Heaven. Lord Jesus, I surrender my rights to self-representation and summon You as my Advocate to help me plead my case before the Righteous Judge and prosecute the evil of altar of *witchcraft* that satan planted in my bloodline. I also ask the blessed Holy Spirit, who is the highest officer of the Courts of Heaven here on earth, to make me sensitive to the proceedings of this Court in order to successfully prosecute the evil altar of *witchcraft* in Jesus' name.

4. Summon the Evil Altar and the Idol That Sits on It to Appear in Court

Heavenly Father, even as I stand in Your royal courtroom I present myself as a living sacrifice, holy and acceptable before You according to Romans 12:1. Heavenly Father, Righteous Judge, I summon the altar of *witchcraft* in my bloodline and the idol that sits on it to appear in Your royal courtroom to face prosecution in Jesus' name. For it is written in First Corinthians 6:3, *"Do you not know that we [believers] will judge angels? How much more then [as to] matters of this life?"* Heavenly Father, I exercise my God-given authority in Christ Jesus to judge demons and principalities, in Jesus' name I pray. Righteous Judge, it is also written in the Constitution of Your Kingdom in First John 3:8, *"For this purpose the Son of God was manifested, that He might destroy the works of the devil"* (NKJV).

5. Address Satan's Accusations and Agree with the Adversary

Heavenly Father, I know that until the end of the age of sin, satan still has legal access to the Courts of Heaven to level accusations against the children of men; for it is written in the book of Revelation 12:10:

> *Then I heard a loud voice in heaven, saying, "Now the salvation, and the power, and the kingdom (dominion, reign) of our God, and the authority of His Christ have come; for the accuser of our [believing] brothers and sisters has been thrown down [at last], he who accuses them and keeps bringing charges [of sinful behavior] against them before our God day and night."*

Heavenly Father, the Lord Jesus also said in the book of Matthew 5:25:

Come to terms quickly [at the earliest opportunity] with your opponent at law while you are with him on the way [to court], so that your opponent does not hand you over to the judge, and the judge to the guard, and you are thrown into prison.

Heavenly Father, in all humility, while renouncing the spirit of pride, I choose to quickly agree with the legal accusations of my adversary, satan. Righteous Judge, every accusation that satan has filed against me and my bloodline in this Court is true.

6. Repent

Heavenly Father, I repent for my personal transgressions, and for the sins and iniquities of my forefathers that opened the door for the spirit and altar of *witchcraft* to oppress my life, in Jesus' name I pray. Lord, every sin of my forefathers that the enemy is using as a legal right to build cases against me and to deny me my destiny, I ask that the blood of Jesus would just wash them away. I repent for any time I have celebrated Halloween; consulted a medium, fortune-teller, tarot card reader, or psychic; or watched movies that were dedicated for the single purpose of glorying witchcraft. I repent for anytime I fantasied about being a witch or consulted with a necromancer in order to talk to dead loved ones, in Jesus' name I pray. I also repent for *witch-craft* that comes in the form of rebellion and not listening to the truth of the gospel of Christ. I also repent for self-inflicted word curses and all covenants with demons that have existed in my ancestral bloodline. I am asking that every covenant with demonic powers will now be revoked and that their right to claim me and my bloodline would now be dismissed before Your court, in Jesus' name. Thank You, Lord, for revoking these demonic cove-nants and evil altars in Jesus' mighty name! Heavenly Father, in my heartfelt desire to divorce myself from the spirit and altar of *witchcraft*, I give back everything and anything that the devil would say came from his kingdom. I only want what the blood of Jesus has secured for me.

7. *Appeal to the Blood of Jesus to Wipe Out All Sin (Satan's Evidence)*

Lord Jesus, thank You for cleansing me by Your blood so satan has no legal footing against me in Your courtroom. It is written in First John 1:9:

> *If we [freely] admit that we have sinned and confess our sins,*
> *He is faithful and just [true to His own nature and promises],*
> *and will forgive our sins and cleanse us continually from all*
> *unrighteousness [our wrongdoing, everything not in confor-*
> *mity with His will and purpose].*

Righteous Judge, I appeal to the blood of Jesus to wipe out all my short-comings, transgressions, and iniquities, in Jesus' name, I pray. I receive by faith the cleansing power of the blood of Jesus.

8. *Ask the Court to Dismiss All of Satan's Accusations and Charges*

Heavenly Father, based upon Jesus' finished work and my heartfelt repentance, I now move on the Court of Heaven to dismiss all of satan's accusations and charges against me and my bloodline in Jesus' name. For it is written that the accuser of the brethren has been cast down. So, I ask You Father to cast down all of satan's accusations against me, in Jesus' name, I pray.

9. *Ask the Lord to Send Angels to Destroy the Evil Altar and Execute the Lord's Judgment Against It*

Heavenly Father, Righteous Judge, I ask that You send high-ranking angelic officers of the Courts who excel in strength to execute the judgment of Your supreme court and destroy the evil altar of *witchcraft* and the idol that sits on it that satan planted in my bloodline, in Jesus' name I pray. By the spirit of prophecy, I prophesy the complete destruction of the evil altar of *witchcraft* in my life, in Jesus' name. For it is written in Psalm 91:11-12, *"For He will command His angels in regard to you, to protect and defend and guard you in all your ways [of obedience and service]. They will lift you up in their hands, so that you do not [even] strike your foot against a stone."* I receive angelic assistance, right now, in Jesus' name.

10. Present Scriptures That Will Be Used in Issuing a Divine Restraining Order

Heavenly Father, I present before Your Supreme Court the following scriptures as my rock-solid evidence against the spirit and altar of *witchcraft* in my life. It is written:

> *For there is no enchantment or omen against Jacob, nor is there any divination against Israel. At the proper time it shall be said to Jacob and to Israel, what has God done!* (Numbers 23:23)
>
> *You shall not allow a woman who practices sorcery to live* (Exodus 22:18).

Righteous Judge, based upon the aforementioned scriptures, it is clear that the spirit and altar of *witchcraft*, if allowed to succeed, would cause great injury to my life, destiny, and also inflict irreparable damage to the purposes of God. I ask that that every legal right the spirit and altar of *witchcraft* is holding be revoked in Jesus' glorious name. Righteous Judge, based upon the aforementioned scriptures, it is clear that I qualify for a divine restraining order against the altar of *witchcraft* and the idol that sits on it, in Jesus' name.

11. Ask the Court to Issue a Divine Restraining Order and Receive the Divine Restraining Order by Faith

Heavenly Father, Righteous Judge, I now ask that a divine restraining order and a permanent injunction against the spirit and altar of *witchcraft* in my life would now be issued by the authority of Your Supreme Court, in Jesus' name. Heavenly Father, I decree and declare that any form of *witchcraft*, whether it be white or black magic or enchantments, the devil has issued or is orchestrating against my life are now cancelled in Jesus' glorious name. Heavenly Father, I receive this divine restraining order and permanent injunction by faith, in Jesus' name. For it is written in the Constitution of Your Kingdom in Hebrews 11:6, *"But without faith it is impossible to [walk with God and] please Him, for whoever comes [near] to God must [necessarily] believe that God exists and that He rewards those who [earnestly and diligently] seek Him."* I believe and declare by faith that the spirit and altar of *witchcraft* in my life has been judged, in Jesus' name!

12. Ask the Lord to Seal Your Righteous Verdict and Court Proceedings in the Blood of Jesus

Heavenly Father, Righteous Judge, I now ask You to seal my righteous verdict against the spirit and altar of *witchcraft* in the precious blood of Jesus. May You also cover with the blood of Jesus all my legal proceedings in this Court in Jesus' name. I decree and declare that my righteous verdict of release and breakthrough from the evil altar of *witchcraft* is now secured in the documents of the Courts of Heaven. For it is written in John's Gospel, chapter 8:36, *"So if the Son makes you free, then you are unquestionably free."* I decree and declare that I am free of the evil altar of *witchcraft* in Jesus' name, amen!

Prayer #8

Uprooting the
Altar of Familiar Spirits

Regard not them that have familiar spirits, neither seek after wizards, to be defiled by them: I am the Lord your God.
—Leviticus 19:31 KJV

In the realm of spiritual warfare and deliverance, there are fewer things that are as sinister as familiar spirits. The reason is simple but deeply profound. As the name suggests, familiar spirits are derived from the phrase "family spirits." These are demonic spirits that are unique to a particular family or ancestry. These demonic spirits are very familiar with the history, character traits, idiosyncrasies, strengths, and weaknesses of a particular bloodline. Consequently, familiar spirits are also known as "surveillance spirits." They place the family under satanic surveillance, so that the intelligence gathered can be used against members of that family to keep them addicted or loyal to evil altars unique to that family bloodline or lineage. This is why so many people struggle to break certain habits or addictions, because as soon as they purpose to do so, these malicious familiar spirits go to work to inflame and exploit their weaknesses. Thankfully, these malicious spirits can be destroyed by destroying the evil altar they operate from. The following prayer is designed to do just that!

Prayer of Activation

1. Address the Father in Praise and Worship

Heavenly Father, holy is Your name and greatly to be praised. I worship and adore You in Jesus' name. May Your Kingdom manifest in my life as it is in Heaven. Plead my cause, O Lord, with those who strive with me; fight against any entity or person who is contending against me. Heavenly Father, it is written in Psalm 27:6, *"And now my head will be lifted up above my enemies around me, in His tent I will offer sacrifices with shouts of joy; I will sing, yes, I will sing praises to the Lord."* Abba, I enjoin my worship to the heavenly chorus of worship of Your holy angels and the crowd of witnesses, in Jesus' name.

2. Ask for the Court to Be Seated

Heavenly Father, Righteous Judge, I ask that the Courts of Heaven be seated according to Daniel 7:9-10. I ask this in Jesus' mighty name. It is written:

> *I kept looking until thrones were set up, and the Ancient of Days (God) took His seat; His garment was white as snow and the hair of His head like pure wool. His throne was flames of fire; its wheels were a burning fire. A river of fire was flowing and coming out from before Him; a thousand thousands were attending Him, and ten thousand times ten thousand were standing before Him; the court was seated, and the books were opened.*

Heavenly Father, I am requesting the privilege of standing before the courtroom of the Ancient of Days according to what was revealed to the prophet Daniel, in Jesus' name, I pray. Heavenly Father, I stand in Your royal

courtroom because of the blood and finished work of Jesus on the cross. I have come to receive Your righteous judgment over my life against the spirit and altar of *familiar spirits* that satan planted in my generational bloodline. Heavenly Father, I call upon Your holy angels to be witnesses to my lawsuit and righteous prosecution of the evil altar of *familiar spirits*. I decree and declare that this evil altar of *familiar spirits* will not subvert my God-given destiny or that of my family members, in Jesus' name I pray.

3. Surrender Your Rights to Self-Representation to the Lord as Your Advocate

Heavenly Father, Your Word in First John 2:1-2 says, "*My little children, these things I write to you, so that you may not sin. And if anyone sins, we have an Advocate with the Father, Jesus Christ the righteous. And He Himself is the propitiation for our sins, and not for ours only but also for the whole world*" (NKJV). I thank You that Jesus is my faithful Advocate before the Righteous Judge in the Courts of Heaven. Lord Jesus, I surrender my rights to self-representation and summon You as my Advocate to help me plead my case before the Righteous Judge and prosecute the evil of altar of *familiar spirits* that satan planted in my bloodline. I also ask the blessed Holy Spirit, who is the highest officer of the Courts of Heaven here on earth, to make me sensitive to the proceedings of this Court in order to successfully prosecute the evil altar of *familiar spirits* in Jesus' name.

4. Summon the Evil Altar and the Idol That Sits on It to Appear in Court

Heavenly Father, even as I stand in Your royal courtroom I present myself as a living sacrifice, holy and acceptable before You according to Romans 12:1. Heavenly Father, Righteous Judge, I summon the altar of *familiar spirits* in my bloodline and the idol that sits on it to appear in Your royal courtroom to face prosecution in Jesus' name. For it is written in

First Corinthians 6:3, *"Do you not know that we [believers] will judge angels? How much more then [as to] matters of this life?"* Heavenly Father, I exercise my God-given authority in Christ Jesus to judge demons and principalities, in Jesus' name I pray. Righteous Judge, it is also written in the constitution of Your Kingdom in First John 3:8, *"For this purpose the Son of God was manifested, that He might destroy the works of the devil"* (NKJV).

5. *Address Satan's Accusations and Agree with the Adversary*

Heavenly Father, I know that until the end of the age of sin, satan still has legal access to the Courts of Heaven to level accusations against the children of men; for it is written in the book of Revelation 12:10:

> *Then I heard a loud voice in heaven, saying, "Now the salvation, and the power, and the kingdom (dominion, reign) of our God, and the authority of His Christ have come; for the accuser of our [believing] brothers and sisters has been thrown down [at last], he who accuses them and keeps bringing charges [of sinful behavior] against them before our God day and night."*

Heavenly Father, the Lord Jesus also said in the book of Matthew 5:25:

> *Come to terms quickly [at the earliest opportunity] with your opponent at law while you are with him on the way [to court], so that your opponent does not hand you over to the judge, and the judge to the guard, and you are thrown into prison.*

Heavenly Father, in all humility, while renouncing the spirit of pride and all familiar spirits, I choose to quickly agree with the legal accusations of my adversary, satan. Righteous Judge, every accusation that satan has filed against me and my bloodline in this Court is true.

6. Repent

Heavenly Father, I repent for my personal transgressions, and for the sins and iniquities of my forefathers that opened the door for the spirit and altar of *familiar spirits* to oppress my life, in Jesus' name I pray. Lord, every sin of my forefathers that the enemy is using as a legal right to build cases against me and to deny me my destiny, I ask that the blood of Jesus would just wash them away. I repent for anything that I have in common with any familiar spirits in my bloodline. I also repent for self-inflicted word curses and all covenants with demons that have existed in my ancestral bloodline. I am asking that every covenant with demonic powers will now be revoked and that their right to claim me and my bloodline would now be dismissed before Your court, in Jesus' name. Thank You, Lord, for revoking these demonic covenants and evil altars in Jesus' mighty name! Heavenly Father, in my heartfelt desire to divorce myself from the spirit and altar of *familiar spirits*, I give back everything and anything that the devil would say came from his kingdom. I only want what the blood of Jesus has secured for me.

7. Appeal to the Blood of Jesus to Wipe Out All Sin (Satan's Evidence)

Lord Jesus, thank You for cleansing me by Your blood so satan has no legal footing against me in Your courtroom. It is written in First John 1:9:

> *If we [freely] admit that we have sinned and confess our sins,*
> *He is faithful and just [true to His own nature and promises],*
> *and will forgive our sins and cleanse us continually from all*
> *unrighteousness [our wrongdoing, everything not in confor-*
> *mity with His will and purpose].*

Righteous Judge, I appeal to the blood of Jesus to wipe out all my short-comings, transgressions, and iniquities, in Jesus' name, I pray. I ask that the blood of Jesus would wipe out all of satan's evidence gathered against me by *familiar spirits*. I receive by faith the cleansing power of the blood of Jesus.

8. Ask the Court to Dismiss All of Satan's Accusations and Charges

Heavenly Father, based upon Jesus' finished work and my heartfelt repentance, I now move on the Court of Heaven to dismiss all of satan's accusations and charges against me and my bloodline in Jesus' name. For it is written that the accuser of the brethren has been cast down. So, I ask You Father to cast down all of satan's accusations against me, in Jesus' name, I pray.

9. Ask the Lord to Send Angels to Destroy the Evil Altar and Execute the Lord's Judgment Against It

Heavenly Father, Righteous Judge, I ask that You send high-ranking angelic officers of the Courts who excel in strength to execute the judgment of Your supreme court and destroy the evil altar of *familiar spirits* and the idol that sits on it that satan planted in my bloodline, in Jesus' name I pray. By the spirit of prophecy, I prophesy the complete destruction of the evil altar of *familiar spirits* in my life, in Jesus' name. For it is written in Psalm 91:11-12, *"For He will command His angels in regard to you, to protect and defend and guard you in all your ways [of obedience and service]. They will lift you up in their hands, so that you do not [even] strike your foot against a stone."* I receive angelic assistance, right now, in Jesus' name.

10. Present Scriptures That Will Be Used in Issuing a Divine Restraining Order

Heavenly Father, I present before Your Supreme Court the following scriptures as my rock-solid evidence against the spirit and altar of *familiar spirits* in my life. It is written:

There shall not be found among you anyone who makes his son or daughter pass through the fire [as a sacrifice], one who uses divination and fortune-telling, one who practices witchcraft, or one who interprets omens, or a sorcerer (Deuteronomy 18:10).

"No weapon that is formed against you will succeed; and every tongue that rises against you in judgment you will condemn. This [peace, righteousness, security, and triumph over opposition] is the heritage of the servants of the Lord, and this is their vindication from Me," says the Lord (Isaiah 54:17).

Righteous Judge, based upon the aforementioned scriptures, it is clear that the spirit and altar of *familiar spirits*, if allowed to succeed, would cause great injury to my life, destiny, and also inflict irreparable damage to the purposes of God. I ask that that every legal right the spirit and altar of *familiar spirits* is holding be revoked in Jesus' glorious name. Righteous Judge, based upon the aforementioned scriptures, it is clear that I qualify for a divine restraining order against the altar of *familiar spirits* and the idol that sits on it, in Jesus' name.

11. Ask the Court to Issue a Divine Restraining Order and Receive the Divine Restraining Order by Faith

Heavenly Father, Righteous Judge, I now ask that a divine restraining order and a permanent injunction against the spirit and altar of *familiar spirits* in my life would now be issued by the authority of Your Supreme Court, in Jesus' name. Heavenly Father, I decree and declare that the assignment of every *familiar spirit* the devil has assigned against my life is now cancelled in Jesus' glorious name. Heavenly Father, I receive this divine restraining order and permanent injunction by faith, in Jesus' name. For it is written in the Constitution of Your Kingdom in Hebrews 11:6, *"But without faith it is impossible to [walk with God and] please Him, for whoever comes [near] to*

God must [necessarily] believe that God exists and that He rewards those who [earnestly and diligently] seek Him." I believe and declare by faith that the spirit and altar of *familiar spirits* in my life has been judged, in Jesus' name!

12. Ask the Lord to Seal Your Righteous Verdict and Court Proceedings in the Blood of Jesus

Heavenly Father, Righteous Judge, I now ask You to seal my righteous verdict against the spirit and altar of *familiar spirits* in the precious blood of Jesus. May You also cover with the blood of Jesus all my legal proceedings in this Court in Jesus' name. I decree and declare that my righteous verdict of release and breakthrough from the evil altar of *familiar spirits* is now secured in the documents of the Courts of Heaven. For it is written in John's Gospel, chapter 8:36, *"So if the Son makes you free, then you are unquestionably free."* I decree and declare that I am free of the evil altar of *familiar spirits* in Jesus' name, amen!

Prayer #9

Uprooting the Altar of Abuse

A soft and gentle and thoughtful answer turns away wrath, but harsh and painful and careless words stir up anger.

—Proverbs 15:1

God is not an abusive God! Nevertheless, there are many people, most especially women, who are living under this spirit's oppressive regime. Nowhere is this spirit more prominent than in marriages, even among so-called Christian marriages, where it transforms husbands into tyrannical dictators who treat their wives as though they are second-class citizens. Some wives or girlfriends are physically abused (beaten) under the influence of this tyrannical spirit. I have also seen husbands who are suffering under the banner of an abusive wife. According to Proverbs 15:1, the spirit of abuse usually manifests itself in harsh and painful words that are designed to injure and malign the soul of its victim. It can also manifest itself in the painful and willful neglect of children who are defenseless against the parent, guardian, or teacher who occupies a place of authority over them. While living in America, I came across several children who were being raised in very abusive foster homes. It's so sad. I have also been to countries that are suffering under a tyrannical, abusive government. The prayer below is designed to help you overthrow the evil altar of the abuser.

Prayer of Activation

1. *Address the Father in Praise and Worship*

Heavenly Father, holy is Your name and greatly to be praised. I worship and adore You in Jesus' name. May Your Kingdom manifest in my life as it is in Heaven. Plead my cause, O Lord, with those who strive with me; fight against any entity or person who is contending against me. Heavenly Father, it is written in Psalm 27:6, *"And now my head will be lifted up above my enemies around me, in His tent I will offer sacrifices with shouts of joy; I will sing, yes, I will sing praises to the Lord."* Abba, I enjoin my worship to the heavenly chorus of worship of Your holy angels and the crowd of witnesses, in Jesus' name.

2. *Ask for the Court to Be Seated*

Heavenly Father, Righteous Judge, I ask that the Courts of Heaven be seated according to Daniel 7:9-10. I ask this in Jesus' mighty name. It is written:

> *I kept looking until thrones were set up, and the Ancient of Days (God) took His seat; His garment was white as snow and the hair of His head like pure wool. His throne was flames of fire; its wheels were a burning fire. A river of fire was flowing and coming out from before Him; a thousand thousands were attending Him, and ten thousand times ten thousand were standing before Him; the court was seated, and the books were opened.*

Heavenly Father, I am requesting the privilege of standing before the courtroom of the Ancient of Days according to what was revealed to the prophet Daniel, in Jesus' name, I pray. Heavenly Father, I stand in Your royal

courtroom because of the blood and finished work of Jesus on the cross. I have come to receive Your righteous judgment over my life against the spirit and altar of *abuse* that satan planted in my generational bloodline. Heavenly Father, I call upon Your holy angels to be witnesses to my lawsuit and righteous prosecution of the evil altar of *abuse*. I decree and declare that this evil altar of *abuse* will not continue to control my will, mind, and emotions; neither will it control my responses to divine relationships that I need to achieve my God-given destiny here on earth, in Jesus' name I pray.

3. Surrender Your Rights to Self-Representation to the Lord as Your Advocate

Heavenly Father, Your Word in First John 2:1-2 says, "*My little children, these things I write to you, so that you may not sin. And if anyone sins, we have an Advocate with the Father, Jesus Christ the righteous. And He Himself is the propitiation for our sins, and not for ours only but also for the whole world*" (NKJV). I thank You that Jesus is my faithful Advocate before the Righteous Judge in the Courts of Heaven. Lord Jesus, I surrender my rights to self-representation and summon You as my Advocate to help me plead my case before the Righteous Judge and prosecute the evil of altar of *abuse* that satan planted in my bloodline. I also ask the blessed Holy Spirit, who is the highest officer of the Courts of Heaven here on earth, to make me sensitive to the proceedings of this Court in order to successfully prosecute the evil altar of *abuse* in Jesus' name.

4. Summon the Evil Altar and the Idol That Sits on It to Appear in Court

Heavenly Father, even as I stand in your royal courtroom I present myself as a living sacrifice, holy and acceptable before You according to Romans 12:1. Heavenly Father, Righteous Judge I summon the altar of *abuse* in my bloodline and the idol that sits on it to appear in your royal courtroom to face prosecution in Jesus' name. For it is written in First Corinthians 6:3, *"Do you not know that we [believers] will judge angels? How much more then [as to] matters of this life?"* Heavenly Father, I exercise my God-given authority in Christ Jesus to judge demons and principalities, in Jesus' name I pray. Righteous Judge it is also written in the Constitution of your Kingdom in First John 3:8, *"For this purpose the Son of God was manifested, that He might destroy the works of the devil"* (NKJV).

5. Address Satan's Accusations and Agree with the Adversary

Heavenly Father, I know that until the end of the age of sin, satan still has legal access to the Courts of Heaven to level accusations against the children of men; for it is written in the book of Revelation 12:10:

> *Then I heard a loud voice in heaven, saying, "Now the salvation, and the power, and the kingdom (dominion, reign) of our God, and the authority of His Christ have come; for the accuser of our [believing] brothers and sisters has been thrown down [at last], he who accuses them and keeps bringing charges [of sinful behavior] against them before our God day and night."*

Heavenly Father, the Lord Jesus also said in the book of Matthew 5:25:

> *Come to terms quickly [at the earliest opportunity] with your opponent at law while you are with him on the way [to court], so that your opponent does not hand you over to the judge, and the judge to the guard, and you are thrown into prison."*

Heavenly Father, in all humility, while renouncing the spirit of pride, I choose to quickly agree with the legal accusations of my adversary, satan. Righteous Judge, every accusation that satan has filed against me and my bloodline in this Court is true.

147

6. Repent

Heavenly Father, I repent for my personal transgressions, and for the sins and iniquities of my forefathers that opened the door for the spirit and altar of *abuse* to oppress my life, in Jesus' name I pray. Lord, every sin of my forefathers that the enemy is using as a legal right to build cases against me and to deny me my destiny, I ask that the blood of Jesus would just wash them away. I repent for any time I have operated in the spirit of *abuse*. I repent for every harsh word that injured another person's soul. I also repent for self-inflicted word curses and all covenants with demons that have existed in my ancestral bloodline. I am asking that every covenant with demonic powers will now be revoked and that their right to claim me and my bloodline would now be dismissed before Your court, in Jesus' name. Thank You, Lord, for revoking these demonic covenants and evil altars in Jesus' mighty name! Heavenly Father, in my heartfelt desire to divorce myself from the spirit and altar of *abuse*, I give back everything and anything that the devil would say came from his kingdom. I only want what the blood of Jesus has secured for me. I also forgive every person who ever abused me spiritually, emotionally and physically in Jesus name.

7. Appeal to the Blood of Jesus to Wipe Out All Sin (Satan's Evidence)

Lord Jesus, thank You for cleansing me by Your blood so satan has no legal footing against me in Your courtroom. It is written in First John 1:9:

> *If we [freely] admit that we have sinned and confess our sins, He is faithful and just [true to His own nature and promises], and will forgive our sins and cleanse us continually from all unrighteousness [our wrongdoing, everything not in conformity with His will and purpose].*

Righteous Judge, I appeal to the blood of Jesus to wipe out all my short-comings, transgressions, and iniquities, in Jesus' name, I pray. I receive by faith the cleansing power of the blood of Jesus.

8. *Ask the Court to Dismiss All of Satan's Accusations and Charges*

Heavenly Father, based upon Jesus' finished work and my heartfelt repentance, I now move on the Court of Heaven to dismiss all of satan's accusations and charges against me and my bloodline in Jesus' name. For it is written that the accuser of the brethren has been cast down. So, I ask You Father to cast down all of satan's accusations against me, in Jesus' name, I pray.

9. *Ask the Lord to Send Angels to Destroy the Evil Altar and Execute the Lord's Judgment Against It*

Heavenly Father, Righteous Judge, I ask that You send high-ranking angelic officers of the Courts who excel in strength to execute the judgment of Your supreme court and destroy the evil altar of *abuse* and the idol that sits on it that satan planted in my bloodline, in Jesus' name I pray. By the spirit of prophecy, I prophesy the complete destruction of the evil altar of *abuse* in my life, in Jesus' name. For it is written in Psalm 91:11-12, *"For He will command His angels in regard to you, to protect and defend and guard you in all your ways [of obedience and service]. They will lift you up in their hands, so that you do not [even] strike your foot against a stone."* I receive angelic assistance, right now, in Jesus' name.

10. Present Scriptures That Will Be Used in Issuing a Divine Restraining Order

Heavenly Father, I present before Your Supreme Court the following scriptures as my rock-solid evidence against the spirit and altar of *abuse* in my life. It is written:

> *I will give thanks and praise to You, for I am fearfully and wonderfully made; wonderful are Your works, and my soul knows it very well* (Psalm 139:14).
>
> *"For I will restore health to you and I will heal your wounds,"* says the Lord, *"because they have called you an outcast, saying: 'This is Zion; no one seeks her and no one cares for her'"* (Jeremiah 30:17).

Righteous Judge, based upon the aforementioned scriptures, it is clear that the spirit and altar of *abuse*, if allowed to succeed, would cause great injury to my life, destiny, and also inflict irreparable damage to the purposes of God. I ask that that every legal right the spirit and altar of *abuse* is holding on to be revoked in Jesus' glorious name. Righteous Judge, based upon the aforementioned scriptures, it is clear that I qualify for a divine restraining order against the altar of *abuse* and the idol that sits on it, in Jesus' name.

11. Ask the Court to Issue a Divine Restraining Order and Receive the Divine Restraining Order by Faith

Heavenly Father, Righteous Judge, I now ask that a divine restraining order and a permanent injunction against the spirit and altar of *abuse* in my life would now be issued by the authority of Your Supreme Court, in Jesus' name. Heavenly Father, I decree and declare that any and all forms of *abuse* plans the devil has issued or is orchestrating against my life are now cancelled in Jesus' glorious name. Heavenly Father, I receive this divine restraining order and permanent injunction by faith, in Jesus' name. For it is written in the Constitution of Your Kingdom in Hebrews 11:6, *"But without faith it is impossible to [walk with God and] please Him, for whoever comes [near] to God must [necessarily] believe that God exists and that He rewards those who [earnestly and diligently] seek Him."* I believe and declare by faith that the spirit and altar of *abuse* in my life has been judged, in Jesus' name!

12. Ask the Lord to Seal Your Righteous Verdict and Court Proceedings in the Blood of Jesus

Heavenly Father, Righteous Judge, I now ask You to seal my righteous verdict against the spirit and altar of *abuse* in the precious blood of Jesus. May You also cover with the blood of Jesus all my legal proceedings in this Court in Jesus' name. I decree and declare that my righteous verdict of release and breakthrough from the evil altar of *abuse* is now secured in the documents of the Courts of Heaven. For it is written in John's Gospel, chapter 8:36, *"So if the Son makes you free, then you are unquestionably free."* I decree and declare that I am free of the evil altar of *abuse* in Jesus' name, amen!

Prayer #10

Uprooting the Altar of Marriage Breakers

For this reason a man shall leave his father and his mother, and shall be joined to his wife; and they shall become one flesh. And the man and his wife were both naked and were not ashamed or embarrassed.

—**Genesis 2:24-25**

No human institution is more important this side of Heaven than the institution of marriage. God designed it to model the deepest level of intimacy and covenant that can exist between two people. Marriage was also designed to be a reflection of the relationship between Christ and the Church (see Eph. 5:31). Unfortunately, satan knows the mystery that marriage was ordained to carry, so satan has unleashed demonic entities to destroy this sacred institution. Divorce is as rampart among God's people as it is in the world. One of the demonic entities satan uses to destroy godly marriages is the altar of marriage breakers. This evil altar is serviced by mistresses, prostitutes, and sellers of pornography. God wants you to know how to insulate your marriage from this altar of marriage breakers. The prayer below was specifically designed to help you destroy the evil altars of marriage breakers in the Courts of Heaven. I am trusting God to turn your marriage around, in Jesus' name!

Prayer of Activation

1. Address the Father in Praise and Worship

Heavenly Father, holy is Your name and greatly to be praised. I worship and adore You in Jesus' name. May Your Kingdom manifest in my life as it is in Heaven. Plead my cause, O Lord, with those who strive with me; fight against any entity or person who is contending against me. Heavenly Father, it is written in Psalm 27:6, *"And now my head will be lifted up above my enemies around me, in His tent I will offer sacrifices with shouts of joy; I will sing, yes, I will sing praises to the Lord."* Abba, I enjoin my worship to the heavenly chorus of worship of Your holy angels and the crowd of witnesses, in Jesus' name.

2. Ask for the Court to Be Seated

Heavenly Father, Righteous Judge, I ask that the Courts of Heaven be seated according to Daniel 7:9-10. I ask this in Jesus' mighty name. It is written:

> *I kept looking until thrones were set up, and the Ancient of Days (God) took His seat; His garment was white as snow and the hair of His head like pure wool. His throne was flames of fire; its wheels were a burning fire. A river of fire was flowing and coming out from before Him; a thousand thousands were attending Him, and ten thousand times ten thousand were standing before Him; the court was seated, and the books were opened.*

Heavenly Father, I am requesting the privilege of standing before the courtroom of the Ancient of Days according to what was revealed to the prophet Daniel, in Jesus' name, I pray. Heavenly Father, I stand in Your royal

courtroom because of the blood and finished work of Jesus on the cross. I have come to receive Your righteous judgment over my life against the spirit and altar of *marriage breakers* that satan planted in my generational bloodline. Heavenly Father, I call upon Your holy angels to be witnesses to my lawsuit and righteous prosecution of the evil altar of *marriage breakers*. I decree and declare that this evil altar of *marriage breakers* will not break my marriage or the marriages of my family members, in Jesus' name I pray.

3. Surrender Your Rights to Self-Representation to the Lord as Your Advocate

Heavenly Father, Your Word in First John 2:1-2 says, *"My little children, these things I write to you, so that you may not sin. And if anyone sins, we have an Advocate with the Father, Jesus Christ the righteous. And He Himself is the propitiation for our sins, and not for ours only but also for the whole world"* (NKJV). I thank You that Jesus is my faithful Advocate before the Righteous Judge in the Courts of Heaven. Lord Jesus, I surrender my rights to self-representation and summon You as my Advocate to help me plead my case before the Righteous Judge and prosecute the evil of altar of *marriage breakers* that satan planted in my bloodline. I also ask the blessed Holy Spirit, who is the highest officer of the Courts of Heaven here on earth, to make me sensitive to the proceedings of this Court in order to successfully prosecute the evil altar of *marriage breakers* in Jesus' name.

4. Summon the Evil Altar and the Idol That Sits on It to Appear in Court

Heavenly Father, even as I stand in Your royal courtroom I present myself as a living sacrifice, holy and acceptable before You according to Romans 12:1. Heavenly Father, Righteous Judge, I summon the altar of *marriage breakers* in my bloodline and the idol that sits on it to appear in Your royal courtroom to face prosecution in Jesus' name. For it is written in

First Corinthians 6:3, *"Do you not know that we [believers] will judge angels? How much more then [as to] matters of this life?"* Heavenly Father, I exercise my God-given authority in Christ Jesus to judge demons and principalities, in Jesus' name I pray. Righteous Judge, it is also written in the Constitution of Your Kingdom in First John 3:8, *"For this purpose the Son of God was manifested, that He might destroy the works of the devil"* (NKJV).

5. Address Satan's Accusations and Agree with the Adversary

Heavenly Father, I know that until the end of the age of sin, satan still has legal access to the Courts of Heaven to level accusations against the children of men; for it is written in the book of Revelation 12:10:

> *Then I heard a loud voice in heaven, saying, "Now the salvation, and the power, and the kingdom (dominion, reign) of our God, and the authority of His Christ have come; for the accuser of our [believing] brothers and sisters has been thrown down [at last], he who accuses them and keeps bringing charges [of sinful behavior] against them before our God day and night."*

Heavenly Father, the Lord Jesus also said in the book of Matthew 5:25:

> *Come to terms quickly [at the earliest opportunity] with your opponent at law while you are with him on the way [to court], so that your opponent does not hand you over to the judge, and the judge to the guard, and you are thrown into prison."*

Heavenly Father, in all humility, while renouncing the spirit of pride, I choose to quickly agree with the legal accusations of my adversary, satan. Righteous Judge, every accusation that satan has filed against me and my bloodline in this Court is true.

6. Repent

Heavenly Father, I repent for my personal transgressions, and for the sins and iniquities of my forefathers that opened the door for the spirit and altar of *marriage breakers* to oppress my life, in Jesus' name I pray. Lord, every sin of my forefathers that the enemy is using as a legal right to build cases against me and to deny me my destiny, I ask that the blood of Jesus would just wash them away. Lord, I repent for sins of fornication and adultery in my life or bloodline. I repent for every moment that I participated in pornography or other sexual sins. I also repent for self-inflicted word curses and all covenants with demons that have existed in my ancestral bloodline. I am asking that every covenant with demonic powers will now be revoked and that their right to claim me and my bloodline would now be dismissed before Your court, in Jesus' name. Thank You, Lord, for revoking these demonic covenants and evil altars in Jesus' mighty name! Heavenly Father, in my heartfelt desire to divorce myself from the spirit and altar of *marriage breakers*, I give back everything and anything that the devil would say came from his kingdom. I only want what the blood of Jesus has secured for me.

7. Appeal to the Blood of Jesus to Wipe Out All Sin (Satan's Evidence)

Lord Jesus, thank You for cleansing me by Your blood so satan has no legal footing against me in Your courtroom. It is written in First John 1:9:

> *If we [freely] admit that we have sinned and confess our sins, He is faithful and just [true to His own nature and promises], and will forgive our sins and cleanse us continually from all unrighteousness [our wrongdoing, everything not in conformity with His will and purpose].*

Righteous Judge, I appeal to the blood of Jesus to wipe out all my short-comings, transgressions, and iniquities, in Jesus' name, I pray. I receive by faith the cleansing power of the blood of Jesus.

8. Ask the Court to Dismiss All of Satan's Accusations and Charges

Heavenly Father, based upon Jesus' finished work and my heartfelt repentance, I now move on the Court of Heaven to dismiss all of satan's accusations and charges against me and my bloodline in Jesus' name. For it is written that the accuser of the brethren has been cast down. So, I ask You Father to cast down all of satan's accusations against me, in Jesus' name, I pray.

9. Ask the Lord to Send Angels to Destroy the Evil Altar and Execute the Lord's Judgment Against It

Heavenly Father, Righteous Judge, I ask that You send high-ranking angelic officers of the Courts who excel in strength to execute the judgment of Your supreme court and destroy the evil altar of *marriage breakers* and the idol that sits on it that satan planted in my bloodline, in Jesus' name I pray. By the spirit of prophecy, I prophesy the complete destruction of the evil altar of *marriage breakers* in my life, in Jesus' name. For it is written in Psalm 91:11-12, *"For He will command His angels in regard to you, to protect and defend and guard you in all your ways [of obedience and service]. They will lift you up in their hands, so that you do not [even] strike your foot against a stone."* I receive angelic assistance, right now, in Jesus' name.

10. Present Scriptures That Will Be Used in Issuing a Divine Restraining Order

Heavenly Father, I present before Your Supreme Court the following scriptures as my rock-solid evidence against the spirit and altar of *marriage breakers* in my life. It is written:

> *So they are no longer two, but one flesh. Therefore, what God has joined together, let no one separate* (Matthew 19:6).
>
> *Marriage is to be held in honor among all [that is, regarded as something of great value], and the marriage bed undefiled [by immorality or by any sexual sin]; for God will judge the sexually immoral and adulterous* (Hebrews 13:4).

Righteous Judge, based upon the aforementioned scriptures, it is clear that the spirit and altar of *marriage breakers*, if allowed to succeed, would cause great injury to my life, destiny, and also inflict irreparable damage to the purposes of God. I ask that that every legal right the spirit and altar of *marriage breakers* is holding be revoked in Jesus' glorious name. Righteous Judge, based upon the aforementioned scriptures, it is clear that I qualify for a divine restraining order against the altar of *marriage breakers* and the idol that sits on it, in Jesus' name.

11. Ask the Court to Issue a Divine Restraining Order and Receive the Divine Restraining Order by Faith

Heavenly Father, Righteous Judge, I now ask that a divine restraining order and a permanent injunction against the spirit and altar of *marriage breakers* in my life would now be issued by the authority of Your Supreme Court, in Jesus' name. Heavenly Father, I decree and declare that any and all forms of *marriage breakers* plans the devil has issued or is orchestrating against my life are now cancelled in Jesus' glorious name. Heavenly Father,

I receive this divine restraining order and permanent injunction by faith, in Jesus' name. For it is written in the Constitution of Your Kingdom in Hebrews 11:6, *"But without faith it is impossible to [walk with God and] please Him, for whoever comes [near] to God must [necessarily] believe that God exists and that He rewards those who [earnestly and diligently] seek Him."* I believe and declare by faith that the spirit and altar of *marriage breakers* in my life has been judged, in Jesus' name!

12. Ask the Lord to Seal Your Righteous Verdict and Court Proceedings in the Blood of Jesus

Heavenly Father, Righteous Judge, I now ask You to seal my righteous verdict against the spirit and altar of *marriage breakers* in the precious blood of Jesus. May You also cover with the blood of Jesus all my legal proceedings in this Court in Jesus' name. I decree and declare that my righteous verdict of release and breakthrough from the evil altar of *marriage breakers* is now secured in the documents of the Courts of Heaven. For it is written in John's Gospel, chapter 8:36, *"So if the Son makes you free, then you are unquestionably free."* I decree and declare that I am free of the evil altar of *marriage breakers* in Jesus' name, amen!

Prayer #11

Uprooting the Altar of Infirmity

And behold, there was a woman who had a spirit of infirmity eighteen years, and was bent over and could in no way raise herself up.
—Luke 13:11 NKJV

In the above passage of Scripture, Jesus healed a woman who had a spirit of infirmity for eighteen years. This is a long time to be sick. The word *infirmity* in the passage literally means sickness caused by a demon. This is a clear biblical admission that some diseases are demonically engineered. For the most part, demonically engineered diseases do not respond to natural medicines because they are spiritual in nature. The most important aspects of this passage are the two phrases Jesus uses in effecting this woman's healing and deliverance. Jesus said, "Woman, you are loosed from your infirmity." Then He argued:

> So ought not this woman, being a daughter of Abraham, whom Satan has bound—think of it—for eighteen years, be loosed from this bond on the Sabbath?

The word "loosed" is a legal expression of law, which is often used when someone is released of their legal obligation by a judge. It becomes obvious that this demonically engineered disease came upon her because of an accusation satan brought against her in the Courts of Heaven. The name *satan* means "accuser" and carries the connation of one who brings a lawsuit. The most powerful phrase Jesus used, which placed this woman's lingering sickness under the jurisdiction of the Courts of Heaven, is the phrase "loosed from this bond." Legally speaking, a "bond" is usually a formal written agreement by which a person undertakes to perform a certain act such as appear in court or fulfill the obligations of a contract. So the spirit of infirmity came upon this woman because of a spiritual bond satan had placed her under that she couldn't pay. So Jesus, being a judge in the Courts of Heaven, "loosed her" from this terrible bond so He could heal her body. The prayer below is designed to do just that for you!

Prayer of Activation

1. Address the Father in Praise and Worship

Heavenly Father, holy is Your name and greatly to be praised. I worship and adore You in Jesus' name. May Your Kingdom manifest in my life as it is in Heaven. Plead my cause, O Lord, with those who strive with me; fight against any entity or person who is contending against me. Heavenly Father, it is written in Psalm 27:6, *"And now my head will be lifted up above my enemies around me, in His tent I will offer sacrifices with shouts of joy; I will sing, yes, I will sing praises to the Lord."* Abba, I enjoin my worship to the heavenly chorus of worship of Your holy angels and the crowd of witnesses, in Jesus' name.

2. Ask for the Court to Be Seated

Heavenly Father, Righteous Judge, I ask that the Courts of Heaven be seated according to Daniel 7:9-10. I ask this in Jesus' mighty name. It is written:

> *I kept looking until thrones were set up, and the Ancient of Days (God) took His seat; His garment was white as snow and the hair of His head like pure wool. His throne was flames of fire; its wheels were a burning fire. A river of fire was flowing and coming out from before Him; a thousand thousands were attending Him, and ten thousand times ten thousand were standing before Him; the court was seated, and the books were opened.*

Heavenly Father, I am requesting the privilege of standing before the courtroom of the Ancient of Days according to what was revealed to the prophet Daniel, in Jesus' name, I pray. Heavenly Father, I stand in Your royal courtroom because of the blood and finished work of Jesus on the cross. I have come to receive Your righteous judgment over my life against the spirit and altar of *infirmity* that satan planted in my generational bloodline. Heavenly Father, I call upon Your holy angels to be witnesses to my lawsuit and righteous prosecution of the evil altar of *infirmity*. I decree and declare that this evil altar of *infirmity* will not kill me or my family members before our appointed time, in Jesus' name I pray.

3. Surrender Your Rights to Self-Representation to the Lord as Your Advocate

Heavenly Father, Your Word in First John 2:1-2 says, "*My little children, these things I write to you, so that you may not sin. And if anyone sins, we have an Advocate with the Father, Jesus Christ the righteous. And He Himself is the propitiation for our sins, and not for ours only but also for the whole world*" (NKJV). I thank You that Jesus is my faithful Advocate before the Righteous Judge in the Courts of Heaven. Lord Jesus, I surrender my rights to self-representation and summon You as my Advocate to help me plead my case before the Righteous Judge and prosecute the evil of altar of *infirmity* that satan planted in my bloodline. I also ask the blessed Holy Spirit, who is the highest officer of the Courts of Heaven here on earth, to make me sensitive to the proceedings of this Court in order to successfully prosecute the evil altar of *infirmity* in Jesus' name.

4. Summon the Evil Altar and the Idol That Sits on It to Appear in Court

Heavenly Father, even as I stand in Your royal courtroom I present myself as a living sacrifice, holy and acceptable before You according to Romans 12:1. Heavenly Father, Righteous Judge, I summon the altar of *infirmity* in my bloodline and the idol that sits on it to appear in Your royal courtroom to face prosecution in Jesus' name. For it is written in First Corinthians 6:3, *"Do you not know that we [believers] will judge angels? How much more then [as to] matters of this life?"* Heavenly Father, I exercise my God-given authority in Christ Jesus to judge demons and principalities, in Jesus' name I pray. Righteous Judge, it is also written in the Constitution of Your Kingdom in First John 3:8, *"For this purpose the Son of God was manifested, that He might destroy the works of the devil"* (NKJV).

5. Address Satan's Accusations and Agree with the Adversary

Heavenly Father, I know that until the end of the age of sin, satan still has legal access to the Courts of Heaven to level accusations against the children of men; for it is written in the book of Revelation 12:10:

> *Then I heard a loud voice in heaven, saying, "Now the salvation, and the power, and the kingdom (dominion, reign) of our God, and the authority of His Christ have come; for the accuser of our [believing] brothers and sisters has been thrown down [at last], he who accuses them and keeps bringing charges [of sinful behavior] against them before our God day and night."*

Heavenly Father, the Lord Jesus also said in the book of Matthew 5:25:

Come to terms quickly [at the earliest opportunity] with your opponent at law while you are with him on the way [to court], so that your opponent does not hand you over to the judge, and the judge to the guard, and you are thrown into prison.

Heavenly Father, in all humility, while renouncing the spirit of pride, I choose to quickly agree with the legal accusations of my adversary, satan. Righteous Judge, every accusation that satan has filed against me and my bloodline in this Court is true.

6. Repent

Heavenly Father, I repent for my personal transgressions, and for the sins and iniquities of my forefathers that opened the door for the spirit and altar of *infirmity* to oppress my life, in Jesus' name I pray. Lord, every sin of my forefathers that the enemy is using as a legal right to build cases against me and to deny me my destiny, I ask that the blood of Jesus would just wash them away. I also repent for self-inflicted word curses and all covenants with demons of *infirmity* that have existed in my ancestral bloodline. I am asking that every covenant with demonic powers will now be revoked and that their right to claim me and my bloodline would now be dismissed before Your court, in Jesus' name. Thank You, Lord, for revoking these demonic covenants and evil altars in Jesus' mighty name! Heavenly Father, in my heartfelt desire to divorce myself from the spirit and altar of *infirmity*, I give back everything and anything that the devil would say came from his kingdom. I only want what the blood of Jesus has secured for me.

7. Appeal to the Blood of Jesus to Wipe Out All Sin (Satan's Evidence)

Lord Jesus, thank You for cleansing me by Your blood so satan has no legal footing against me in Your courtroom. It is written in First John 1:9:

If we [freely] admit that we have sinned and confess our sins, He is faithful and just [true to His own nature and promises], and will forgive our sins and cleanse us continually from all unrighteousness [our wrongdoing, everything not in conformity with His will and purpose].

Righteous Judge, I appeal to the blood of Jesus to wipe out all my shortcomings, transgressions, and iniquities, in Jesus' name, I pray. I receive by faith the cleansing power of the blood of Jesus.

8. Ask the Court to Dismiss All of Satan's Accusations and Charges

Heavenly Father, based upon Jesus' finished work and my heartfelt repentance, I now move on the Court of Heaven to dismiss all of satan's accusations and charges against me and my bloodline in Jesus' name. For it is written that the accuser of the brethren has been cast down. So, I ask You Father to cast down all of satan's accusations against me, in Jesus' name, I pray.

9. Ask the Lord to Send Angels to Destroy the Evil Altar and Execute the Lord's Judgment Against It

Heavenly Father, Righteous Judge, I ask that You send high-ranking angelic officers of the Courts who excel in strength to execute the judgment of Your supreme court and destroy the evil altar of *infirmity* and the idol that sits on it that satan planted in my bloodline, in Jesus' name I pray. By the spirit of prophecy, I prophesy the complete destruction of the evil altar of *infirmity* in my life, in Jesus' name. For it is written in Psalm 91:11-12, *"For He will command His angels in regard to you, to protect and defend and guard you in all your ways [of obedience and service]. They will lift you up in their hands, so that you do not [even] strike your foot against a stone."* I receive angelic assistance, right now, in Jesus' name.

10. Present Scriptures That Will Be Used in Issuing a Divine Restraining Order

Heavenly Father, I present before Your Supreme Court the following scriptures as my rock-solid evidence against the spirit and altar of *infirmity* in my life. It is written:

> But when Jesus saw her, He called her to Him and said to her, *"Woman, you are loosed from your infirmity."* And He laid His hands on her, and immediately she was made straight, and glorified God (Luke 13:12-13 NKJV).
>
> But He was wounded for our transgressions, He was crushed for our wickedness [our sin, our injustice, our wrongdoing]; the punishment [required] for our well-being fell on Him, and by His stripes (wounds) we are healed (Isaiah 53:5).

Righteous Judge, based upon the aforementioned scriptures, it is clear that the spirit and altar of *infirmity*, if allowed to succeed, would cause great injury to my life, destiny, and also inflict irreparable damage to the purposes of God. I ask that that every legal right the spirit and altar of *infirmity* is holding be revoked in Jesus' glorious name. Righteous Judge, based upon the aforementioned scriptures, it is clear that I qualify for a divine restraining order against the altar of *infirmity* and the idol that sits on it, in Jesus' name.

11. Ask the Court to Issue a Divine Restraining Order and Receive the Divine Restraining Order by Faith

Heavenly Father, Righteous Judge, I now ask that a divine restraining order and a permanent injunction against the spirit and altar of *infirmity* in my life would now be issued by the authority of Your Supreme Court, in Jesus' name. Heavenly Father, I decree and declare that any and all forms of *infirmity* plans the devil has issued or is orchestrating against my life are now cancelled in Jesus' glorious name. Heavenly Father, I receive this divine restraining order and permanent injunction by faith, in Jesus' name. For it is written in the Constitution of Your Kingdom in Hebrews 11:6, *"But without faith it is impossible to [walk with God and] please Him, for whoever comes [near] to God must [necessarily] believe that God exists and that He rewards those who [earnestly and diligently] seek Him."* I believe and declare by faith that the spirit and altar of *infirmity* in my life has been judged, in Jesus' name!

12. Ask the Lord to Seal Your Righteous Verdict and Court Proceedings in the Blood of Jesus

Heavenly Father, Righteous Judge, I now ask You to seal my righteous verdict against the spirit and altar of *infirmity* in the precious blood of Jesus. May You also cover with the blood of Jesus all my legal proceedings in this Court in Jesus' name. I decree and declare that my righteous verdict of release and breakthrough from the evil altar of *infirmity* is now secured in the documents of the Courts of Heaven. For it is written in John's Gospel, chapter 8:36, *"So if the Son makes you free, then you are unquestionably free."* I decree and declare that I am free of the evil altar of *infirmity* in Jesus' name, amen!

Prayer #12

Uprooting the Altar of Forgetfulness

For he who lacks these things is shortsighted, even to blindness, and has forgotten that he was cleansed from his old sins.

—2 Peter 1:9 NKJV

Have you ever forgotten a piece of priceless jewelry, such as a wedding ring, and found yourself searching frantically for it? The emotional relief you feel when you find it is only surpassed by the pain of not finding it. A while back I went to take my clothes to my neighborhood dry cleaners. I parked my truck, then placed my latest Galaxy 10 phone on the roof of my truck while I pulled my dirty clothes from the back seat. Unfortunately for me, when I went back to my truck, I drove off and forgot that my new phone was still on the roof. Miles away it suddenly dawned on me that I had forgotten my phone. I panicked and a sinking feeling came over me. I called my missing phone several times, hoping that a good Samaritan had picked it up. No one answered the phone, which was not a good sign. I drove back to the cleaners but never found it. I was so upset with myself for forgetting to take it off the roof of my truck. I ended up paying more money for another phone. I know people who lost out of very important business opportunities just because they forgot the time of their appointment. I have heard horror stories of mothers whose children were kidnapped at shopping malls just because in the busyness of shopping they forgot to look in the direction of their children for a few minutes. What about people who missed important flights to strategic assignments because when they got to the counter they suddenly realized they had forgotten their passports? A certain dear sister I know would have been very wealthy by now, because she was one of the first people to invest in Bitcoin to the tune of thousands. Her returns would have been more than 1,000 percent except for the fact that she forgot where she placed the username and password to her Bitcoin account. For years she searched frantically for this piece of paper and never found it. She recently died without having found the key to her secret wealth. Without a shadow of a doubt, the altar of forgetfulness has cost many people life, fortunes, relationships, opportunities, and so forth. The prayer below is the antidote you need.

Prayer of Activation

1. Address the Father in Praise and Worship

Heavenly Father, holy is Your name and greatly to be praised. I worship and adore You in Jesus' name. May Your Kingdom manifest in my life as it is in Heaven. Plead my cause, O Lord, with those who strive with me; fight against any entity or person who is contending against me. Heavenly Father, it is written in Psalm 27:6, *"And now my head will be lifted up above my enemies around me, in His tent I will offer sacrifices with shouts of joy; I will sing, yes, I will sing praises to the Lord."* Abba, I enjoin my worship to the heavenly chorus of worship of Your holy angels and the crowd of witnesses, in Jesus' name.

2. Ask for the Court to Be Seated

Heavenly Father, Righteous Judge, I ask that the Courts of Heaven be seated according to Daniel 7:9-10. I ask this in Jesus' mighty name. It is written:

I kept looking until thrones were set up, and the Ancient of Days (God) took His seat; His garment was white as snow and the hair of His head like pure wool. His throne was flames of fire; its wheels were a burning fire. A river of fire was flowing and coming out from before Him; a thousand thousands were attending Him, and ten thousand times ten thousand were standing before Him; the court was seated, and the books were opened.

Heavenly Father, I am requesting the privilege of standing before the courtroom of the Ancient of Days according to what was revealed to the prophet Daniel, in Jesus' name, I pray. Heavenly Father, I stand in Your royal courtroom because of the blood and finished work of Jesus on the cross. I have come to receive Your righteous judgment over my life against the spirit and altar of *forgetfulness* that satan planted in my generational bloodline. Heavenly Father, I call upon Your holy angels to be witnesses to my lawsuit and righteous prosecution of the evil altar of *forgetfulness*. I decree and declare that this evil altar of *forgetfulness* will not control my life anymore or arrest the remembrance of memories that I need to achieve my God-given destiny here on earth, in Jesus' name I pray.

3. Surrender Your Rights to Self-Representation to the Lord as Your Advocate

Heavenly Father, Your Word in First John 2:1-2 says, "*My little children, these things I write to you, so that you may not sin. And if anyone sins, we have an Advocate with the Father, Jesus Christ the righteous. And He Himself is the propitiation for our sins, and not for ours only but also for the whole world*" (NKJV). I thank You that Jesus is my faithful Advocate before the Righteous Judge in the Courts of Heaven. Lord Jesus, I surrender my rights to self-representation and summon You as my Advocate to help me plead my case before the Righteous Judge and prosecute the evil of altar of *forgetfulness* that satan planted in my bloodline. I also ask the blessed Holy Spirit, who is the highest officer of the Courts of Heaven here on earth, to make me sensitive to the proceedings of this Court in order to successfully prosecute the evil altar of *forgetfulness* in Jesus' name.

4. Summon the Evil Altar and the Idol That Sits on It to Appear in Court

Heavenly Father, even as I stand in Your royal courtroom I present myself as a living sacrifice, holy and acceptable before You according to Romans 12:1. Heavenly Father, Righteous Judge, I summon the altar of *forgetfulness* in my bloodline and the idol that sits on it to appear in Your royal courtroom to face prosecution in Jesus' name. For it is written in First Corinthians 6:3, *"Do you not know that we [believers] will judge angels? How much more then [as to] matters of this life?"* Heavenly Father, I exercise my God-given authority in Christ Jesus to judge demons and principalities, in Jesus' name I pray. Righteous Judge, it is also written in the constitution of Your Kingdom in First John 3:8, *"For this purpose the Son of God was manifested, that He might destroy the works of the devil"* (NKJV).

5. Address Satan's Accusations and Agree with the Adversary

Heavenly Father, I know that until the end of the age of sin, satan still has legal access to the Courts of Heaven to level accusations against the children of men; for it is written in the book of Revelation 12:10:

> *Then I heard a loud voice in heaven, saying, "Now the salvation, and the power, and the kingdom (dominion, reign) of our God, and the authority of His Christ have come; for the accuser of our [believing] brothers and sisters has been thrown down [at last], he who accuses them and keeps bringing charges [of sinful behavior] against them before our God day and night."*

Heavenly Father, the Lord Jesus also said in the book of Matthew 5:25:

> *Come to terms quickly [at the earliest opportunity] with your opponent at law while you are with him on the way [to court], so that your opponent does not hand you over to the judge, and the judge to the guard, and you are thrown into prison."*

Heavenly Father, in all humility, while renouncing the spirit of pride, I choose to quickly agree with the legal accusations of my adversary, satan. Righteous Judge, every accusation that satan has filed against me and my bloodline in this Court is true.

6. Repent

Heavenly Father, I repent for my personal transgressions, and for the sins and iniquities of my forefathers that opened the door for the spirit and altar of *forgetfulness* to oppress my life, in Jesus' name I pray. Lord, every sin of my forefathers that the enemy is using as a legal right to build cases against me and to deny me my destiny, I ask that the blood of Jesus would just wash them away. I repent for anyone who has been hurt by my forgetfulness. I also repent for self-inflicted word curses and all covenants with demons that have existed in my ancestral bloodline. I am asking that every covenant with demonic powers will now be revoked and that their right to claim me and my bloodline would now be dismissed before Your court, in Jesus' name. Thank You, Lord, for revoking these demonic covenants and evil altars in Jesus' mighty name! Heavenly Father, in my heartfelt desire to divorce myself from the spirit and altar of *forgetfulness*, I give back everything and anything that the devil would say came from his kingdom. I only want what the blood of Jesus has secured for me.

7. *Appeal to the Blood of Jesus to Wipe Out All Sin (Satan's Evidence)*

Lord Jesus, thank You for cleansing me by Your blood so satan has no legal footing against me in Your courtroom. It is written in First John 1:9:

> *If we [freely] admit that we have sinned and confess our sins, He is faithful and just [true to His own nature and promises], and will forgive our sins and cleanse us continually from all unrighteousness [our wrongdoing, everything not in conformity with His will and purpose].*

Righteous Judge, I appeal to the blood of Jesus to wipe out all my shortcomings, transgressions, and iniquities, in Jesus' name, I pray. I receive by faith the cleansing power of the blood of Jesus.

8. *Ask the Court to Dismiss All of Satan's Accusations and Charges*

Heavenly Father, based upon Jesus' finished work and my heartfelt repentance, I now move on the Court of Heaven to dismiss all of satan's accusations and charges against me and my bloodline in Jesus' name. For it is written that the accuser of the brethren has been cast down. So, I ask You Father to cast down all of satan's accusations against me, in Jesus' name, I pray.

9. *Ask the Lord to Send Angels to Destroy the Evil Altar and Execute the Lord's Judgment Against It*

Heavenly Father, Righteous Judge, I ask that You send high-ranking angelic officers of the Courts who excel in strength to execute the judgment of Your supreme court and destroy the evil altar of *forgetfulness* and the idol that sits on it that satan planted in my bloodline, in Jesus' name I pray. By the spirit of prophecy, I prophesy the complete destruction of the evil altar of *forgetfulness* in my life, in Jesus' name. For it is written in Psalm 91:11-12, *"For He will command His angels in regard to you, to protect and defend and guard you in all your ways [of obedience and service]. They will lift you up in their hands, so that you do not [even] strike your foot against a stone."* I receive angelic assistance, right now, in Jesus' name.

10. Present Scriptures That Will Be Used in Issuing a Divine Restraining Order

Heavenly Father, I present before Your Supreme Court the following scriptures as my rock-solid evidence against the spirit and altar of *forgetfulness* in my life. It is written:

> But the Comforter, which is the Holy Ghost, whom the Father will send in my name, he shall teach you all things, and bring all things to your remembrance, whatsoever I have said unto you (John 14:26 KJV).
>
> The memory of the just is blessed: but the name of the wicked shall rot (Proverbs 10:7 KJV).

Righteous Judge, based upon the aforementioned scriptures, it is clear that the spirit and altar of *forgetfulness*, if allowed to succeed, would cause great injury to my life, destiny, and also inflict irreparable damage to the purposes of God. I ask that that every legal right the spirit and altar of *forgetfulness* is holding be revoked in Jesus' glorious name. Righteous Judge, based upon the aforementioned scriptures, it is clear that I qualify for a divine restraining order against the altar of *forgetfulness* and the idol that sits on it, in Jesus' name.

11. Ask the Court to Issue a Divine Restraining Order and Receive the Divine Restraining Order by Faith

Heavenly Father, Righteous Judge, I now ask that a divine restraining order and a permanent injunction against the spirit and altar of *forgetfulness* in my life would now be issued by the authority of Your Supreme Court, in Jesus' name. Heavenly Father, I decree and declare that any and all forms of *forgetfulness* plans the devil has issued or is orchestrating against my life are now cancelled in Jesus' glorious name. Heavenly Father, I receive this divine restraining order and permanent injunction by faith, in Jesus' name. For it is written in the Constitution of Your Kingdom in Hebrews 11:6, *"But without faith it is impossible to [walk with God and] please Him, for whoever comes [near] to God must [necessarily] believe that God exists and that He rewards those who [earnestly and diligently] seek Him."* I believe and declare by faith that the spirit and altar of *forgetfulness* in my life has been judged, in Jesus' name!

12. Ask the Lord to Seal Your Righteous Verdict and Court Proceedings in the Blood of Jesus

Heavenly Father, Righteous Judge, I now ask You to seal my righteous verdict against the spirit and altar of *forgetfulness* in the precious blood of Jesus. May You also cover with the blood of Jesus all my legal proceedings in this Court in Jesus' name. I decree and declare that my righteous verdict of release and breakthrough from the evil altar of *forgetfulness* is now secured in the documents of the Courts of Heaven. For it is written in John's Gospel, chapter 8:36, *"So if the Son makes you free, then you are unquestionably free."* I decree and declare that I am free of the evil altar of *forgetfulness* in Jesus' name, amen!

Prayer #13

Uprooting the Altar of Failure

So Saul died for his trespass which he committed against the Lord, for his *failure* to keep the word of the Lord; and also because he consulted a medium [regarding a spirit of the dead], to inquire of her.
—1 Chronicles 10:13

No one really wants to fail and yet failure is a common human experience. To fail means to flounder at something you were supposed to succeed at. Even though failure is a common human experience, for some people failure is tragically systemic and borderline demonic. It seems everything that they put their hands on ends in abject failure. Failure at a business venture, for instance, could lead to massive financial losses and even bankruptcy. Failure at the relationship of marriage is the reason there are so many divorces in the world, even among some Christians who sincerely love Jesus. Some failures can also be catastrophic. Nevertheless, no failure is more tragic than the failure to believe and apply God's Word! This is because nothing changes on earth without digesting the engrafted Word of God, which is able to save our souls. The following prayer is designed to help you destroy the evil altar of failure.

Prayer of Activation

1. Address the Father in Praise and Worship

Heavenly Father, holy is Your name and greatly to be praised. I worship and adore You in Jesus' name. May Your Kingdom manifest in my life as it is in Heaven. Plead my cause, O Lord, with those who strive with me; fight against any entity or person who is contending against me. Heavenly Father, it is written in Psalm 27:6, *"And now my head will be lifted up above my enemies around me, in His tent I will offer sacrifices with shouts of joy; I will sing, yes, I will sing praises to the Lord."* Abba, I enjoin my worship to the heavenly chorus of worship of Your holy angels and the crowd of witnesses, in Jesus' name.

2. Ask for the Court to Be Seated

Heavenly Father, Righteous Judge, I ask that the Courts of Heaven be seated according to Daniel 7:9-10. I ask this in Jesus' mighty name. It is written:

> *I kept looking until thrones were set up, and the Ancient of Days (God) took His seat; His garment was white as snow and the hair of His head like pure wool. His throne was flames of fire; its wheels were a burning fire. A river of fire was flowing and coming out from before Him; a thousand thousands were attending Him, and ten thousand times ten thousand were standing before Him; the court was seated, and the books were opened.*

Heavenly Father, I am requesting the privilege of standing before the courtroom of the Ancient of Days according to what was revealed to the prophet Daniel, in Jesus' name, I pray. Heavenly Father, I stand in Your royal

courtroom because of the blood and finished work of Jesus on the cross. I have come to receive Your righteous judgment over my life against the spirit and altar of *failure* that satan planted in my generational bloodline. Heavenly Father, I call upon Your holy angels to be witnesses to my lawsuit and righteous prosecution of the evil altar of *failure*. I decree and declare that this evil altar of *failure* will not continue to control my life or destroy divine opportunities that I need to achieve my God-given destiny here on earth, in Jesus' name I pray.

3. Surrender Your Rights to Self-Representation to the Lord as Your Advocate

Heavenly Father, Your Word in First John 2:1-2 says, *"My little children, these things I write to you, so that you may not sin. And if anyone sins, we have an Advocate with the Father, Jesus Christ the righteous. And He Himself is the propitiation for our sins, and not for ours only but also for the whole world"* (NKJV). I thank You that Jesus is my faithful Advocate before the Righteous Judge in the Courts of Heaven. Lord Jesus, I surrender my rights to self-representation and summon You as my Advocate to help me plead my case before the Righteous Judge and prosecute the evil of altar of *failure* that satan planted in my bloodline. I also ask the blessed Holy Spirit, who is the highest officer of the Courts of Heaven here on earth, to make me sensitive to the proceedings of this Court in order to successfully prosecute the evil altar of *failure* in Jesus' name.

4. Summon the Evil Altar and the Idol That Sits on It to Appear in Court

Heavenly Father, even as I stand in Your royal courtroom I present myself as a living sacrifice, holy and acceptable before You according to Romans 12:1. Heavenly Father, Righteous Judge, I summon the altar of *failure* in my bloodline and the idol that sits on it to appear in Your royal courtroom to face prosecution in Jesus' name. For it is written in First Corinthians 6:3, *"Do you not know that we [believers] will judge angels? How much more then [as to] matters of this life?"* Heavenly Father, I exercise my God-given authority in Christ Jesus to judge demons and principalities, in Jesus' name I pray. Righteous Judge, it is also written in the constitution of Your Kingdom in First John 3:8, *"For this purpose the Son of God was manifested, that He might destroy the works of the devil"* (NKJV).

5. Address Satan's Accusations and Agree with the Adversary

Heavenly Father, I know that until the end of the age of sin, satan still has legal access to the Courts of Heaven to level accusations against the children of men; for it is written in the book of Revelation 12:10:

> *Then I heard a loud voice in heaven, saying, "Now the salvation, and the power, and the kingdom (dominion, reign) of our God, and the authority of His Christ have come; for the accuser of our [believing] brothers and sisters has been thrown down [at last], he who accuses them and keeps bringing charges [of sinful behavior] against them before our God day and night."*

Heavenly Father, the Lord Jesus also said in the book of Matthew 5:25:

> *Come to terms quickly [at the earliest opportunity] with your opponent at law while you are with him on the way [to court], so that your opponent does not hand you over to the judge, and the judge to the guard, and you are thrown into prison."*

Heavenly Father, in all humility, while renouncing the spirit of pride, I choose to quickly agree with the legal accusations of my adversary, satan. Righteous Judge, every accusation that satan has filed against me and my bloodline in this Court is true.

6. Repent

Heavenly Father, I repent for my personal transgressions, and for the sins and iniquities of my forefathers that opened the door for the spirit and altar of *failure* to oppress my life, in Jesus' name I pray. Lord, every sin of my forefathers that the enemy is using as a legal right to build cases against me and to deny me my destiny, I ask that the blood of Jesus would just wash them away. I repent for failure to obey and apply the word of God. I also repent for self-inflicted word curses and all covenants with demons that have existed in my ancestral bloodline. I am asking that every covenant with demonic powers will now be revoked and that their right to claim me and my bloodline would now be dismissed before Your court, in Jesus' name. Thank You, Lord, for revoking these demonic covenants and evil altars in Jesus' mighty name! Heavenly Father, in my heartfelt desire to divorce myself from the spirit and altar of *failure*, I give back everything and anything that the devil would say came from his kingdom. I only want what the blood of Jesus has secured for me.

7. Appeal to the Blood of Jesus to Wipe Out All Sin (Satan's Evidence)

Lord Jesus, thank You for cleansing me by Your blood so satan has no legal footing against me in Your courtroom. It is written in First John 1:9:

> If we [freely] admit that we have sinned and confess our sins,
> He is faithful and just [true to His own nature and promises],
> and will forgive our sins and cleanse us continually from all
> unrighteousness [our wrongdoing, everything not in confor-
> mity with His will and purpose].

Righteous Judge, I appeal to the blood of Jesus to wipe out all my short-comings, transgressions, and iniquities, in Jesus' name, I pray. I receive by faith the cleansing power of the blood of Jesus.

8. Ask the Court to Dismiss All of Satan's Accusations and Charges

Heavenly Father, based upon Jesus' finished work and my heartfelt repentance, I now move on the Court of Heaven to dismiss all of satan's accusations and charges against me and my bloodline in Jesus' name. For it is written that the accuser of the brethren has been cast down. So, I ask You Father to cast down all of satan's accusations against me, in Jesus' name, I pray.

9. Ask the Lord to Send Angels to Destroy the Evil Altar and Execute the Lord's Judgment Against It

Heavenly Father, Righteous Judge, I ask that You send high-ranking angelic officers of the Courts who excel in strength to execute the judgment of Your supreme court and destroy the evil altar of *failure* and the idol that sits on it that satan planted in my bloodline, in Jesus' name I pray. By the spirit of prophecy, I prophesy the complete destruction of the evil altar of *failure* in my life, in Jesus' name. For it is written in Psalm 91:11-12, *"For He will command His angels in regard to you, to protect and defend and guard you in all your ways [of obedience and service]. They will lift you up in their hands, so that you do not [even] strike your foot against a stone."* I receive angelic assistance, right now, in Jesus' name.

10. Present Scriptures That Will Be Used in Issuing a Divine Restraining Order

Heavenly Father, I present before Your Supreme Court the following scriptures as my rock-solid evidence against the spirit and altar of *failure* in my life. It is written:

For though the righteous fall seven times, they rise again, but the wicked stumble when calamity strikes (Proverbs 24:16 NIV).

I can do all things [which He has called me to do] through Him who strengthens and empowers me [to fulfill His purpose—I am self-sufficient in Christ's sufficiency; I am ready for anything and equal to anything through Him who infuses me with inner strength and confident peace] (Philippians 4:13).

Righteous Judge, based upon the aforementioned scriptures, it is clear that the spirit and altar of *failure*, if allowed to succeed, would cause great injury to my life, destiny, and also inflict irreparable damage to the purposes of God. I ask that that every legal right the spirit and altar of *failure* is holding be revoked in Jesus' glorious name. Righteous Judge, based upon the aforementioned scriptures, it is clear that I qualify for a divine restraining order against the altar of *failure* and the idol that sits on it, in Jesus' name.

11. Ask the Court to Issue a Divine Restraining Order and Receive the Divine Restraining Order by Faith

Heavenly Father, Righteous Judge, I now ask that a divine restraining order and a permanent injunction against the spirit and altar of *failure* in my life would now be issued by the authority of Your Supreme Court, in Jesus' name. Heavenly Father, I decree and declare that any form of *failure* the devil is orchestrating against my life is now cancelled in Jesus' glorious name. Heavenly Father, I receive this divine restraining order and permanent injunction by faith, in Jesus' name. For it is written in the Constitution of Your Kingdom in Hebrews 11:6, *"But without faith it is impossible to [walk with God and] please Him, for whoever comes [near] to God must [necessarily] believe that God exists and that He rewards those who [earnestly and diligently] seek Him."* I believe and declare by faith that the spirit and altar of *failure* in my life has been judged, in Jesus' name!

12. Ask the Lord to Seal Your Righteous Verdict and Court Proceedings in the Blood of Jesus

Heavenly Father, Righteous Judge, I now ask You to seal my righteous verdict against the spirit and altar of *failure* in the precious blood of Jesus. May You also cover with the blood of Jesus all my legal proceedings in this Court in Jesus' name. I decree and declare that my righteous verdict of release and breakthrough from the evil altar of *failure* is now secured in the documents of the Courts of Heaven. For it is written in John's Gospel, chapter 8:36, *"So if the Son makes you free, then you are unquestionably free."* I decree and declare that I am free of the evil altar of *failure* in Jesus' name, amen!

Prayer #14

Uprooting the Altar of Pride

Now I, Nebuchadnezzar, praise and exalt and honor the King of heaven, for all His works are true and faithful and His ways are just, and He is able to humiliate and humble those who walk in [self-centered, self-righteous] pride.

—Daniel 4:37

Perhaps there is no sin God hates more than pride, and yet pride is something most humans struggle with. Pride is lucifer's primordial sin. It was his undoing. Before lucifer became satan, the devil as we know him now, he was one of the most exalted of all the angels in Heaven. His celestial body was a thing of immense beauty. God built music instruments for worship inside him so he could lead all of heaven in the worship of God. However, the scripture says in the book of Ezekiel 28 that he corrupted his wisdom by being impressed by his own beauty and influence. He became so self-absorbed (which is the root of pride) that he wanted other angels to worship him as God! So in his pride lucifer staged the historic and catastrophic rebellion of one third of the angels of heaven who aligned themselves with him against their own creator. It's no wonder the writer of the book of Proverbs declares that "pride" comes before a fall. I have seen so many great ministers of the gospel, business leaders, and politicians fall due to pride. Most scary is the fact that God resists the proud while giving grace to the humble (see James 4:6)! The *dangerous prayer* below is designed to help you destroy the altars of pride in your life so you can attract the favor of God.

Prayer of Activation

1. Address the Father in Praise and Worship

Heavenly Father, holy is Your name and greatly to be praised. I worship and adore You in Jesus' name. May Your Kingdom manifest in my life as it is in Heaven. Plead my cause, O Lord, with those who strive with me; fight against any entity or person who is contending against me. Heavenly Father, it is written in Psalm 27:6, *"And now my head will be lifted up above my enemies around me, in His tent I will offer sacrifices with shouts of joy; I will sing, yes, I will sing praises to the Lord."* Abba, I enjoin my worship to the heavenly chorus of worship of Your holy angels and the crowd of witnesses, in Jesus' name.

2. Ask for the Court to Be Seated

Heavenly Father, Righteous Judge, I ask that the Courts of Heaven be seated according to Daniel 7:9-10. I ask this in Jesus' mighty name. It is written:

> *I kept looking until thrones were set up, and the Ancient of Days (God) took His seat; His garment was white as snow and the hair of His head like pure wool. His throne was flames of fire; its wheels were a burning fire. A river of fire was flowing and coming out from before Him; a thousand thousands were attending Him, and ten thousand times ten thousand were standing before Him; the court was seated, and the books were opened.*

Heavenly Father, I am requesting the privilege of standing before the courtroom of the Ancient of Days according to what was revealed to the prophet Daniel, in Jesus' name, I pray. Heavenly Father, I stand in Your royal courtroom because of the blood and finished work of Jesus on the cross. I have come to receive Your righteous judgment over my life against the spirit and altar of *pride* that satan planted in my generational bloodline. Heavenly Father, I call upon Your holy angels to be witnesses to my lawsuit and righteous prosecution of the evil altar of *pride*. I decree and declare that this evil altar of *pride* will not continue to control my will, mind and emotions nor kill divine relationships I need to achieve my God-given destiny here on earth, in Jesus' name I pray.

3. Surrender Your Rights to Self-Representation to the Lord as Your Advocate

Heavenly Father, Your Word in First John 2:1-2 says, "*My little children, these things I write to you, so that you may not sin. And if anyone sins, we have an Advocate with the Father, Jesus Christ the righteous. And He Himself is the propitiation for our sins, and not for ours only but also for the whole world*" (NKJV). I thank You that Jesus is my faithful Advocate before the Righteous Judge in the Courts of Heaven. Lord Jesus, I surrender my rights to self-representation and summon You as my Advocate to help me plead my case before the Righteous Judge and prosecute the evil of altar of *pride* that satan planted in my soul and bloodline. I also ask the blessed Holy Spirit, who is the highest officer of the Courts of Heaven here on earth, to make me sensitive to the proceedings of this Court in order to successfully prosecute the evil altar of *pride* in Jesus' name.

4. Summon the Evil Altar and the Idol That Sits on It to Appear in Court

Heavenly Father, even as I stand in Your royal courtroom I present myself as a living sacrifice, holy and acceptable before You according to Romans 12:1. Heavenly Father, Righteous Judge, I summon the altar of *pride* in my bloodline and the idol that sits on it to appear in Your royal courtroom to face prosecution in Jesus' name. For it is written in First Corinthians 6:3, *"Do you not know that we [believers] will judge angels? How much more then [as to] matters of this life?"* Heavenly Father, I exercise my God-given authority in Christ Jesus to judge demons and principalities, in Jesus' name I pray. Righteous Judge, it is also written in the constitution of Your Kingdom in First John 3:8, *"For this purpose the Son of God was manifested, that He might destroy the works of the devil"* (NKJV).

5. Address Satan's Accusations and Agree with the Adversary

Heavenly Father, I know that until the end of the age of sin, satan still has legal access to the Courts of Heaven to level accusations against the children of men; for it is written in the book of Revelation 12:10:

> *Then I heard a loud voice in heaven, saying, "Now the salvation, and the power, and the kingdom (dominion, reign) of our God, and the authority of His Christ have come; for the accuser of our [believing] brothers and sisters has been thrown down [at last], he who accuses them and keeps bringing charges [of sinful behavior] against them before our God day and night."*

Heavenly Father, the Lord Jesus also said in the book of Matthew 5:25:

> *Come to terms quickly [at the earliest opportunity] with your opponent at law while you are with him on the way [to court],*

so that your opponent does not hand you over to the judge, and
the judge to the guard, and you are thrown into prison.

Heavenly Father, in all humility, while renouncing the spirit of pride, I choose to quickly agree with the legal accusations of my adversary, satan. Righteous Judge, every accusation that satan has filed against me and my bloodline in this Court is true.

6. Repent

Heavenly Father, I repent for my personal transgressions, and for the sins and iniquities of my forefathers that opened the door for the spirit and altar of *pride* to oppress my life, in Jesus' name I pray. Lord, every sin of my forefathers that the enemy is using as a legal right to build cases against me and to deny me my destiny, I ask that the blood of Jesus would just wash them away. I repent for each instance I have operated in the spirit of *pride*. I also repent for self-inflicted word curses due to *pride* and all covenants with demons that have existed in my ancestral bloodline. I am asking that every covenant with the spirit of *pride* will now be revoked and its legal right to claim me and my bloodline would now be dismissed before Your court, in Jesus' name. Thank You, Lord, for revoking these demonic covenants and evil altars in Jesus' mighty name! Heavenly Father, in my heartfelt desire to divorce myself from the spirit and altar of *pride*, I give back everything and anything that the devil would say came from his kingdom. I only want what the blood of Jesus has secured for me.

7. Appeal to the Blood of Jesus to Wipe Out All Sin (Satan's Evidence)

Lord Jesus, thank You for cleansing me by Your blood so satan has no legal footing against me in Your courtroom. It is written in First John 1:9:

If we [freely] admit that we have sinned and confess our sins,
He is faithful and just [true to His own nature and promises],
and will forgive our sins and cleanse us continually from all
unrighteousness [our wrongdoing, everything not in confor-
mity with His will and purpose].

Righteous Judge, I appeal to the blood of Jesus to wipe out all my short-comings, transgressions, and iniquities, in Jesus' name, I pray. I receive by faith the cleansing power of the blood of Jesus.

8. Ask the Court to Dismiss All of Satan's Accusations and Charges

Heavenly Father, based upon Jesus' finished work and my heartfelt repentance, I now move on the Court of Heaven to dismiss all of satan's accusations and charges against me and my bloodline in Jesus' name. For it is written that the accuser of the brethren has been cast down. So, I ask You Father to cast down all of satan's accusations against me, in Jesus' name, I pray.

9. Ask the Lord to Send Angels to Destroy the Evil Altar and Execute the Lord's Judgment Against It

Heavenly Father, Righteous Judge, I ask that You send high-ranking angelic officers of the Courts who excel in strength to execute the judgment of Your supreme court and destroy the evil altar of *pride* and the idol that sits on it that satan planted in my bloodline, in Jesus' name I pray. By the spirit of prophecy, I prophesy the complete destruction of the evil altar of *pride* in my life, in Jesus' name. For it is written in Psalm 91:11-12, *"For He will com-mand His angels in regard to you, to protect and defend and guard you in all your ways [of obedience and service]. They will lift you up in their hands, so that you do not [even] strike your foot against a stone."* I receive angelic assistance, right now, in Jesus' name.

10. Present Scriptures That Will Be Used in Issuing a Divine Restraining Order

Heavenly Father, I present before Your Supreme Court the following scriptures as my rock-solid evidence against the spirit and altar of *pride* in my life. It is written:

> But He gives us more and more grace [through the power of the Holy Spirit to defy sin and live an obedient life that reflects both our faith and our gratitude for our salvation]. Therefore, it says, "God is opposed to the proud and haughty, but [continually] gives [the gift of] grace to the humble [who turn away from self-righteousness]" (James 4:6).
>
> Before disaster the heart of a man is haughty and filled with self-importance, but humility comes before honor (Proverbs 18:12).

Righteous Judge, based upon the aforementioned scriptures, it is clear that the spirit and altar of *pride*, if allowed to succeed, would cause great injury to my life, destiny, and also inflict irreparable damage to the purposes of God. I ask that that every legal right the spirit and altar of *pride* is holding be revoked in Jesus' glorious name. Righteous Judge, based upon the aforementioned scriptures, it is clear that I qualify for a divine restraining order against the altar of *pride* and the idol that sits on it, in Jesus' name.

11. Ask the Court to Issue a Divine Restraining Order and Receive the Divine Restraining Order by Faith

Heavenly Father, Righteous Judge, I now ask that a divine restraining order and a permanent injunction against the spirit and altar of *pride* in my life would now be issued by the authority of Your Supreme Court, in Jesus' name. Heavenly Father, I decree and declare that any and all forms of *pride* that the devil is orchestrating in my life is now cancelled in Jesus' glorious name. Heavenly Father, I receive this divine restraining order and permanent injunction by faith, in Jesus' name. For it is written in the Constitution of Your Kingdom in Hebrews 11:6, *"But without faith it is impossible to [walk with God and] please Him, for whoever comes [near] to God must [necessarily] believe that God exists and that He rewards those who [earnestly and diligently] seek Him."* I believe and declare by faith that the spirit and altar of *pride* in my life has been judged, in Jesus' name!

12. Ask the Lord to Seal Your Righteous Verdict and Court Proceedings in the Blood of Jesus

Heavenly Father, Righteous Judge, I now ask You to seal my righteous verdict against the spirit and altar of *pride* in the precious blood of Jesus. May You also cover with the blood of Jesus all my legal proceedings in this Court in Jesus' name. I decree and declare that my righteous verdict of release and breakthrough from the evil altar of *pride* is now secured in the documents of the Courts of Heaven. For it is written in John's Gospel, chapter 8:36, *"So if the Son makes you free, then you are unquestionably free."* I decree and declare that I am free of the evil altar of *pride* in Jesus' name, amen!

Prayer #15

Uprooting the Altar of Jezebel

But I have this [charge] against you, that you tolerate the woman
Jezebel, who calls herself a prophetess [claiming to be inspired],
and she teaches and misleads My bond-servants so that they commit [acts of sexual] immorality and eat food sacrificed to idols.
—**Revelation 2:20**

It goes without saying that God hates the spirit of Jezebel! In the above
passage of scripture, Jesus rebukes one of His churches, which was flirting
with the spirit of Jezebel. Based upon the above passage of scripture, the
spirit of Jezebel is the spirit that teaches children of God to commit acts of
sexual immorality and eat food sacrificed to idols. The Jezebel spirit is also
presented in the Bible as a spirit of manipulation, witchcraft, and control.
Most importantly, it's a spirit that hates true prophets of God and also hates
the presence of God.

This is why there was a showdown between Jezebel and Elijah! If you
struggle internally with wanting to control everything or manipulate people
around you, you probably have the altar of Jezebel in your ancestral bloodline. This is true also of people, including Christians, who hate the prophetic
for no obvious reason. The good news is that God is able to destroy this
evil altar of seduction, manipulation, and control. Perhaps you are under
someone (a spouse or spiritual leader) who exhibits this spirit of control and

manipulation toward you. You can also use the *dangerous prayer* below to destroy the evil altar of Jezebel in your bloodline or over you.

Prayer of Activation

1. Address the Father in Praise and Worship

Heavenly Father, holy is Your name and greatly to be praised. I worship and adore You in Jesus' name. May Your Kingdom manifest in my life as it is in Heaven. Plead my cause, O Lord, with those who strive with me; fight against any entity or person who is contending against me. Heavenly Father, it is written in Psalm 27:6, *"And now my head will be lifted up above my enemies around me, in His tent I will offer sacrifices with shouts of joy; I will sing, yes, I will sing praises to the Lord."* Abba, I enjoin my worship to the heavenly chorus of worship of Your holy angels and the crowd of witnesses, in Jesus' name.

2. Ask for the Court to Be Seated

Heavenly Father, Righteous Judge, I ask that the Courts of Heaven be seated according to Daniel 7:9-10. I ask this in Jesus' mighty name. It is written:

> *I kept looking until thrones were set up, and the Ancient of Days (God) took His seat; His garment was white as snow and the hair of His head like pure wool. His throne was flames of fire; its wheels were a burning fire. A river of fire was flowing and coming out from before Him; a thousand thousands were attending Him, and ten thousand times ten thousand were standing before Him; the court was seated, and the books were opened.*

Heavenly Father, I am requesting the privilege of standing before the courtroom of the Ancient of Days according to what was revealed to the prophet Daniel, in Jesus' name, I pray. Heavenly Father, I stand in Your royal courtroom because of the blood and finished work of Jesus on the cross. I have come to receive Your righteous judgment over my life against the spirit and altar of *Jezebel* that satan planted in my generational bloodline. Heavenly Father, I call upon Your holy angels to be witnesses to my lawsuit and righteous prosecution of the evil altar of *Jezebel*. I decree and declare that this evil altar of *Jezebel* will not kill the prophetic in my life or control my life and the divine relationships I need to achieve my God-given destiny here on earth, in Jesus' name I pray.

3. Surrender Your Rights to Self-Representation to the Lord as Your Advocate

Heavenly Father, Your Word in First John 2:1-2 says, "*My little children, these things I write to you, so that you may not sin. And if anyone sins, we have an Advocate with the Father, Jesus Christ the righteous. And He Himself is the propitiation for our sins, and not for ours only but also for the whole world*" (NKJV). I thank You that Jesus is my faithful Advocate before the Righteous Judge in the Courts of Heaven. Lord Jesus, I surrender my rights to self-representation and summon You as my Advocate to help me plead my case before the Righteous Judge and prosecute the evil of altar of *Jezebel* that satan planted in my bloodline or he is using in my life. I also ask the blessed Holy Spirit, who is the highest officer of the Courts of Heaven here on earth, to make me sensitive to the proceedings of this Court in order to successfully prosecute the evil altar of *Jezebel* in Jesus' name.

4. Summon the Evil Altar and the Idol That Sits on It to Appear in Court

Heavenly Father, even as I stand in Your royal courtroom I present myself as a living sacrifice, holy and acceptable before You according to Romans 12:1. Heavenly Father, Righteous Judge, I summon the altar of *Jezebel* in my bloodline and the idol that sits on it to appear in Your royal courtroom to face prosecution in Jesus' name. For it is written in First Corinthians 6:3, *"Do you not know that we [believers] will judge angels? How much more then [as to] matters of this life?"* Heavenly Father, I exercise my God-given authority in Christ Jesus to judge demons and principalities, in Jesus' name I pray. Righteous Judge, it is also written in the constitution of Your Kingdom in First John 3:8, *"For this purpose the Son of God was manifested, that He might destroy the works of the devil"* (NKJV).

5. Address Satan's Accusations and Agree with the Adversary

Heavenly Father, I know that until the end of the age of sin, satan still has legal access to the Courts of Heaven to level accusations against the children of men; for it is written in the book of Revelation 12:10:

> *Then I heard a loud voice in heaven, saying, "Now the salvation, and the power, and the kingdom (dominion, reign) of our God, and the authority of His Christ have come; for the accuser of our [believing] brothers and sisters has been thrown down [at last], he who accuses them and keeps bringing charges [of sinful behavior] against them before our God day and night."*

Heavenly Father, the Lord Jesus also said in the book of Matthew 5:25:

> *Come to terms quickly [at the earliest opportunity] with your opponent at law while you are with him on the way [to court],*

so that your opponent does not hand you over to the judge, and
the judge to the guard, and you are thrown into prison.

Heavenly Father, in all humility, while renouncing the spirit of pride, I choose to quickly agree with the legal accusations of my adversary, satan. Righteous Judge, every accusation that satan has filed against me and my bloodline in this Court is true.

6. Repent

Heavenly Father, I repent for my personal transgressions, and for the sins and iniquities of my forefathers that opened the door for the spirit and altar of *Jezebel* to oppress my life, in Jesus' name I pray. Lord, every sin of my forefathers that the enemy is using as a legal right to build cases against me and to deny me my destiny, I ask that the blood of Jesus would just wash them away. I repent for each time I have operated in this spirit of manipulation, witchcraft, and control. I also repent for self-inflicted word curses and all covenants with demons that have existed in my ancestral bloodline. I am asking that every covenant with demonic powers will now be revoked and that their right to claim me and my bloodline would now be dismissed before Your court, in Jesus' name. Thank You, Lord, for revoking these demonic covenants and evil altars in Jesus' mighty name! Heavenly Father, in my heartfelt desire to divorce myself from the spirit and altar of *Jezebel*, I give back everything and anything that the devil would say came from his kingdom. I only want what the blood of Jesus has secured for me.

7. Appeal to the Blood of Jesus to Wipe Out All Sin (Satan's Evidence)

Lord Jesus, thank You for cleansing me by Your blood so satan has no legal footing against me in Your courtroom. It is written in First John 1:9:

If we [freely] admit that we have sinned and confess our sins,
He is faithful and just [true to His own nature and promises],
and will forgive our sins and cleanse us continually from all
unrighteousness [our wrongdoing, everything not in confor-
mity with His will and purpose].

Righteous Judge, I appeal to the blood of Jesus to wipe out all my short-comings, transgressions, and iniquities, in Jesus' name, I pray. I receive by faith the cleansing power of the blood of Jesus.

8. Ask the Court to Dismiss All of Satan's Accusations and Charges

Heavenly Father, based upon Jesus' finished work and my heartfelt repentance, I now move on the Court of Heaven to dismiss all of satan's accusations and charges against me and my bloodline in Jesus' name. For it is written that the accuser of the brethren has been cast down. So, I ask You Father to cast down all of satan's accusations against me, in Jesus' name, I pray.

9. Ask the Lord to Send Angels to Destroy the Evil Altar and Execute the Lord's Judgment Against It

Heavenly Father, Righteous Judge, I ask that You send high-ranking angelic officers of the Courts who excel in strength to execute the judgment of Your supreme court and destroy the evil altar of *Jezebel* and the idol that sits on it that satan planted in my bloodline, in Jesus' name I pray. By the spirit of prophecy, I prophesy the complete destruction of the evil altar of *Jezebel* in my life, in Jesus' name. For it is written in Psalm 91:11-12, *"For He will command His angels in regard to you, to protect and defend and guard you in all your ways [of obedience and service]. They will lift you up in their hands, so that you do not [even] strike your foot against a stone."* I receive angelic assistance, right now, in Jesus' name.

10. Present Scriptures That Will Be Used in Issuing a Divine Restraining Order

Heavenly Father, I present before Your Supreme Court the following scriptures as my rock-solid evidence against the spirit and altar of *Jezebel* in my life. It is written:

> *And he said, "Throw her down." So they threw her down, and some of her blood spattered on the wall and on the horses, and he trampled her underfoot* (2 Kings 9:33).
>
> *The corpse of **Jezebel** will be like dung on the surface of the field in the property of Jezreel, so they cannot say, "This is **Jezebel"** (2 Kings 9:37).

Righteous Judge, based upon the aforementioned scriptures, it is clear that the spirit and altar of *Jezebel*, if allowed to succeed, would cause great injury to my life, destiny, and also inflict irreparable damage to the purposes of God. I ask that that every legal right the spirit and altar of *Jezebel* is holding be revoked in Jesus' glorious name. Righteous Judge, based upon the aforementioned scriptures, it is clear that I qualify for a divine restraining order against the altar of *Jezebel* and the idol that sits on it, in Jesus' name.

11. Ask the Court to Issue a Divine Restraining Order and Receive the Divine Restraining Order by Faith

Heavenly Father, Righteous Judge, I now ask that a divine restraining order and a permanent injunction against the spirit and altar of *Jezebel* in my life would now be issued by the authority of Your Supreme Court, in Jesus' name. Heavenly Father, I decree and declare that any manifestation of *Jezebel* the devil is orchestrating against my life is now cancelled in Jesus' glorious name. Heavenly Father, I receive this divine restraining order and permanent injunction by faith, in Jesus' name. For it is written in the Constitution of Your Kingdom in Hebrews 11:6, *"But without faith it is impossible to [walk with God and] please Him, for whoever comes [near] to God must [necessarily] believe that God exists and that He rewards those who [earnestly and diligently] seek Him."* I believe and declare by faith that the spirit and altar of *Jezebel* in my life has been judged, in Jesus' name!

12. Ask the Lord to Seal Your Righteous Verdict and Court Proceedings in the Blood of Jesus

Heavenly Father, Righteous Judge, I now ask You to seal my righteous verdict against the spirit and altar of *Jezebel* in the precious blood of Jesus. May You also cover with the blood of Jesus all my legal proceedings in this Court in Jesus' name. I decree and declare that my righteous verdict of release and breakthrough from the evil altar of *Jezebel* is now secured in the documents of the Courts of Heaven. For it is written in John's Gospel, chapter 8:36, *"So if the Son makes you free, then you are unquestionably free."* I decree and declare that I am free of the evil altar of *Jezebel* in Jesus' name, amen!

Prayer #16

Uprooting the Altar of Marine or Water Spirits

In that day the Lord will punish *Leviathan* the fleeing serpent with His fierce and great and mighty sword [rescuing Israel from her enemy], even *Leviathan* the twisted serpent; and He will kill the dragon who lives in the sea.

—Isaiah 27:1

M ost of the nightmares and sexual (wet) dreams most people suffer from are due to marine or water spirits. I have received correspondence from Christians from all over the world who write to me seeking deliverance because they are tired of having sexual dreams with men or women who are not their husbands or wives. One of the most powerful of these water spirits is a fierce sea serpent the Bible calls Leviathan. The Bible has much to say about this marine spirit in the book of Job. The book of Job lets us know that Leviathan is the king of all the children of pride. Since Leviathan is a water spirit, it is safe to say that the most of the pride we struggle with is due to the influence of water spirits over the water in our bodies.

Isaiah 27:1 gives us two key things we need to know about this water spirit. Number one, it's a "twisted serpent"—this means that this marine spirit is responsible for all the twisting of truth that happens on earth. Water spirits are responsible for evil now being called good and good being called evil, due to Leviathan's ability to twist the truth. I am convinced this spirit is over most of the gender confusion that is plaguing our world today. Number two, it's a sea dragon, meaning that the evil altar of this demonic principality is found in the sea (water). As our bodies are 70 percent water, we are very vulnerable to the influence of water spirits due to our sin-infected bodies. This kind of demonic influence will only stop after our physical bodies put on immortality. The good news is that we can take Leviathan and any other water spirit into the Courts of Heaven to be prosecuted by God Himself. The dangerous prayer below is designed to help you break free and destroy the evil altar of marine or water spirits!

Prayer of Activation

1. Address the Father in Praise and Worship

Heavenly Father, holy is Your name and greatly to be praised. I worship and adore You in Jesus' name. May Your Kingdom manifest in my life as it is in Heaven. Plead my cause, O Lord, with those who strive with me; fight against any entity or person who is contending against me. Heavenly Father, it is written in Psalm 27:6, *"And now my head will be lifted up above my enemies around me, in His tent I will offer sacrifices with shouts of joy; I will sing, yes, I will sing praises to the Lord."* Abba, I enjoin my worship to the heavenly chorus of worship of Your holy angels and the crowd of witnesses, in Jesus' name.

2. Ask for the Court to Be Seated

Heavenly Father, Righteous Judge, I ask that the Courts of Heaven be seated according to Daniel 7:9-10. I ask this in Jesus' mighty name. It is written:

I kept looking until thrones were set up, and the Ancient of Days (God) took His seat; His garment was white as snow and the hair of His head like pure wool. His throne was flames of fire; its wheels were a burning fire. A river of fire was flowing and coming out from before Him; a thousand thousands were attending Him, and ten thousand times ten thousand were standing before Him; the court was seated, and the books were opened.

Heavenly Father, I am requesting the privilege of standing before the courtroom of the Ancient of Days according to what was revealed to the prophet Daniel, in Jesus' name, I pray. Heavenly Father, I stand in Your royal courtroom because of the blood and finished work of Jesus on the cross. I have come to receive Your righteous judgment over my life against the altar of *marine or water spirits* that satan planted in my generational bloodline. Righteous Judge, I am asking this Court to set me free from the power of Leviathan, that twisted serpent, or any other water spirit. Heavenly Father, I call upon Your holy angels to be witnesses to my lawsuit and righteous prosecution of the evil altar of *marine or water spirits*. I decree and declare that this evil altar of *marine or water spirits* will not control me through the water in my body or destroy the divine relationships I need to achieve my God-given destiny here on earth, in Jesus' name I pray.

3. Surrender Your Rights to Self-Representation to the Lord as Your Advocate

Heavenly Father, Your Word in First John 2:1-2 says, "*My little children, these things I write to you, so that you may not sin. And if anyone sins, we have an Advocate with the Father, Jesus Christ the righteous. And He Himself is the propitiation for our sins, and not for ours only but also for the whole world*" (NKJV). I thank You that Jesus is my faithful Advocate before the Righteous Judge in the Courts of Heaven. Lord Jesus, I surrender my rights to self-representation and summon You as my Advocate to help me plead my case before the Righteous Judge and prosecute the evil of altar of *marine or water spirits* that satan planted in my bloodline. I also ask the blessed Holy Spirit, who is the highest officer of the Courts of Heaven here on earth, to make me sensitive to the proceedings of this Court in order to successfully prosecute the evil altar of *marine or water spirits* in Jesus' name.

4. Summon the Evil Altar and the Idol That Sits on It to Appear in Court

Heavenly Father, even as I stand in Your royal courtroom I present myself as a living sacrifice, holy and acceptable before You according to Romans 12:1. Heavenly Father, Righteous Judge, I summon the altar of *marine or water spirits* in my bloodline and the idol that sits on it to appear in Your royal courtroom to face prosecution in Jesus' name. For it is written in First Corinthians 6:3, *"Do you not know that we [believers] will judge angels? How much more then [as to] matters of this life?"* Heavenly Father, I exercise my God-given authority in Christ Jesus to judge demons and principalities, in Jesus' name I pray. Righteous Judge, it is also written in the Constitution of Your Kingdom in First John 3:8, *"For this purpose the Son of God was manifested, that He might destroy the works of the devil"* (NKJV).

5. Address Satan's Accusations and Agree with the Adversary

Heavenly Father, I know that until the end of the age of sin, satan still has legal access to the Courts of Heaven to level accusations against the children of men; for it is written in the book of Revelation 12:10:

> *Then I heard a loud voice in heaven, saying, "Now the salvation, and the power, and the kingdom (dominion, reign) of our God, and the authority of His Christ have come; for the accuser of our [believing] brothers and sisters has been thrown down [at last], he who accuses them and keeps bringing*

charges [of sinful behavior] against them before our God day and night."

Heavenly Father, the Lord Jesus also said in the book of Matthew 5:25:

Come to terms quickly [at the earliest opportunity] with your opponent at law while you are with him on the way [to court], so that your opponent does not hand you over to the judge, and the judge to the guard, and you are thrown into prison.

Heavenly Father, in all humility, while renouncing the spirit of pride, I choose to quickly agree with the legal accusations of my adversary, satan. Righteous Judge, every accusation that satan has filed against me and my bloodline in this Court is true.

6. Repent

Heavenly Father, I repent for my personal transgressions, and for the sins and iniquities of my forefathers that opened the door for the altar of *marine or water spirits* to oppress my life, in Jesus' name I pray. Lord, every sin of my forefathers that the enemy is using as a legal right to build cases against me and to deny me my destiny, I ask that the blood of Jesus would just wash them away. I repent for every sexual fantasy, sin, or wet dream that I have ever had. I also repent for self-inflicted word curses and all covenants with *marine spirits* that have existed in my ancestral bloodline. I am asking that every covenant with these demonic powers will now be revoked and that their legal right to claim me and my bloodline would now be dismissed before Your court, in Jesus' name. Thank You, Lord, for revoking these demonic covenants and evil marine altars in Jesus' mighty name! Heavenly Father, in my heartfelt desire to divorce myself from the altar of *marine or water spirits*, I give back everything and anything that the devil would say came from his kingdom. I only want what the blood of Jesus has secured for me.

7. *Appeal to the Blood of Jesus to Wipe Out All Sin (Satan's Evidence)*

Lord Jesus, thank You for cleansing me by Your blood so satan has no legal footing against me in Your courtroom. It is written in First John 1:9:

> *If we [freely] admit that we have sinned and confess our sins, He is faithful and just [true to His own nature and promises], and will forgive our sins and cleanse us continually from all unrighteousness [our wrongdoing, everything not in conformity with His will and purpose].*

Righteous Judge, I appeal to the blood of Jesus to wipe out all my shortcomings, transgressions, and iniquities, in Jesus' name, I pray. I receive by faith the cleansing power of the blood of Jesus.

8. *Ask the Court to Dismiss All of Satan's Accusations and Charges*

Heavenly Father, based upon Jesus' finished work and my heartfelt repentance, I now move on the Court of Heaven to dismiss all of satan's accusations and charges against me and my bloodline in Jesus' name. For it is written that the accuser of the brethren has been cast down. So, I ask You Father to cast down all of satan's accusations against me, in Jesus' name, I pray.

9. *Ask the Lord to Send Angels to Destroy the Evil Altar and Execute the Lord's Judgment Against It*

Heavenly Father, Righteous Judge, I ask that You send high-ranking angelic officers of the Courts who excel in strength to execute the judgment of Your supreme court and destroy the evil altar of *marine or water spirits* and the idol that sits on it that satan planted in my bloodline, in Jesus' name

I pray. By the spirit of prophecy, I prophesy the complete destruction of the evil altar of *marine or water spirits* in my life, in Jesus' name. For it is written in Psalm 91:11-12, *"For He will command His angels in regard to you, to protect and defend and guard you in all your ways [of obedience and service]. They will lift you up in their hands, so that you do not [even] strike your foot against a stone."* I receive angelic assistance, right now, in Jesus' name.

10. *Present Scriptures That Will Be Used in Issuing a Divine Restraining Order*

Heavenly Father, I present before Your Supreme Court the following scriptures as my rock-solid evidence against the altar of *marine or water spirits* in my life. It is written:

> *You crushed the heads of* **Leviathan** *(Egypt); you gave him as food for the creatures of the wilderness* (Psalm 74:14).
>
> *Little children (believers, dear ones), you are of God and you belong to Him and have [already] overcome them [the agents of the antichrist]; because He who is in you is greater than he (Satan) who is in the world [of sinful mankind]* (First John 4:4).

Righteous Judge, based upon the aforementioned scriptures, it is clear that the altar of *marine or water spirits*, if allowed to succeed, would cause great injury to my life, destiny, and also inflict irreparable damage to the purposes of God. I ask that that every legal right the altar of *marine or water spirits* is holding be revoked in Jesus' glorious name. Righteous Judge, based upon the aforementioned scriptures, it is clear that I qualify for a divine restraining order against the altar of *marine or water spirits* and the idol that sits on it, in Jesus' name.

11. Ask the Court to Issue a Divine Restraining Order and Receive the Divine Restraining Order by Faith

Heavenly Father, Righteous Judge, I now ask that a divine restraining order and a permanent injunction against the altar of *marine or water spirits* in my life would now be issued by the authority of Your Supreme Court, in Jesus' name. Heavenly Father, I decree and declare that any *marine or water spirits* the devil has unleashed against my life are now arrested in Jesus' glorious name. Heavenly Father, I receive this divine restraining order and permanent injunction by faith, in Jesus' name. For it is written in the constitution of Your Kingdom in Hebrews 11:6, *"But without faith it is impossible to [walk with God and] please Him, for whoever comes [near] to God must [necessarily] believe that God exists and that He rewards those who [earnestly and diligently] seek Him."* I believe and declare by faith that the altar of *marine or water spirits* in my life has been judged, in Jesus' name!

12. Ask the Lord to Seal Your Righteous Verdict and Court Proceedings in the Blood of Jesus

Heavenly Father, Righteous Judge, I now ask You to seal my righteous verdict against the altar of *marine or water spirits* in the precious blood of Jesus. May You also cover with the blood of Jesus all my legal proceedings in this Court in Jesus' name. I decree and declare that my righteous verdict of release and breakthrough from the evil altar of *marine or water spirits* is now secured in the documents of the Courts of Heaven. For it is written in John's Gospel, chapter 8:36, *"So if the Son makes you free, then you are unquestionably free."* I decree and declare that I am free of the evil altar of *marine or water spirits* in Jesus' name, amen!

Prayer #17

Uprooting the Altar of the Delilah Spirit

Then Delilah realized that he had told her everything in his heart, so she sent and called for the Philistine lords, saying, "Come up this once, because he has told me everything in his heart." Then the Philistine lords came up to her and brought the money [they had promised] in their hands. She made Samson sleep on her knees, and she called a man and had him shave off the seven braids of his head. Then she began to abuse Samson, and his strength left him.
—Judges 16:18-19

The evil altar of the Delilah spirit is an altar of seduction that is designed to cause men and women of God (children of God) who carry higher callings in God to compromise themselves. This evil altar is behind much of the sexual and financial scandals that have rocked the body of Christ over the years. A Philistine woman by the name of Delilah became the face of this evil spirit and its altar. Delilah is famous for bringing down the mighty Samson by seducing him into exposing the secret to his supernatural abilities and forcing him to break his Nazirite vow of consecration to God. If you have ever compromised the anointing and calling upon your life for any reason, it's due to the operations of the evil altar of Delilah. Delilah did not love Samson; she was hired to discover the secret of his strength in God in order to sway him from his devotion to God. The first thing that happened to Samson after he exposed his connection to God to Delilah was that Philistine lords gouged his eyes and he became blind. So the altar of the Delilah spirit is behind why some gifted people lose their original vision of what God called them to do. Whether you have been a victim of this evil altar of the Delilah spirit or not, the *dangerous prayer* below is designed for you to destroy the altar of the Delilah spirit in your life or bloodline!

Prayer of Activation

1. Address the Father in Praise and Worship

Heavenly Father, holy is Your name and greatly to be praised. I worship and adore You in Jesus' name. May Your Kingdom manifest in my life as it is in Heaven. Plead my cause, O Lord, with those who strive with me; fight against any entity or person who is contending against me. Heavenly Father, it is written in Psalm 27:6, *"And now my head will be lifted up above my enemies around me, in His tent I will offer sacrifices with shouts of joy; I will sing, yes, I will sing praises to the Lord."* Abba, I enjoin my worship to the heavenly chorus of worship of Your holy angels and the crowd of witnesses, in Jesus' name.

2. Ask for the Court to Be Seated

Heavenly Father, Righteous Judge, I ask that the Courts of Heaven be seated according to Daniel 7:9-10. I ask this in Jesus' mighty name. It is written:

> *I kept looking until thrones were set up, and the Ancient of Days (God) took His seat; His garment was white as snow and the hair of His head like pure wool. His throne was flames of fire; its wheels were a burning fire. A river of fire was flowing*

and coming out from before Him; a thousand thousands were attending Him, and ten thousand times ten thousand were standing before Him; the court was seated, and the books were opened.

Heavenly Father, I am requesting the privilege of standing before the courtroom of the Ancient of Days according to what was revealed to the prophet Daniel, in Jesus' name, I pray. Heavenly Father, I stand in Your royal courtroom because of the blood and finished work of Jesus on the cross. I have come to receive Your righteous judgment over my life against the altar of the *Delilah spirit* that satan planted in my generational blood-line. Heavenly Father, I call upon Your holy angels to be witnesses to my lawsuit and righteous prosecution of the evil altar of the *Delilah spirit*. I decree and declare that this evil altar of the *Delilah spirit* will not force me to compromise and destroy my consecration to the Lord, in Jesus' name I pray.

3. Surrender Your Rights to Self-Representation to the Lord as Your Advocate

Heavenly Father, Your Word in First John 2:1-2 says, "*My little children, these things I write to you, so that you may not sin. And if anyone sins, we have an Advocate with the Father, Jesus Christ the righteous. And He Himself is the propitiation for our sins, and not for ours only but also for the whole world*" (NKJV). I thank You that Jesus is my faithful Advocate before the Righteous Judge in the Courts of Heaven. Lord Jesus, I surrender my rights to self-representation and summon You as my Advocate to help me plead my case before the Righteous Judge and prosecute the evil of altar of the *Delilah* spirit that satan planted in my bloodline. I also ask the blessed Holy Spirit, who is the highest officer of the Courts of Heaven here on earth, to make me sensitive to the proceedings of this Court in order to successfully prosecute the evil altar of the *Delilah* spirit in Jesus' name.

4. Summon the Evil Altar and the Idol That Sits on It to Appear in Court

Heavenly Father, even as I stand in Your royal courtroom I present myself as a living sacrifice, holy and acceptable before You according to Romans 12:1. Heavenly Father, Righteous Judge, I summon the altar of the *Delilah* spirit in my bloodline and the idol that sits on it to appear in Your royal courtroom to face prosecution in Jesus' name. For it is written in First Corinthians 6:3, *"Do you not know that we [believers] will judge angels? How much more then [as to] matters of this life?"* Heavenly Father, I exercise my God-given authority in Christ Jesus to judge demons and principalities, in Jesus' name I pray. Righteous Judge, it is also written in the Constitution of Your Kingdom in First John 3:8, *"For this purpose the Son of God was manifested, that He might destroy the works of the devil"* (NKJV).

5. Address Satan's Accusations and Agree with the Adversary

Heavenly Father, I know that until the end of the age of sin, satan still has legal access to the Courts of Heaven to level accusations against the children of men; for it is written in the book of Revelation 12:10:

> *Then I heard a loud voice in heaven, saying, "Now the salvation, and the power, and the kingdom (dominion, reign) of our God, and the authority of His Christ have come; for the accuser of our [believing] brothers and sisters has been thrown down [at last], he who accuses them and keeps bringing charges [of sinful behavior] against them before our God day and night."*

Heavenly Father, the Lord Jesus also said in the book of Matthew 5:25:

> *Come to terms quickly [at the earliest opportunity] with your opponent at law while you are with him on the way [to court],*

211

so that your opponent does not hand you over to the judge, and
the judge to the guard, and you are thrown into prison.

Heavenly Father, in all humility, while renouncing the spirit of pride, I choose to quickly agree with the legal accusations of my adversary, satan. Righteous Judge, every accusation that satan has filed against me and my bloodline in this Court is true.

6. Repent

Heavenly Father, I repent for my personal transgressions, and for the sins and iniquities of my forefathers that opened the door for the altar of the *Delilah* spirit to oppress my life, in Jesus' name I pray. Lord, every sin of my forefathers that the enemy is using as a legal right to build cases against me and to deny me my destiny, I ask that the blood of Jesus would just wash them away. I repent for each time I have fraternized with the *Delilah* spirit. I repent for each time I have compromised what you called me to do, Heavenly Father. I also repent for self-inflicted word curses and all covenants with demons that have existed in my ancestral bloodline. I am asking that every covenant with demonic powers will now be revoked and that their right to claim me and my bloodline would now be dismissed before Your court, in Jesus' name. Thank You, Lord, for revoking these demonic covenants and evil altars in Jesus' mighty name! Heavenly Father, in my heartfelt desire to divorce myself from the altar of the *Delilah* spirit, I give back everything and anything that the devil would say came from his kingdom. I only want what the blood of Jesus has secured for me.

7. Appeal to the Blood of Jesus to Wipe Out All Sin (Satan's Evidence)

Lord Jesus, thank You for cleansing me by Your blood so satan has no legal footing against me in Your courtroom. It is written in First John 1:9:

*If we [freely] admit that we have sinned and confess our sins,
He is faithful and just [true to His own nature and promises],
and will forgive our sins and cleanse us continually from all
unrighteousness [our wrongdoing, everything not in conformity with His will and purpose].*

Righteous Judge, I appeal to the blood of Jesus to wipe out all my short-
comings, transgressions, and iniquities, in Jesus' name, I pray. I receive by
faith the cleansing power of the blood of Jesus.

8. Ask the Court to Dismiss All of Satan's Accusations and Charges

Heavenly Father, based upon Jesus' finished work and my heartfelt
repentance, I now move on the Court of Heaven to dismiss all of satan's
accusations and charges against me and my bloodline in Jesus' name. For it
is written that the accuser of the brethren has been cast down. So, I ask You
Father to cast down all of satan's accusations against me, in Jesus' name, I
pray.

9. Ask the Lord to Send Angels to Destroy the Evil Altar and Execute the Lord's Judgment Against It

Heavenly Father, Righteous Judge, I ask that You send high-ranking
angelic officers of the Courts who excel in strength to execute the judgment
of Your supreme court and destroy the evil altar of the *Delilah* spirit and the
idol that sits on it that satan planted in my bloodline, in Jesus' name I pray.
By the spirit of prophecy, I prophesy the complete destruction of the evil
altar of the *Delilah* spirit in my life, in Jesus' name. For it is written in Psalm
91:11-12, *"For He will command His angels in regard to you, to protect and
defend and guard you in all your ways [of obedience and service]. They will lift
you up in their hands, so that you do not [even] strike your foot against a stone."*
I receive angelic assistance, right now, in Jesus' name.

10. Present Scriptures That Will Be Used in Issuing a Divine Restraining Order

Heavenly Father, I present before Your Supreme Court the following scriptures as my rock-solid evidence against the altar of the *Delilah* spirit in my life. It is written:

> So submit to [the authority of] God. Resist the devil [stand firm against him] and he will flee from you (James 4:7).
>
> For the lips of an immoral woman drip honey [like a honeycomb] and her speech is smoother than oil; but in the end she is bitter like [the extract of] wormwood, sharp as a two-edged sword. Her feet go down to death; her steps take hold of Sheol (the nether world, the place of the dead) (Proverbs 5:3-5).

Righteous Judge, based upon the aforementioned scriptures, it is clear that the altar of the *Delilah* spirit, if allowed to succeed, would cause great injury to my life, destiny, and also inflict irreparable damage to the purposes of God. I ask that that every legal right the altar of the *Delilah* spirit is holding be revoked in Jesus' glorious name. Righteous Judge, based upon the aforementioned scriptures, it is clear that I qualify for a divine restraining order against the altar of the *Delilah* spirit and the idol that sits on it, in Jesus' name.

11. Ask the Court to Issue a Divine Restraining Order and Receive the Divine Restraining Order by Faith

Heavenly Father, Righteous Judge, I now ask that a divine restraining order and a permanent injunction against the altar of the *Delilah* spirit in my life would now be issued by the authority of Your Supreme Court, in Jesus' name. Heavenly Father, I decree and declare that any plan of the *Delilah* spirit to compromise or destroy my anointing are now cancelled in Jesus' glorious name. Heavenly Father, I receive this divine restraining order and permanent injunction by faith, in Jesus' name. For it is written in the constitution of Your Kingdom in Hebrews 11:6, *"But without faith it is impossible to [walk with God and] please Him, for whoever comes [near] to God must [necessarily] believe that God exists and that He rewards those who [earnestly and diligently] seek Him."* I believe and declare by faith that the altar of the *Delilah* spirit in my life has been judged, in Jesus' name!

12. Ask the Lord to Seal Your Righteous Verdict and Court Proceedings in the Blood of Jesus

Heavenly Father, Righteous Judge, I now ask You to seal my righteous verdict against the altar of the *Delilah* spirit in the precious blood of Jesus. May You also cover with the blood of Jesus all my legal proceedings in this Court in Jesus' name. I decree and declare that my righteous verdict of release and breakthrough from the evil altar of the *Delilah* spirit is now secured in the documents of the Courts of Heaven. For it is written in John's Gospel, chapter 8:36, *"So if the Son makes you free, then you are unquestionably free."* I decree and declare that I am free of the evil altar of the *Delilah* spirit in Jesus' name, amen!

Prayer #18

Uprooting the Altar of Delay

The Lord our God spoke to us at Horeb, saying, " You have stayed long enough on this mountain. Turn and resume your journey, and go to the hill country of the Amorites, and to all their neighbors in the Arabah, in the hill country and in the lowland (the Shephelah), in the Negev (South country) and on the coast of the [Mediterranean] Sea, the land of the Canaanites, and Lebanon, as far as the great river, the river Euphrates."
—**Deuteronomy 1:6-7**

I once heard a man of God declare that if the devil cannot stop you from fulfilling your destiny, he will do his best to delay the manifestation of your destiny! After many years of apostolic service to the Lord, I have also come to the same sobering conclusion. Delay is the number-one complaint I get all over the world from Christians. From the look of pain and frustration in their eyes it's abundantly clear that the "delay" in entering into what God promised has taken a toll. In the above passage of Scripture, God deals with the subject of "delay" head-on. "You have stayed long enough on this mountain. Turn and resume your journey!" This one statement unmasks the mystery behind all "delayed destinies"—it's due to lingering around the same mountain or problem. The mountain is a metaphor for anything we are allowing satan to use as a tool of delaying our forward advancement in the Kingdom by getting us distracted by focusing on the problem rather than on God and His faithfulness to His word!

I know of anointed people of destiny who are stuck and can't get past the fact that their spouse filed for divorce. They are Christians who went through bankruptcy who are still traumatized by it; they are constantly rehearsing what they could have done differently and also feeling sorry for themselves. However, the one thing that they are not doing is moving forward—they are stuck! In my study of evil altars, I have discovered that there are predictable rituals around "delay." Wherever there are "rituals," there is an altar; in this case it's an evil altar of delay! The *dangerous prayer* below will help you prosecute and destroy this evil altar of delay. It's time for you to experience supernatural acceleration—no more delays and no more postponements concerning what God has called you to do!

Prayer of Activation

1. Address the Father in Praise and Worship

Heavenly Father, holy is Your name and greatly to be praised. I worship and adore You in Jesus' name. May Your Kingdom manifest in my life as it is in Heaven. Plead my cause, O Lord, with those who strive with me; fight against any entity or person who is contending against me. Heavenly Father, it is written in Psalm 27:6, *"And now my head will be lifted up above my enemies around me, in His tent I will offer sacrifices with shouts of joy; I will sing, yes, I will sing praises to the Lord."* Abba, I enjoin my worship to the heavenly chorus of worship of Your holy angels and the crowd of witnesses, in Jesus' name.

2. Ask for the Court to Be Seated

Heavenly Father, Righteous Judge, I ask that the Courts of Heaven be seated according to Daniel 7:9-10. I ask this in Jesus' mighty name. It is written:

> I kept looking until thrones were set up, and the Ancient of Days (God) took His seat; His garment was white as snow and the hair of His head like pure wool. His throne was flames of fire; its wheels were a burning fire. A river of fire was flowing and coming out from before Him; a thousand thousands were attending Him, and ten thousand times ten thousand were standing before Him; the court was seated, and the books were opened.

Heavenly Father, I am requesting the privilege of standing before the courtroom of the Ancient of Days according to what was revealed to the prophet Daniel, in Jesus' name, I pray. Heavenly Father, I stand in Your royal courtroom because of the blood and finished work of Jesus on the cross. I have come to receive Your righteous judgment over my life against the spirit and altar of *delay* that satan planted in my generational bloodline. Heavenly Father, I call upon Your holy angels to be witnesses to my lawsuit and righteous prosecution of the evil altar of *delay*. I decree and declare that this evil altar of *delay* will not postpone or delay breakthroughs and divine opportunities the Lord has ordained for me, in Jesus' name I pray.

3. Surrender Your Rights to Self-Representation to the Lord as Your Advocate

Heavenly Father, Your Word in First John 2:1-2 says, "*My little children, these things I write to you, so that you may not sin. And if anyone sins, we have an Advocate with the Father, Jesus Christ the righteous. And He Himself is the propitiation for our sins, and not for ours only but also for the whole world*"

(NKJV). I thank You that Jesus is my faithful Advocate before the Righteous Judge in the Courts of Heaven. Lord Jesus, I surrender my rights to self-representation and summon You as my Advocate to help me plead my case before the Righteous Judge and prosecute the evil of altar of *delay* that satan planted in my bloodline. I also ask the blessed Holy Spirit, who is the highest officer of the Courts of Heaven here on earth, to make me sensitive to the proceedings of this Court in order to successfully prosecute the evil altar of *delay* in Jesus' name.

4. Summon the Evil Altar and the Idol That Sits on It to Appear in Court

Heavenly Father, even as I stand in Your royal courtroom I present myself as a living sacrifice, holy and acceptable before You according to Romans 12:1. Heavenly Father, Righteous Judge, I summon the altar of *delay* in my bloodline and the idol that sits on it to appear in Your royal courtroom to face prosecution in Jesus' name. For it is written in First Corinthians 6:3, *"Do you not know that we [believers] will judge angels? How much more then [as to] matters of this life?"* Heavenly Father, I exercise my God-given authority in Christ Jesus to judge demons and principalities, in Jesus' name I pray. Righteous Judge, it is also written in the Constitution of Your Kingdom in First John 3:8, *"For this purpose the Son of God was manifested, that He might destroy the works of the devil"* (NKJV).

5. Address Satan's Accusations and Agree with the Adversary

Heavenly Father, I know that until the end of the age of sin, satan still has legal access to the Courts of Heaven to level accusations against the children of men; for it is written in the book of Revelation 12:10:

> *Then I heard a loud voice in heaven, saying, "Now the salvation, and the power, and the kingdom (dominion, reign) of our God, and the authority of His Christ have come; for*

*the accuser of our [believing] brothers and sisters has been
thrown down [at last], he who accuses them and keeps bringing charges [of sinful behavior] against them before our God
day and night."*

Heavenly Father, the Lord Jesus also said in the book of Matthew 5:25:

*Come to terms quickly [at the earliest opportunity] with your
opponent at law while you are with him on the way [to court],
so that your opponent does not hand you over to the judge, and
the judge to the guard, and you are thrown into prison.*

Heavenly Father, in all humility, while renouncing the spirit of pride,
I choose to quickly agree with the legal accusations of my adversary, satan.
Righteous Judge, every accusation that satan has filed against me and my
bloodline in this Court is true.

6. Repent

Heavenly Father, I repent for my personal transgressions, and for the
sins and iniquities of my forefathers that opened the door for the spirit and
altar of *delay* to oppress my life, in Jesus' name I pray. Lord, every sin of
my forefathers that the enemy is using as a legal right to build cases against
me and to delay my destiny, I ask that the blood of Jesus would just wash
them away. I also repent for self-inflicted word curses and all covenants with
demons that have existed in my ancestral bloodline. I am asking that every
covenant with demonic powers will now be revoked and that their right to
claim me and my bloodline would now be dismissed before Your court, in
Jesus' name. Thank You, Lord, for revoking these demonic covenants and
arresting the evil altar of delay in Jesus' mighty name! Heavenly Father, in
my heartfelt desire to divorce myself from the spirit and altar of *delay*, I give
back everything and anything that the devil would say came from his kingdom. I only want what the blood of Jesus has secured for me.

7. *Appeal to the Blood of Jesus to Wipe Out All Sin (Satan's Evidence)*

Lord Jesus, thank You for cleansing me by Your blood so satan has no legal footing against me in Your courtroom. It is written in First John 1 :9:

> *If we [freely] admit that we have sinned and confess our sins, He is faithful and just [true to His own nature and promises], and will forgive our sins and cleanse us continually from all unrighteousness [our wrongdoing, everything not in conformity with His will and purpose].*

Righteous Judge, I appeal to the blood of Jesus to wipe out all my shortcomings, transgressions, and iniquities, in Jesus' name, I pray. I receive by faith the cleansing power of the blood of Jesus.

8. *Ask the Court to Dismiss All of Satan's Accusations and Charges*

Heavenly Father, based upon Jesus' finished work and my heartfelt repentance, I now move on the Court of Heaven to dismiss all of satan's accusations and charges against me and my bloodline in Jesus' name. For it is written that the accuser of the brethren has been cast down. So, I ask You Father to cast down all of satan's accusations against me, in Jesus' name, I pray.

9. *Ask the Lord to Send Angels to Destroy the Evil Altar and Execute the Lord's Judgment Against It*

Heavenly Father, Righteous Judge, I ask that You send high-ranking angelic officers of the Courts who excel in strength to execute the judgment of Your supreme court and destroy the evil altar of *delay* and the idol that sits on it that satan planted in my bloodline, in Jesus' name I pray. By the spirit of prophecy, I prophesy the complete destruction of the evil altar of *delay* in my life, in Jesus' name. For it is written in Psalm 91:11-12, *"For He will command His angels in regard to you, to protect and defend and guard you in all your ways [of obedience and service]. They will lift you up in their hands, so that you do not [even] strike your foot against a stone."* I receive angelic assistance, right now, in Jesus' name.

10. Present Scriptures That Will Be Used in Issuing a Divine Restraining Order

Heavenly Father, I present before Your Supreme Court the following scriptures as my rock-solid evidence against the spirit and altar of *delay* in my life. It is written:

> *Who has heard of such a thing? Who has seen such things? Can a land be born in one day? Or can a nation be brought forth in a moment? As soon as Zion was in labor, she also brought forth her sons* (Isaiah 66:8).

> *"For I the Lord will speak, and whatever word I speak will be accomplished. It will no longer be delayed, for in your days, O rebellious house, I will speak the word and I will fulfill it," says the Lord God. Again the word of the Lord came to me, saying, "Son of man, behold, the house of Israel is saying, 'The vision that Ezekiel sees is for many years from now, and he prophesies of the times that are far off.' Therefore say to them, 'Thus says the Lord God, "None of My words will be delayed any longer. Whatever word I speak will be fulfilled completely,"'" says the Lord God* (Ezekiel 12:25-28).

Righteous Judge, based upon the aforementioned scriptures, it is clear to me that the spirit and altar of *delay*, if allowed to succeed, would cause great injury to my life, destiny, and also inflict irreparable damage to the purposes of God. I ask that that every legal right the spirit and altar of *delay* is holding be revoked in Jesus' glorious name. Righteous Judge, based upon the aforementioned scriptures, it is clear that I qualify for a divine restraining order against the altar of *delay* and the idol that sits on it, in Jesus' name.

11. Ask the Court to Issue a Divine Restraining Order and Receive the Divine Restraining Order by Faith

Heavenly Father, Righteous Judge, I now ask that a divine restraining order and a permanent injunction against the spirit and altar of *delay* in my life would now be issued by the authority of Your Supreme Court, in Jesus' name. Heavenly Father, I decree and declare that any and all forms of *delay* the devil has issued or is orchestrating against my life are now cancelled in Jesus' glorious name. Heavenly Father, I receive this divine restraining order and permanent injunction by faith, in Jesus' name. For it is written in the Constitution of Your Kingdom in Hebrews 11:6, *"But without faith it is impossible to [walk with God and] please Him, for whoever comes [near] to God must [necessarily] believe that God exists and that He rewards those who [earnestly and diligently] seek Him."* I believe and declare by faith that the spirit and altar of *delay* in my life has been judged, in Jesus' name!

12. Ask the Lord to Seal Your Righteous Verdict and Court Proceedings in the Blood of Jesus

Heavenly Father, Righteous Judge, I now ask You to seal my righteous verdict against the spirit and altar of *delay* in the precious blood of Jesus. May You also cover with the blood of Jesus all my legal proceedings in this Court in Jesus' name. I decree and declare that my righteous verdict of release and breakthrough from the evil altar of *delay* is now secured in the documents of the Courts of Heaven. For it is written in John's Gospel, chapter 8:36, *"So if the Son makes you free, then you are unquestionably free."* I decree and declare that I am free of the evil altar of *delay* in Jesus' name, amen!

Prayer #19

Uprooting the Altar of Self-Sabotage

If you have been snared with the words of your lips, If you have been trapped by the speech of your mouth, do this now, my son, and release yourself [from the obligation]; since you have come into the hand of your neighbor, go humble yourself, and plead with your neighbor [to pay his debt and release you].

—**Proverbs 6:2-3**

There is nothing more dangerous than self-sabotage, because in this scenario you literally become your own worst enemy. It's unnatural for anyone to work against their own interests. So it goes without saying that self-sabotage is driven by demons. After observing human behavior and studying many kinds of spiritual phenomenon, I have discovered that there are people who attend to an evil altar of self-sabotage. Just when you begin to think that their time of breakthrough has come, they do something stupid or foolish that completely derails and sabotages the very thing God wanted to give or do for them. Some people don't even know why they end up sabotaging themselves. The truth of the matter is that at some point, satan was given the legal right by one of their forefathers to plant an altar of self-sabotage in their bloodline. Take the case of Esau, for instance—he was Isaac's firstborn. As the firstborn of Isaac, the "double portion" blessing of the firstborn was his to enjoy. However, one unfortunate day, Esau came back from hunting wild animals and he was famished. He found his younger brother Jacob cooking porridge. He asked for a cup of porridge and Jacob told him he could have it in exchange for his firstborn birthright, and Esau sold this priceless spiritual blessing for a mere pot of porridge! Who does this? A person who is possessed by an altar of self-sabotage! The *dangerous prayer* below is designed to help you destroy the evil altar of self-sabotage.

Prayer of Activation

1. *Address the Father in Praise and Worship*

Heavenly Father, holy is Your name and greatly to be praised. I worship and adore You in Jesus' name. May Your Kingdom manifest in my life as it is in Heaven. Plead my cause, O Lord, with those who strive with me; fight against any entity or person who is contending against me. Heavenly Father, it is written in Psalm 27:6, *"And now my head will be lifted up above my enemies around me, in His tent I will offer sacrifices with shouts of joy; I will sing, yes, I will sing praises to the Lord."* Abba, I enjoin my worship to the heavenly chorus of worship of Your holy angels and the crowd of witnesses, in Jesus' name.

2. *Ask for the Court to Be Seated*

Heavenly Father, Righteous Judge, I ask that the Courts of Heaven be seated according to Daniel 7:9-10. I ask this in Jesus' mighty name. It is written:

> *I kept looking until thrones were set up, and the Ancient of Days (God) took His seat; His garment was white as snow and the hair of His head like pure wool. His throne was flames of fire; its wheels were a burning fire. A river of fire was flowing*

and coming out from before Him; a thousand thousands were attending Him, and ten thousand times ten thousand were standing before Him; the court was seated, and the books were opened.

Heavenly Father, I am requesting the privilege of standing before the courtroom of the Ancient of Days according to what was revealed to the prophet Daniel, in Jesus' name, I pray. Heavenly Father, I stand in Your royal courtroom because of the blood and finished work of Jesus on the cross. I have come to receive Your righteous judgment over my life against the spirit and altar of *self-sabotage* that satan planted in my generational bloodline. Heavenly Father, I call upon Your holy angels to be witnesses to my lawsuit and righteous prosecution of the evil altar of *self-sabotage*. I decree and declare that this evil altar of *self-sabotage* will not deceive me into becoming my own worst enemy or sabotage divine relationships I need to achieve my God-given destiny here on earth, in Jesus' name I pray.

3. Surrender Your Rights to Self-Representation to the Lord as Your Advocate

Heavenly Father, Your Word in First John 2:1-2 says, *"My little children, these things I write to you, so that you may not sin. And if anyone sins, we have an Advocate with the Father, Jesus Christ the righteous. And He Himself is the propitiation for our sins, and not for ours only but also for the whole world"* (NKJV). I thank You that Jesus is my faithful Advocate before the Righteous Judge in the Courts of Heaven. Lord Jesus, I surrender my rights to self-representation and summon You as my Advocate to help me plead my case before the Righteous Judge and prosecute the evil of altar of *self-sabotage* that satan planted in my bloodline. I also ask the blessed Holy Spirit, who is the highest officer of the Courts of Heaven here on earth, to make me sensitive to the proceedings of this Court in order to successfully prosecute the evil altar of *self-sabotage* in Jesus' name.

4. Summon the Evil Altar and the Idol That Sits on It to Appear in Court

Heavenly Father, even as I stand in Your royal courtroom I present myself as a living sacrifice, holy and acceptable before You according to Romans 12:1. Heavenly Father, Righteous Judge, I summon the altar of *self-sabotage* in my bloodline and the idol that sits on it to appear in Your royal courtroom to face prosecution in Jesus' name. For it is written in First Corinthians 6:3, *"Do you not know that we [believers] will judge angels? How much more then [as to] matters of this life?"* Heavenly Father, I exercise my God-given authority in Christ Jesus to judge demons and principalities, in Jesus' name I pray. Righteous Judge, it is also written in the Constitution of Your Kingdom in First John 3:8, *"For this purpose the Son of God was manifested, that He might destroy the works of the devil"* (NKJV).

5. Address Satan's Accusations and Agree with the Adversary

Heavenly Father, I know that until the end of the age of sin, satan still has legal access to the Courts of Heaven to level accusations against the children of men; for it is written in the book of Revelation 12:10:

> *Then I heard a loud voice in heaven, saying, "Now the salvation, and the power, and the kingdom (dominion, reign) of our God, and the authority of His Christ have come; for the accuser of our [believing] brothers and sisters has been thrown down [at last], he who accuses them and keeps bringing charges [of sinful behavior] against them before our God day and night."*

Heavenly Father, the Lord Jesus also said in the book of Matthew 5:25:

> *Come to terms quickly [at the earliest opportunity] with your opponent at law while you are with him on the way [to court],*

so that your opponent does not hand you over to the judge, and the judge to the guard, and you are thrown into prison.

Heavenly Father, in all humility, while renouncing the spirit of pride, I choose to quickly agree with the legal accusations of my adversary, satan. Righteous Judge, every accusation that satan has filed against me and my bloodline in this Court is true.

6. Repent

Heavenly Father, I repent for my personal transgressions, and for the sins and iniquities of my forefathers that opened the door for the spirit and altar of *self-sabotage* to oppress my life, in Jesus' name I pray. Lord, every sin of my forefathers that the enemy is using as a legal right to build cases against me and *sabotage* my destiny, I ask that the blood of Jesus would just wash them away. I also repent for self-inflicted word curses and all covenants with demons that have existed in my ancestral bloodline that satan is using to *sabotage* my life. I am asking that every covenant with demonic powers will now be revoked and that their right to claim me and my bloodline would now be dismissed before Your court, in Jesus' name. Thank You, Lord, for revoking these demonic covenants and evil altars of *sabotage* in Jesus' mighty name! Heavenly Father, in my heartfelt desire to divorce myself from the spirit and altar of *self-sabotage,* I give back everything and anything that the devil would say came from his kingdom. I only want what the blood of Jesus has secured for me.

7. Appeal to the Blood of Jesus to Wipe Out All Sin (Satan's Evidence)

Lord Jesus, thank You for cleansing me by Your blood so satan has no legal footing against me in Your courtroom. It is written in First John 1:9:

*If we [freely] admit that we have sinned and confess our sins,
He is faithful and just [true to His own nature and promises],
and will forgive our sins and cleanse us continually from all
unrighteousness [our wrongdoing, everything not in conformity with His will and purpose].*

Righteous Judge, I appeal to the blood of Jesus to wipe out all my short-comings, transgressions, and iniquities, in Jesus' name, I pray. I receive by faith the cleansing power of the blood of Jesus.

8. Ask the Court to Dismiss All of Satan's Accusations and Charges

Heavenly Father, based upon Jesus' finished work and my heartfelt repentance, I now move on the Court of Heaven to dismiss all of satan's accusations and charges against me and my bloodline in Jesus' name. For it is written that the accuser of the brethren has been cast down. So, I ask You Father to cast down all of satan's accusations against me, in Jesus' name, I pray.

9. Ask the Lord to Send Angels to Destroy the Evil Altar and Execute the Lord's Judgment Against It

Heavenly Father, Righteous Judge, I ask that You send high-ranking angelic officers of the Courts who excel in strength to execute the judgment of Your supreme court and destroy the evil altar of *self-sabotage* and the idol that sits on it that satan planted in my bloodline, in Jesus' name I pray. By the spirit of prophecy, I prophesy the complete destruction of the evil altar of *self-sabotage* in my life, in Jesus' name. For it is written in Psalm 91:11-12, *"For He will command His angels in regard to you, to protect and defend and guard you in all your ways [of obedience and service]. They will lift you up in their hands, so that you do not [even] strike your foot against a stone."* I receive angelic assistance, right now, in Jesus' name.

10. Present Scriptures That Will Be Used in Issuing a Divine Restraining Order

Heavenly Father, I present before Your Supreme Court the following scriptures as my rock-solid evidence against the spirit and altar of *self-sabotage* in my life. It is written:

> *He shall call upon Me, and I will answer him; I will be with him in trouble; I will deliver him and honor him. With long life I will satisfy him, and show him My salvation* (Psalm 91:15-16 NKJV).

> *The thief does not come except to steal, and to kill, and to destroy. I have come that they may have life, and that they may have it more abundantly* (John 10:10 NKJV).

> *I will not die, but live, and declare the works and recount the illustrious acts of the Lord* (Psalm 118:17).

Righteous Judge, based upon the aforementioned scriptures, it is clear to me that the spirit and altar of *self-sabotage*, if allowed to succeed, would cause great injury to my life, destiny, and also inflict irreparable damage to the purposes of God. I ask that that every legal right the spirit and altar of *self-sabotage* is holding be revoked in Jesus' glorious name. Righteous Judge, based upon the aforementioned scriptures, it is clear that I qualify for a divine restraining order against the altar of *self-sabotage* and the idol that sits on it, in Jesus' name.

11. Ask the Court to Issue a Divine Restraining Order and Receive the Divine Restraining Order by Faith

Heavenly Father, Righteous Judge, I now ask that a divine restraining order and a permanent injunction against the spirit and altar of *self-sabotage* in my life would now be issued by the authority of Your Supreme Court, in

Jesus' name. Heavenly Father, I decree and declare that any and all forms of *self-sabotage* the devil is orchestrating against my life are now cancelled in Jesus' glorious name. Heavenly Father, I receive this divine restraining order and permanent injunction by faith, in Jesus' name. For it is written in the Constitution of Your Kingdom in Hebrews 11:6, *"But without faith it is impossible to [walk with God and] please Him, for whoever comes [near] to God must [necessarily] believe that God exists and that He rewards those who [earnestly and diligently] seek Him."* I believe and declare by faith that the spirit and altar of *self-sabotage* in my life has been judged, in Jesus' name!

12. Ask the Lord to Seal Your Righteous Verdict and Court Proceedings in the Blood of Jesus

Heavenly Father, Righteous Judge, I now ask You to seal my righteous verdict against the spirit and altar of *self-sabotage* in the precious blood of Jesus. May You also cover with the blood of Jesus all my legal proceedings in this Court in Jesus' name. I decree and declare that my righteous verdict of release and breakthrough from the evil altar of *self-sabotage* is now secured in the documents of the Courts of Heaven. For it is written in John's Gospel, chapter 8:36, *"So if the Son makes you free, then you are unquestionably free."* I decree and declare that I am free of the evil altar of *self-sabotage* in Jesus' name, amen!

Prayer #20

Uprooting the Altar of Abortion Spirits

Samuel said to Saul, "You have acted foolishly; you have not kept the commandment of the Lord your God, which He commanded you, for [if you had obeyed] the Lord would have established your kingdom over Israel forever. But now your kingdom shall not endure. The Lord has sought out for Himself a man (David) after His own heart, and the Lord has appointed him as leader and ruler over His people, because you have not kept (obeyed) what the Lord commanded you."

—1 Samuel 13:13-14

Perhaps there is nothing more common to the human experience, ever since the fall of man in the garden of Eden, than the evil ministry of abortion spirits. I am ashamed to say that I live in a country (USA) that leads the world in the number of aborted babies per year. When a baby is aborted, everything it contained in terms of both purpose and potential is declared null and void. Heaven weeps because some of these aborted babies were carrying medicines and vaccines for the diseases of tomorrow. The *dangerous prayer* below is also designed to destroy the evil altar of abortion spirits in your bloodline that have been killing babies.

Notwithstanding the importance of stopping the abortion of babies, there is another very common and tragic aspect to the operation of the evil altar of abortion spirits. Let us first define the word *abortion*. According to Dictionary.com the word *abortion* means to "fail, cease, or stop at an early or premature stage." This is the aspect of the evil altar of abortion spirits that I have seen all over the world. There are Christians whose businesses, aspirations, and promising careers died prematurely for some minuscule reason. Many have prematurely disconnected with their God-given spiritual fathers or destiny helpers because they got offended or sidetracked just before these people released the spiritual and natural deposits they were carrying from God for the people they were assigned to. If you are one of those people who have been suffering abortion of opportunities, relationships, careers, and projects, then the following *dangerous prayer* for destroying the evil altar of abortion spirits is for you.

Prayer of Activation

1. *Address the Father in Praise and Worship*

Heavenly Father, holy is Your name and greatly to be praised. I worship and adore You in Jesus' name. May Your Kingdom manifest in my life as it is in Heaven. Plead my cause, O Lord, with those who strive with me; fight against any entity or person who is contending against me. Heavenly Father, it is written in Psalm 27:6, *"And now my head will be lifted up above my enemies around me, in His tent I will offer sacrifices with shouts of joy; I will sing, yes, I will sing praises to the Lord."* Abba, I enjoin my worship to the heavenly chorus of worship of Your holy angels and the crowd of witnesses, in Jesus' name.

2. Ask for the Court to Be Seated

Heavenly Father, Righteous Judge, I ask that the Courts of Heaven be seated according to Daniel 7:9-10. I ask this in Jesus' mighty name. It is written:

> I kept looking until thrones were set up, and the Ancient of Days (God) took His seat; His garment was white as snow and the hair of His head like pure wool. His throne was flames of fire; its wheels were a burning fire. A river of fire was flowing and coming out from before Him; a thousand thousands were attending Him, and ten thousand times ten thousand were standing before Him; the court was seated, and the books were opened.

Heavenly Father, I am requesting the privilege of standing before the courtroom of the Ancient of Days according to what was revealed to the prophet Daniel, in Jesus' name, I pray. Heavenly Father, I stand in Your royal courtroom because of the blood and finished work of Jesus on the cross. I have come to receive Your righteous judgment over my life against the altar of *abortion spirits* that satan planted in my generational bloodline. Heavenly Father, I call upon Your holy angels to be witnesses to my lawsuit and righteous prosecution of the evil altar of *abortion spirits*. I decree and declare that this evil altar of *abortion spirits* will not abort my God-given destiny or the divine relationships I need to achieve my God-given destiny here on earth, in Jesus' name I pray.

3. Surrender Your Rights to Self-Representation to the Lord as Your Advocate

Heavenly Father, Your Word in First John 2:1-2 says, "*My little children, these things I write to you, so that you may not sin. And if anyone sins, we have an Advocate with the Father, Jesus Christ the righteous. And He Himself is the propitiation for our sins, and not for ours only but also for the whole world"* (NKJV). I thank You that Jesus is my faithful Advocate before the Righteous Judge in the Courts of Heaven. Lord Jesus, I surrender my rights to self-representation and summon You as my Advocate to help me plead my case before the Righteous Judge and prosecute the evil of altar of *abortion spirits* that satan planted in my bloodline. I also ask the blessed Holy Spirit, who is the highest officer of the Courts of Heaven here on earth, to make me sensitive to the proceedings of this Court in order to successfully prosecute the evil altar of *abortion spirits* in Jesus' name.

4. Summon the Evil Altar and the Idol That Sits on It to Appear in Court

Heavenly Father, even as I stand in Your royal courtroom I present myself as a living sacrifice, holy and acceptable before You according to Romans 12:1. Heavenly Father, Righteous Judge, I summon the altar of *abortion spirits* in my bloodline and the idol that sits on it to appear in Your royal courtroom to face prosecution in Jesus' name. For it is written in First Corinthians 6:3, *"Do you not know that we [believers] will judge angels? How much more then [as to] matters of this life?"* Heavenly Father, I exercise my God-given authority in Christ Jesus to judge demons and principalities, in Jesus' name I pray. Righteous Judge, it is also written in the Constitution of Your Kingdom in First John 3:8, *"For this purpose the Son of God was manifested, that He might destroy the works of the devil"* (NKJV).

5. Address Satan's Accusations and Agree with the Adversary

Heavenly Father, I know that until the end of the age of sin, satan still has legal access to the Courts of Heaven to level accusations against the children of men; for it is written in the book of Revelation 12:10:

> *Then I heard a loud voice in heaven, saying, "Now the salvation, and the power, and the kingdom (dominion, reign)*

of our God, and the authority of His Christ have come; for the accuser of our [believing] brothers and sisters has been thrown down [at last], he who accuses them and keeps bringing charges [of sinful behavior] against them before our God day and night."

Heavenly Father, the Lord Jesus also said in the book of Matthew 5:25:

Come to terms quickly [at the earliest opportunity] with your opponent at law while you are with him on the way [to court], so that your opponent does not hand you over to the judge, and the judge to the guard, and you are thrown into prison.

Heavenly Father, in all humility, while renouncing the spirit of pride, I choose to quickly agree with the legal accusations of my adversary, satan. Righteous Judge, every accusation that satan has filed against me and my bloodline in this Court is true.

6. Repent

Heavenly Father, I repent for my personal transgressions, and for the sins and iniquities of my forefathers that opened the door for the altar of *abortion spirits* to oppress my life, in Jesus' name I pray. Lord, every sin of my forefathers that *abortion spirits* are using as a legal right to build cases against me and to abort my destiny, I ask that the blood of Jesus would just wash them away. I repent for anyone in my bloodline who has ever committed an abortion. I also repent for self-inflicted word curses and all covenants with demons that have existed in my ancestral bloodline. I am asking that every covenant with demonic powers will now be revoked and that their right to claim me and my bloodline would now be dismissed before Your court, in Jesus' name. Thank You, Lord, for revoking these demonic covenants and evil altars in Jesus' mighty name! Heavenly Father, in my heartfelt desire to divorce myself from the altar of *abortion spirits*, I give back everything and anything that the devil would say came from his kingdom. I only want what the blood of Jesus has secured for me.

7. *Appeal to the Blood of Jesus to Wipe Out All Sin (Satan's Evidence)*

Lord Jesus, thank You for cleansing me by Your blood so satan has no legal footing against me in Your courtroom. It is written in First John 1:9:

If we [freely] admit that we have sinned and confess our sins, He is faithful and just [true to His own nature and promises], and will forgive our sins and cleanse us continually from all unrighteousness [our wrongdoing, everything not in conformity with His will and purpose].

Righteous Judge, I appeal to the blood of Jesus to wipe out all my shortcomings, transgressions, and iniquities, in Jesus' name, I pray. I receive by faith the cleansing power of the blood of Jesus.

8. *Ask the Court to Dismiss All of Satan's Accusations and Charges*

Heavenly Father, based upon Jesus' finished work and my heartfelt repentance, I now move on the Court of Heaven to dismiss all of satan's accusations and charges against me and my bloodline in Jesus' name. For it is written that the accuser of the brethren has been cast down. So, I ask You Father to cast down all of satan's accusations against me, in Jesus' name, I pray.

9. *Ask the Lord to Send Angels to Destroy the Evil Altar and Execute the Lord's Judgment Against It*

Heavenly Father, Righteous Judge, I ask that You send high-ranking angelic officers of the Courts who excel in strength to execute the judgment of Your supreme court and destroy the evil altar of *abortion spirits* and the idol that sits on it that satan planted in my bloodline, in Jesus' name I pray. By the spirit of prophecy, I prophesy the complete destruction of the evil altar of *abortion spirits* in my life, in Jesus' name. For it is written in Psalm 91:11-12, *"For He will command His angels in regard to you, to protect and defend and guard you in all your ways [of obedience and service]. They will lift you up in their hands, so that you do not [even] strike your foot against a stone."* I receive angelic assistance, right now, in Jesus' name.

10. Present Scriptures That Will Be Used in Issuing a Divine Restraining Order

Heavenly Father, I present before Your Supreme Court the following scriptures as my rock-solid evidence against the altar of *abortion spirits* in my life. It is written:

> *"Then I will rebuke the devourer (insects, plague) for your sake and he will not destroy the fruits of the ground, nor will your vine in the field drop its grapes [before harvest],"* says the Lord of hosts. *"All nations shall call you happy and blessed, for you shall be a land of delight,"* says the Lord of hosts (Malachi 3:11-12).
>
> *I will not die, but live, and declare the works and recount the illustrious acts of the Lord* (Psalm 118:17).

Righteous Judge, based upon the aforementioned scriptures, it is clear that the altar of *abortion spirits,* if allowed to succeed, would cause great injury to my life, destiny, and also inflict irreparable damage to the purposes of God. I ask that that every legal right the altar of *abortion spirits* is holding be revoked in Jesus' glorious name. Righteous Judge, based upon the aforementioned scriptures, it is clear that I qualify for a divine restraining order against the altar of *abortion spirits* and the idol that sits on it, in Jesus' name.

11. Ask the Court to Issue a Divine Restraining Order and Receive the Divine Restraining Order by Faith

Heavenly Father, Righteous Judge, I now ask that a divine restraining order and a permanent injunction against the altar of *abortion spirits* n my life would now be issued by the authority of Your Supreme Court, in Jesus' name. Heavenly Father, I decree and declare that any and all forms of *abortion spirits* the devil has unleashed against my life, ministry or business are now cancelled in Jesus' glorious name. Heavenly Father, I receive this divine restraining order and permanent injunction by faith, in Jesus' name. For it is written in the Constitution of Your Kingdom in Hebrews 11:6, *"But without faith it is impossible to [walk with God and] please Him, for whoever comes [near] to God must [necessarily] believe that God exists and that He rewards those who [earnestly and diligently] seek Him."* I believe and declare by faith that the altar of *abortion spirits* in my life has been judged, in Jesus' name!

12. Ask the Lord to Seal Your Righteous Verdict and Court Proceedings in the Blood of Jesus

Heavenly Father, Righteous Judge, I now ask You to seal my righteous verdict against the altar of *abortion spirits* in the precious blood of Jesus. May You also cover with the blood of Jesus all my legal proceedings in this Court in Jesus' name. I decree and declare that my righteous verdict of release and breakthrough from the evil altar of *abortion spirits* is now secured in the documents of the Courts of Heaven. For it is written in John's Gospel, chapter 8:36, *"So if the Son makes you free, then you are unquestionably free."* I decree and declare that I am free of the evil altar of *abortion spirits* in Jesus' name, amen!

Prayer #21

Uprooting the Altar of Strife and Confusion

But if ye have bitter envying and strife in your hearts, glory not, and lie not against the truth. This wisdom descendeth not from above, but is earthly, sensual, devilish. For where envying and strife is, there is confusion and every evil work.

—James 3:14-16 KJV

Every time I see people fighting or quarrelling, especially Christians, the above passage of Scripture quickly comes to mind. The Bible makes it clear that wherever there is envying and strife there's confusion and every evil work! I want that last statement to really sink in. First, it means that the altar of strife is the one that opens the door to all kinds of confusion that is being released in certain atmospheres and in the lives of certain people. Second, the altar of strife and confusion ultimately opens the door for the manifestation of every evil work! To me this is really scary! The term or the phrase *every evil work* means that nothing evil or wicked is left out of the equation. I know families as well as husbands and wives who are always fighting over something. They have endless quarrels over the stupidest of things. I have been to so-called family reunions where I saw the evil altar of strife and confusion take over and destroy the entire gathering. I have also seen churches and businesses that have been destroyed by the altar of strife and confusion. Truly, this is not an evil altar to play with. It must be destroyed in the Courts of Heaven. The following *dangerous prayer* is designed to help you and me destroy the evil altar of strife and confusion.

Prayer of Activation

1. Address the Father in Praise and Worship

Heavenly Father, holy is Your name and greatly to be praised. I worship and adore You in Jesus' name. May Your Kingdom manifest in my life as it is in Heaven. Plead my cause, O Lord, with those who strive with me; fight against any entity or person who is contending against me. Heavenly Father, it is written in Psalm 27:6, *"And now my head will be lifted up above my enemies around me, in His tent I will offer sacrifices with shouts of joy; I will sing, yes, I will sing praises to the Lord."* Abba, I enjoin my worship to the heavenly chorus of worship of Your holy angels and the crowd of witnesses, in Jesus' name.

2. Ask for the Court to Be Seated

Heavenly Father, Righteous Judge, I ask that the Courts of Heaven be seated according to Daniel 7:9-10. I ask this in Jesus' mighty name. It is written:

> *I kept looking until thrones were set up, and the Ancient of Days (God) took His seat; His garment was white as snow and the hair of His head like pure wool. His throne was flames of fire; its wheels were a burning fire. A river of fire was flowing and coming out from before Him; a thousand thousands were attending Him, and ten thousand times ten thousand were standing before Him; the court was seated, and the books were opened.*

Heavenly Father, I am requesting the privilege of standing before the courtroom of the Ancient of Days according to what was revealed to the prophet Daniel, in Jesus' name, I pray. Heavenly Father, I stand in Your royal courtroom because of the blood and finished work of Jesus on the cross. I have come to receive Your righteous judgment over my life against the spirit and altar of *strife and confusion* that satan planted in my generational bloodline. Heavenly Father, I call upon Your holy angels to be witnesses to my lawsuit and righteous prosecution of the evil *strife and confusion*. I decree and declare that this evil altar of *strife and confusion* will not control me nor strain relationship with family members and divine relationships I need to achieve my God-given destiny here on earth, in Jesus' name I pray.

3. Surrender Your Rights to Self-Representation to the Lord as Your Advocate

Heavenly Father, Your Word in First John 2:1-2 says, "*My little children, these things I write to you, so that you may not sin. And if anyone sins, we have an Advocate with the Father, Jesus Christ the righteous. And He Himself is the propitiation for our sins, and not for ours only but also for the whole world*" (NKJV). I thank You that Jesus is my faithful Advocate before the Righteous Judge in the Courts of Heaven. Lord Jesus, I surrender my rights to self-representation and summon You as my Advocate to help me plead my case before the Righteous Judge and prosecute the evil of altar of *strife and confusion* that satan planted in my bloodline. I also ask the blessed Holy Spirit, who is the highest officer of the Courts of Heaven here on earth, to make me sensitive to the proceedings of this Court in order to successfully prosecute the evil altar of *strife and confusion* in Jesus' name.

4. Summon the Evil Altar and the Idol That Sits on It to Appear in Court

Heavenly Father, even as I stand in Your royal courtroom I present myself as a living sacrifice, holy and acceptable before You according to Romans 12:1. Heavenly Father, Righteous Judge, I summon the altar of *strife and confusion* in my bloodline and the idol that sits on it to appear in Your royal courtroom to face prosecution in Jesus' name. For it is written in First Corinthians 6:3, *"Do you not know that we [believers] will judge angels? How much more then [as to] matters of this life?"* Heavenly Father, I exercise my God-given authority in Christ Jesus to judge demons and principalities, in Jesus' name I pray. Righteous Judge, it is also written in the Constitution of Your Kingdom in First John 3:8, *"For this purpose the Son of God was manifested, that He might destroy the works of the devil"* (NKJV).

5. Address Satan's Accusations and Agree with the Adversary

Heavenly Father, I know that until the end of the age of sin, satan still has legal access to the Courts of Heaven to level accusations against the children of men; for it is written in the book of Revelation 12:10:

> *Then I heard a loud voice in heaven, saying, "Now the salvation, and the power, and the kingdom (dominion, reign) of our God, and the authority of His Christ have come; for the accuser of our [believing] brothers and sisters has been thrown down [at last], he who accuses them and keeps bringing charges [of sinful behavior] against them before our God day and night."*

Heavenly Father, the Lord Jesus also said in the book of Matthew 5:25:

> *Come to terms quickly [at the earliest opportunity] with your opponent at law while you are with him on the way [to court],*

so that your opponent does not hand you over to the judge, and
the judge to the guard, and you are thrown into prison.

Heavenly Father, in all humility, while renouncing the spirit of pride, I choose to quickly agree with the legal accusations of my adversary, satan. Righteous Judge, every accusation that satan has filed against me and my bloodline in this Court is true.

6. Repent

Heavenly Father, I repent for my personal transgressions, and for the sins and iniquities of my forefathers that opened the door for the spirit and altar of *strife and confusion* to oppress my life, in Jesus' name I pray. Lord, every sin of my forefathers that the enemy is using as a legal right to build cases against me and to cause me to wallow in endless *strife and confusion,* I ask that the blood of Jesus would just wash them away. I repent for anytime I have been the source of *strife and confusion,* in Jesus' name. I also repent for self-inflicted word curses and all covenants with demons that have existed in my ancestral bloodline. I am asking that every covenant with demonic powers and the altar of *strife and confusion* will now be revoked and that their right to claim me and my bloodline would now be dismissed before Your court, in Jesus' name. Thank You, Lord, for revoking these demonic covenants and evil altars in Jesus' mighty name! Heavenly Father, in my heartfelt desire to divorce myself from the spirit and altar of *strife and confusion*, I give back everything and anything that the devil would say came from his kingdom. I only want what the blood of Jesus has secured for me.

7. Appeal to the Blood of Jesus to Wipe Out All Sin (Satan's Evidence)

Lord Jesus, thank You for cleansing me by Your blood so satan has no legal footing against me in Your courtroom. It is written in First John 1:9:

If we [freely] admit that we have sinned and confess our sins,
He is faithful and just [true to His own nature and promises],
and will forgive our sins and cleanse us continually from all
unrighteousness [our wrongdoing, everything not in confor-
mity with His will and purpose].

Righteous Judge, I appeal to the blood of Jesus to wipe out all my short-comings, transgressions, and iniquities, in Jesus' name, I pray. I receive by faith the cleansing power of the blood of Jesus.

8. *Ask the Court to Dismiss All of Satan's Accusations and Charges*

Heavenly Father, based upon Jesus' finished work and my heartfelt repentance, I now move on the Court of Heaven to dismiss all of satan's accusations and charges against me and my bloodline in Jesus' name. For it is written that the accuser of the brethren has been cast down. So, I ask You Father to cast down all of satan's accusations against me, in Jesus' name, I pray.

9. *Ask the Lord to Send Angels to Destroy the Evil Altar and Execute the Lord's Judgment Against It*

Heavenly Father, Righteous Judge, I ask that You send high-ranking angelic officers of the Courts who excel in strength to execute the judgment of Your supreme court and destroy the evil altar of *strife and confusion* and the idol that sits on it that satan planted in my bloodline, in Jesus' name I pray. By the spirit of prophecy, I prophesy the complete destruction of the evil altar of *strife and confusion* in my life, in Jesus' name. For it is written in Psalm 91:11-12, *"For He will command His angels in regard to you, to protect and defend and guard you in all your ways [of obedience and service]. They will lift you up in their hands, so that you do not [even] strike your foot against a stone."* I receive angelic assistance, right now, in Jesus' name.

10. Present Scriptures That Will Be Used in Issuing a Divine Restraining Order

Heavenly Father, I present before Your Supreme Court the following scriptures as my rock-solid evidence against the spirit and altar of *strife and confusion* in my life. It is written:

> *Continually pursue peace with everyone, and the sanctification without which no one will [ever] see the Lord* (Hebrews 12:14).

> *Make every effort to keep the oneness of the Spirit in the bond of peace [each individual working together to make the whole successful]* (Ephesians 4:3).

Righteous Judge, based upon the aforementioned scriptures, it is clear that the spirit and altar of *strife and confusion,* if allowed to succeed, would cause great injury to my life, destiny, and also inflict irreparable damage to the purposes of God. I ask that that every legal right the spirit and altar of *strife and confusion* is holding be revoked in Jesus' glorious name. Righteous Judge, based upon the aforementioned scriptures, it is clear that I qualify for a divine restraining order against the altar of *strife and confusion* and the idol that sits on it, in Jesus' name.

11. Ask the Court to Issue a Divine Restraining Order and Receive the Divine Restraining Order by Faith

Heavenly Father, Righteous Judge, I now ask that a divine restraining order and a permanent injunction against the spirit and altar of *strife and confusion* in my life would now be issued by the authority of Your Supreme Court, in Jesus' name. Heavenly Father, I decree and declare that any and all forms of *strife and confusion* the devil is orchestrating against my life is now cancelled in Jesus' glorious name. Heavenly Father, I receive this divine restraining order and permanent injunction by faith, in Jesus' name. For it is written in the Constitution of Your Kingdom in Hebrews 11:6, *"But without faith it is impossible to [walk with God and] please Him, for whoever comes [near] to God must [necessarily] believe that God exists and that He rewards those who [earnestly and diligently] seek Him."* I believe and declare by faith that the spirit and altar of *strife and confusion* in my life has been judged, in Jesus' name!

12. Ask the Lord to Seal Your Righteous Verdict and Court Proceedings in the Blood of Jesus

Heavenly Father, Righteous Judge, I now ask You to seal my righteous verdict against the spirit and altar of *strife and confusion* in the precious blood of Jesus. May You also cover with the blood of Jesus all my legal proceedings in this Court in Jesus' name. I decree and declare that my righteous verdict of release and breakthrough from the evil altar of *strife and confusion* is now secured in the documents of the Courts of Heaven. For it is written in John's Gospel, chapter 8:36, *"So if the Son makes you free, then you are unquestionably free."* I decree and declare that I am free of the evil altar of *strife and confusion* in Jesus' name, amen!

Prayer #22

Uprooting the Altar of Lying Spirits

The Lord said to him, "In what way?" So he said, "I will go out and be a lying spirit in the mouth of all his prophets." And the Lord said, "You shall persuade him, and also prevail. Go out and do so."
—1 Kings 22:22 NKJV

Only God knows how many relationships, careers, marriages and businesses have been destroyed because of a lie! Yes, it's abundantly clear from the testimony of scripture that lying is the devil's favorite tool of destruction. Lying is actually a weapon of mass destruction. I remember years ago watching a movie based upon a true story called *Rosewood*. In this movie a married white woman was having an affair with her husband's coworker. When she was about to get caught, she decided to falsely accuse a black man of raping her in order to deflect blame for herself and hide the affair from her unsuspecting husband. By the time the lie she told was discovered, the entire town of Rosewood (a flourishing black neighborhood) was on fire! Several innocent black men and women had been killed.

There is even a pervasive realm of lying that psychiatric doctors label a "pathology." Consequently, a person who suffers from this mental disease is also known as a pathological liar! These people are like Jim Carrey in the movie *Liar, Liar*! However, I now know better. These people are simply human attendants to the evil altar of lying spirits that they are powerless to break away from, especially if they are Christians but struggle with lying. Thankfully, the *dangerous prayer* below was designed to help you destroy the evil altar of lying spirits in the Courts of Heaven.

Prayer of Activation

1. Address the Father in Praise and Worship

Heavenly Father, holy is Your name and greatly to be praised. I worship and adore You in Jesus' name. May Your Kingdom manifest in my life as it is in Heaven. Plead my cause, O Lord, with those who strive with me; fight against any entity or person who is contending against me. Heavenly Father, it is written in Psalm 27:6, *"And now my head will be lifted up above my enemies around me, in His tent I will offer sacrifices with shouts of joy; I will sing, yes, I will sing praises to the Lord."* Abba, I enjoin my worship to the heavenly chorus of worship of Your holy angels and the crowd of witnesses, in Jesus' name.

2. Ask for the Court to Be Seated

Heavenly Father, Righteous Judge, I ask that the Courts of Heaven be seated according to Daniel 7:9-10. I ask this in Jesus' mighty name. It is written:

> *I kept looking until thrones were set up, and the Ancient of Days (God) took His seat; His garment was white as snow and the hair of His head like pure wool. His throne was flames of fire; its wheels were a burning fire. A river of fire was flowing and coming out from before Him; a thousand thousands were attending Him, and ten thousand times ten thousand were standing before Him; the court was seated, and the books were opened.*

Heavenly Father, I am requesting the privilege of standing before the courtroom of the Ancient of Days according to what was revealed to the prophet Daniel, in Jesus' name, I pray. Heavenly Father, I stand in Your royal courtroom because of the blood and finished work of Jesus on the cross. I have come to receive Your righteous judgment over my life against the altar of *lying spirits* that satan planted in my generational bloodline. Heavenly Father, I call upon Your holy angels to be witnesses to my lawsuit and righteous prosecution of the evil altar of *lying spirits*. I decree and declare that this evil altar of *lying spirits* will not compel me to lie for any reason, especially to the divine relationships I need to achieve my God-given destiny here on earth, in Jesus' name I pray.

3. Surrender Your Rights to Self-Representation to the Lord as Your Advocate

Heavenly Father, Your Word in First John 2:1-2 says, "*My little children, these things I write to you, so that you may not sin. And if anyone sins, we have an Advocate with the Father, Jesus Christ the righteous. And He Himself is the propitiation for our sins, and not for ours only but also for the whole world*" (NKJV). I thank You that Jesus is my faithful Advocate before the Righteous Judge in the Courts of Heaven. Lord Jesus, I surrender my rights to self-representation and summon You as my Advocate to help me plead my case before the Righteous Judge and prosecute the evil of altar of *lying spirits* that satan planted in my bloodline. I also ask the blessed Holy Spirit, who is the highest officer of the Courts of Heaven here on earth, to make me sensitive to the proceedings of this Court in order to successfully prosecute the evil altar of *lying spirits* in Jesus' name.

4. Summon the Evil Altar and the Idol That Sits on It to Appear in Court

Heavenly Father, even as I stand in Your royal courtroom I present myself as a living sacrifice, holy and acceptable before You according to Romans 12:1. Heavenly Father, Righteous Judge, I summon the altar of *lying spirits* in my bloodline and the idol that sits on it to appear in Your royal courtroom to face prosecution in Jesus' name. For it is written in First Corinthians 6:3, *"Do you not know that we [believers] will judge angels? How much more then [as to] matters of this life?"* Heavenly Father, I exercise my God-given authority in Christ Jesus to judge demons and principalities, in Jesus' name I pray. Righteous Judge, it is also written in the Constitution of Your Kingdom in First John 3:8, *"For this purpose the Son of God was manifested, that He might destroy the works of the devil"* (NKJV).

5. Address Satan's Accusations and Agree with the Adversary

Heavenly Father, I know that until the end of the age of sin, satan still has legal access to the Courts of Heaven to level accusations against the children of men; for it is written in the book of Revelation 12:10:

> *Then I heard a loud voice in heaven, saying, "Now the salvation, and the power, and the kingdom (dominion, reign) of our God, and the authority of His Christ have come; for the accuser of our [believing] brothers and sisters has been thrown down [at last], he who accuses them and keeps bringing charges [of sinful behavior] against them before our God day and night."*

Heavenly Father, the Lord Jesus also said in the book of Matthew 5:25:

> *Come to terms quickly [at the earliest opportunity] with your opponent at law while you are with him on the way [to court],*

*so that your opponent does not hand you over to the judge, and
the judge to the guard, and you are thrown into prison.*

Heavenly Father, in all humility, while renouncing the spirit of pride, I choose to quickly agree with the legal accusations of my adversary, satan. Righteous Judge, every accusation that satan has filed against me and my bloodline in this Court is true.

6. Repent

Heavenly Father, I repent for my personal transgressions, and for the sins and iniquities of my forefathers that opened the door for the altar of *lying spirits* to oppress my life, in Jesus' name I pray. Lord, every sin of my forefathers that the enemy is using as a legal right to build cases against me and to deny me my destiny, I ask that the blood of Jesus would just wash them away. I repent for any lie that I have ever told, especially the ones that hurt other people. I also repent for self-inflicted word curses and all covenants with demons of lying that have existed in my ancestral bloodline. I am asking that every covenant with demonic powers will now be revoked and that their right to claim me and my bloodline would now be dismissed before Your court, in Jesus' name. Thank You, Lord, for revoking these demonic covenants and the evil altar of *lying spirits* in Jesus' mighty name! Heavenly Father, in my heartfelt desire to divorce myself from the altar of *lying spirits*, I give back everything and anything that the devil would say came from his kingdom. I only want what the blood of Jesus has secured for me.

7. Appeal to the Blood of Jesus to Wipe Out All Sin (Satan's Evidence)

Lord Jesus, thank You for cleansing me by Your blood so satan has no legal footing against me in Your courtroom. It is written in First John 1:9:

If we [freely] admit that we have sinned and confess our sins,
He is faithful and just [true to His own nature and promises],
and will forgive our sins and cleanse us continually from all
unrighteousness [our wrongdoing, everything not in confor-
mity with His will and purpose].

Righteous Judge, I appeal to the blood of Jesus to wipe out all my short-comings, transgressions, and iniquities, in Jesus' name, I pray. I receive by faith the cleansing power of the blood of Jesus.

8. *Ask the Court to Dismiss All of Satan's Accusations and Charges*

Heavenly Father, based upon Jesus' finished work and my heartfelt repentance, I now move on the Court of Heaven to dismiss all of satan's accusations and charges against me and my bloodline in Jesus' name. For it is written that the accuser of the brethren has been cast down. So, I ask You Father to cast down all of satan's accusations against me, in Jesus' name, I pray.

9. *Ask the Lord to Send Angels to Destroy the Evil Altar and Execute the Lord's Judgment Against It*

Heavenly Father, Righteous Judge, I ask that You send high-ranking angelic officers of the Courts who excel in strength to execute the judgment of Your supreme court and destroy the evil altar of *lying spirits* and the idol that sits on it that satan planted in my bloodline, in Jesus' name I pray. By the spirit of prophecy, I prophesy the complete destruction of the evil altar of *lying spirits* in my life, in Jesus' name. For it is written in Psalm 91:11-12, *"For He will command His angels in regard to you, to protect and defend and guard you in all your ways [of obedience and service]. They will lift you up in their hands, so that you do not [even] strike your foot against a stone."* I receive angelic assistance, right now, in Jesus' name.

10. Present Scriptures That Will Be Used in Issuing a Divine Restraining Order

Heavenly Father, I present before Your Supreme Court the following scriptures as my rock-solid evidence against the altar of *lying spirits* in my life. It is written:

> *You shall not testify falsely [that is, lie, withhold, or manip-ulate the truth] against your neighbor (any person)* (Exodus 20:16).
>
> *And you will know the truth [regarding salvation], and the truth will set you free [from the penalty of sin]* (John 8:32).

Righteous Judge, based upon the aforementioned scriptures, it is clear to me that the altar of *lying spirits,* if allowed to succeed, would cause great injury to my life, destiny, and also inflict irreparable damage to the purposes of God. I ask that that every legal right the spirit and altar of *lying spirits* is holding be revoked in Jesus' glorious name. Righteous Judge, based upon the aforementioned scriptures, it is clear that I qualify for a divine restraining order against the altar of *lying spirits* and the idol that sits on it, in Jesus' name.

11. Ask the Court to Issue a Divine Restraining Order and Receive the Divine Restraining Order by Faith

Heavenly Father, Righteous Judge, I now ask that a divine restraining order and a permanent injunction against the altar of *lying spirits* in my life would now be issued by the authority of Your Supreme Court, in Jesus' name. Heavenly Father, I decree and declare that any *lies* or *lying spirit* the devil is orchestrating against my life are now arrested in Jesus' glorious name. Heavenly Father, I receive this divine restraining order and permanent injunction by faith, in Jesus' name. For it is written in the Constitution of

Your Kingdom in Hebrews 11:6, *"But without faith it is impossible to [walk with God and] please Him, for whoever comes [near] to God must [necessarily] believe that God exists and that He rewards those who [earnestly and diligently] seek Him."* I believe and declare by faith that the altar of *lying spirits* in my life has been judged, in Jesus' name!

12. Ask the Lord to Seal Your Righteous Verdict and Court Proceedings in the Blood of Jesus

Heavenly Father, Righteous Judge, I now ask You to seal my righteous verdict against the altar of *lying spirits* in the precious blood of Jesus. May You also cover with the blood of Jesus all my legal proceedings in this Court in Jesus' name. I decree and declare that my righteous verdict of release and breakthrough from the evil altar of *lying spirits* is now secured in the documents of the Courts of Heaven. For it is written in John's Gospel, chapter 8:36, *"So if the Son makes you free, then you are unquestionably free."* I decree and declare that I am free from the evil altar of *lying spirits* in Jesus' name, amen!

Prayer #23

Uprooting the Altar of False Prophecies

The Lord said to him, "How?" And he said, " I will go out and be a deceiving spirit in the mouth of all his prophets." Then the Lord said, "You are to entice him and also succeed. Go and do so." Now then, behold, the Lord has put a deceiving spirit in the mouth of all these prophets; and the Lord has proclaimed disaster against you.
—**1 Kings 22:22-23**

You cannot read the Bible and not come away with the understanding that God hates false prophecies and false prophets. As a matter of fact, the penalty for false prophecy in the Old Testament was actually death. This is how harshly God looked at the sin of leading people astray using false prophecies. So why does God hate the altar of false prophecies so much? The answer lies in understanding the fact that God uses the medium of prophecy to communicate His will to His children on the earth. And there is nothing more important on Earth than discovering God's will. A false prophecy gives satan the power to control and drive people, especially God's children, in the wrong direction. Imagine being told by a false prophet who to marry only to discover later on that God had nothing to do with it!

The entire religion of Islam, which has millions of followers, was due to false prophecies the prophet Muhammad received from an angel that appeared to him in Medina. The only problem with his extra-biblical revelations is that the Koran points lost souls away from Jesus and the message of salvation found only in Jesus. I know of Christians who will never move in their God-given destiny until they renounce the false prophecies they are holding on to. I know of single brothers and sisters in Christ who are still holding on to prophecies of marrying a man or woman who is currently married, but they keep hoping, waiting, and believing things will change! May the Lord use the *dangerous prayer* below to destroy the evil altar of false prophecies that is controlling our life and holding back our destiny.

Prayer of Activation

1. Address the Father in Praise and Worship

Heavenly Father, holy is Your name and greatly to be praised. I worship and adore You in Jesus' name. May Your Kingdom manifest in my life as it is in Heaven. Plead my cause, O Lord, with those who strive with me; fight against any entity or person who is contending against me. Heavenly Father, it is written in Psalm 27:6, *"And now my head will be lifted up above my enemies around me, in His tent I will offer sacrifices with shouts of joy; I will sing, yes, I will sing praises to the Lord."* Abba, I enjoin my worship to the heavenly chorus of worship of Your holy angels and the crowd of witnesses, in Jesus' name.

2. Ask for the Court to Be Seated

Heavenly Father, Righteous Judge, I ask that the Courts of Heaven be seated according to Daniel 7:9-10. I ask this in Jesus' mighty name. It is written:

> *I kept looking until thrones were set up, and the Ancient of Days (God) took His seat; His garment was white as snow*

and the hair of His head like pure wool. His throne was flames of fire; its wheels were a burning fire. A river of fire was flowing and coming out from before Him; a thousand thousands were attending Him, and ten thousand times ten thousand were standing before Him; the court was seated, and the books were opened.

Heavenly Father, I am requesting the privilege of standing before the courtroom of the Ancient of Days according to what was revealed to the prophet Daniel, in Jesus' name, I pray. Heavenly Father, I stand in Your royal courtroom because of the blood and finished work of Jesus on the cross. I have come to receive Your righteous judgment over my life against the spirit and altar of *false prophecies* that satan planted in my generational bloodline. Heavenly Father, I call upon Your holy angels to be witnesses to my lawsuit and righteous prosecution of the evil altar of *false prophecies*. I decree and declare that this evil altar of *false prophecies* will not deceive me nor waste my time on earth chasing false prophecies that God never spoke over my life, in Jesus' name I pray.

3. *Surrender Your Rights to Self-Representation to the Lord as Your Advocate*

Heavenly Father, Your Word in First John 2:1-2 says, *"My little children, these things I write to you, so that you may not sin. And if anyone sins, we have an Advocate with the Father, Jesus Christ the righteous. And He Himself is the propitiation for our sins, and not for ours only but also for the whole world"* (NKJV). I thank You that Jesus is my faithful Advocate before the Righteous Judge in the Courts of Heaven. Lord Jesus, I surrender my rights to self-representation and summon You as my Advocate to help me plead my case before the Righteous Judge and prosecute the evil of altar of *false prophecies* that satan planted in my bloodline. I also ask the blessed Holy Spirit, who is the highest officer of the Courts of Heaven here on earth, to make me sensitive to the proceedings of this Court in order to successfully prosecute the evil altar of *false prophecies* in Jesus' name.

4. *Summon the Evil Altar and the Idol That Sits on It to Appear in Court*

Heavenly Father, even as I stand in Your royal courtroom I present myself as a living sacrifice, holy and acceptable before You according to Romans 12:1. Heavenly Father, Righteous Judge, I summon the altar of *false prophecies* in my bloodline and the idol that sits on it to appear in Your royal courtroom to face prosecution in Jesus' name. For it is written in First Corinthians 6:3, *"Do you not know that we [believers] will judge angels? How much more then [as to] matters of this life?"* Heavenly Father, I exercise my God-given authority in Christ Jesus to judge demons and principalities, in Jesus' name I pray. Righteous Judge, it is also written in the Constitution of Your Kingdom in First John 3:8, *"For this purpose the Son of God was manifested, that He might destroy the works of the devil"* (NKJV).

5. *Address Satan's Accusations and Agree with the Adversary*

Heavenly Father, I know that until the end of the age of sin, satan still has legal access to the Courts of Heaven to level accusations against the children of men; for it is written in the book of Revelation 12:10:

> *Then I heard a loud voice in heaven, saying, "Now the salvation, and the power, and the kingdom (dominion, reign) of our God, and the authority of His Christ have come; for the accuser of our [believing] brothers and sisters has been thrown down [at last], he who accuses them and keeps bringing charges [of sinful behavior] against them before our God day and night."*

Heavenly Father, the Lord Jesus also said in the book of Matthew 5:25:

Come to terms quickly [at the earliest opportunity] with your opponent at law while you are with him on the way [to court], so that your opponent does not hand you over to the judge, and the judge to the guard, and you are thrown into prison.

Heavenly Father, in all humility, while renouncing the spirit of pride, I choose to quickly agree with the legal accusations of my adversary, satan. Righteous Judge, every accusation that satan has filed against me and my bloodline in this Court is true.

6. Repent

Heavenly Father, I repent for my personal transgressions, and for the sins and iniquities of my forefathers that opened the door for the spirit and altar of *false prophecies* to oppress my life, in Jesus' name I pray. Lord, every sin of my forefathers that the enemy is using as a legal right to build cases against me and to deny me my destiny through *false prophecy*, I ask that the blood of Jesus would just wash them away. I repent for holding on to prophesies that I knew not to be true. I also repent for self-inflicted word curses and all covenants with demons that have existed in my ancestral bloodline. I am asking that every covenant with demonic powers will now be revoked and that their right to claim me and my bloodline would now be dismissed before Your court, in Jesus' name. Thank You, Lord, for revoking these demonic covenants and evil altars in Jesus' mighty name! Heavenly Father, in my heartfelt desire to divorce myself from the spirit and altar of *false prophecies*, I give back everything and anything that the devil would say came from his kingdom. I only want what the blood of Jesus has secured for me.

7. Appeal to the Blood of Jesus to Wipe Out All Sin (Satan's Evidence)

Lord Jesus, thank You for cleansing me by Your blood so satan has no legal footing against me in Your courtroom. It is written in First John 1:9:

If we [freely] admit that we have sinned and confess our sins,
He is faithful and just [true to His own nature and promises],
and will forgive our sins and cleanse us continually from all
unrighteousness [our wrongdoing, everything not in confor-
mity with His will and purpose].

Righteous Judge, I appeal to the blood of Jesus to wipe out all my short-comings, transgressions, and iniquities, in Jesus' name, I pray. I receive by faith the cleansing power of the blood of Jesus.

8. Ask the Court to Dismiss All of Satan's Accusations and Charges

Heavenly Father, based upon Jesus' finished work and my heartfelt repentance, I now move on the Court of Heaven to dismiss all of satan's accusations and charges against me and my bloodline in Jesus' name. For it is written that the accuser of the brethren has been cast down. So, I ask You Father to cast down all of satan's accusations against me, in Jesus' name, I pray.

9. Ask the Lord to Send Angels to Destroy the Evil Altar and Execute the Lord's Judgment Against It

Heavenly Father, Righteous Judge, I ask that You send high-ranking angelic officers of the Courts who excel in strength to execute the judgment of Your supreme court and destroy the evil altar of *false prophecies* and the idol that sits on it that satan planted in my bloodline, in Jesus' name I pray. By the spirit of prophecy, I prophesy the complete destruction of the evil altar of *false prophecies* in my life, in Jesus' name. For it is written in Psalm 91:11-12, *"For He will command His angels in regard to you, to protect and defend and guard you in all your ways [of obedience and service]. They will lift you up in their hands, so that you do not [even] strike your foot against a stone."* I receive angelic assistance, right now, in Jesus' name.

10. Present Scriptures That Will Be Used in Issuing a Divine Restraining Order

Heavenly Father, I present before Your Supreme Court the following scriptures as my rock-solid evidence against the spirit and altar of *false prophecies* in my life. It is written:

> "For there will no longer be any false and empty vision or flattering divination within the house of Israel. For I the Lord will speak, and whatever word I speak will be accomplished. It will no longer be delayed, for in your days, O rebellious house, I will speak the word and I will fulfill it," says the Lord God (Ezekiel 12:24-25).

> "For I know the plans and thoughts that I have for you," says the Lord, "plans for peace and well-being and not for disaster, to give you a future and a hope" (Jeremiah 29:11).

Righteous Judge, based upon the aforementioned scriptures, it is clear to me that the spirit and altar of *false prophecies,* if allowed to succeed, would cause great injury to my life, destiny, and also inflict irreparable damage to the purposes of God. I ask that that every legal right the spirit and altar of *false prophecies* is holding be revoked in Jesus' glorious name. Righteous Judge, based upon the aforementioned scriptures, it is clear that I qualify for a divine restraining order against the altar of *false prophecies* and the idol that sits on it, in Jesus' name.

11. Ask the Court to Issue a Divine Restraining Order and Receive the Divine Restraining Order by Faith

Heavenly Father, Righteous Judge, I now ask that a divine restraining order and a permanent injunction against the spirit and altar of *false prophecies* in my life would now be issued by the authority of Your Supreme Court, in Jesus' name. Heavenly Father, I decree and declare that any and all *false prophecies* the devil has engineered against and over my life are now cancelled in Jesus' glorious name. Heavenly Father, I receive this divine restraining order and permanent injunction by faith, in Jesus' name. For it is written in the Constitution of Your Kingdom in Hebrews 11:6, *"But without faith it is impossible to [walk with God and] please Him, for whoever comes [near] to God must [necessarily] believe that God exists and that He rewards those who [earnestly and diligently] seek Him."* I believe and declare by faith that the spirit and altar of *false prophecies* in my life has been judged, in Jesus' name!

12. Ask the Lord to Seal Your Righteous Verdict and Court Proceedings in the Blood of Jesus

Heavenly Father, Righteous Judge, I now ask You to seal my righteous verdict against the spirit and altar of *false prophecies* in the precious blood of Jesus. May You also cover with the blood of Jesus all my legal proceedings in this Court in Jesus' name. I decree and declare that my righteous verdict of release and breakthrough from the evil altar of *false prophecies* is now secured in the documents of the Courts of Heaven. For it is written in John's Gospel, chapter 8:36, *"So if the Son makes you free, then you are unquestionably free."* I decree and declare that I am free from the evil altar of *false prophecies* in Jesus' name, amen!

Prayer #24

Uprooting the Altar of Fear

For the thing which I greatly fear comes upon me, and that of which I am afraid has come upon me.
—Job 3:25

So, first of all, let me assert my firm belief that the only thing we have to fear is fear itself—nameless, unreasoning, unjustified terror, which paralyzes needed efforts to convert retreat into advance." Those were the words that came directly from President Franklin D. Roosevelt's inaugural speech in 1933. The United States was in the middle of the Great Depression and later to enter World War II. No truer statement has ever been spoken outside of the Bible than the words of a famous American president. Fear is truly a menacing and ruthless terrorist! There are so many people, including Christians, who are constantly living in fear. Let us take the case of Job, for instance. Job was deeply beloved of God and blessed beyond human comprehension. However, he lived under constant fear that his children might sin against God and die! His fears eventually opened the door for satan to level accusations against him in the Courts of Heaven. The global COVID-19 pandemic has only accelerated the fearful living of so many people. The Bible says that fear has torment and whosoever lives in fear is not perfected in the love of God! Perhaps this is why satan loves to use fear to control people's lives and choices. Unfortunately, I have seen too many Christians who are attendants to this evil altar of fear. They service this evil altar every day.

Many are crying for freedom from living in fear. The *dangerous prayer* below is your weapon to destroy the evil altar of fear.

Prayer of Activation

1. Address the Father in Praise and Worship

Heavenly Father, holy is Your name and greatly to be praised. I worship and adore You in Jesus' name. May Your Kingdom manifest in my life as it is in Heaven. Plead my cause, O Lord, with those who strive with me; fight against any entity or person who is contending against me. Heavenly Father, it is written in Psalm 27:6, *"And now my head will be lifted up above my enemies around me, in His tent I will offer sacrifices with shouts of joy; I will sing, yes, I will sing praises to the Lord."* Abba, I enjoin my worship to the heavenly chorus of worship of Your holy angels and the crowd of witnesses, in Jesus' name.

2. Ask for the Court to Be Seated

Heavenly Father, Righteous Judge, I ask that the Courts of Heaven be seated according to Daniel 7:9-10. I ask this in Jesus' mighty name. It is written:

> *I kept looking until thrones were set up, and the Ancient of Days (God) took His seat; His garment was white as snow and the hair of His head like pure wool. His throne was flames of fire; its wheels were a burning fire. A river of fire was flowing and coming out from before Him; a thousand thousands were attending Him, and ten thousand times ten thousand were standing before Him; the court was seated, and the books were opened.*

Heavenly Father, I am requesting the privilege of standing before the courtroom of the Ancient of Days according to what was revealed to the prophet Daniel, in Jesus' name, I pray. Heavenly Father, I stand in Your royal courtroom because of the blood and finished work of Jesus on the cross. I have come to receive Your righteous judgment over my life against the spirit and altar of *fear* that satan planted in my generational bloodline. Heavenly Father, I call upon Your holy angels to be witnesses to my lawsuit and righteous prosecution of the evil altar of *fear*. I decree and declare that this evil altar of *fear* will not terrorize me or my family members with endless fears and neither will it kill my ability to trust divine relationships I need to achieve my God-given destiny here on earth, in Jesus' name I pray.

3. Surrender Your Rights to Self-Representation to the Lord as Your Advocate

Heavenly Father, Your Word in First John 2:1-2 says, "*My little children, these things I write to you, so that you may not sin. And if anyone sins, we have an Advocate with the Father, Jesus Christ the righteous. And He Himself is the propitiation for our sins, and not for ours only but also for the whole world*" (NKJV). I thank You that Jesus is my faithful Advocate before the Righteous Judge in the Courts of Heaven. Lord Jesus, I surrender my rights to self-representation and summon You as my Advocate to help me plead my case before the Righteous Judge and prosecute the evil of altar of *fear* that satan planted in my bloodline. I also ask the blessed Holy Spirit, who is the highest officer of the Courts of Heaven here on earth, to make me sensitive to the proceedings of this Court in order to successfully prosecute the evil altar of *fear* in Jesus' name.

4. Summon the Evil Altar and the Idol That Sits on It to Appear in Court

Heavenly Father, even as I stand in Your royal courtroom I present myself as a living sacrifice, holy and acceptable before You according to Romans 12:1. Heavenly Father, Righteous Judge, I summon the altar of *fear* in my bloodline and the idol that sits on it to appear in Your royal courtroom to face prosecution in Jesus' name. For it is written in First Corinthians 6:3, *"Do you not know that we [believers] will judge angels? How much more then [as to] matters of this life?"* Heavenly Father, I exercise my God-given authority in Christ Jesus to judge demons and principalities, in Jesus' name I pray. Righteous Judge, it is also written in the Constitution of Your Kingdom in First John 3:8, *"For this purpose the Son of God was manifested, that He might destroy the works of the devil"* (NKJV).

5. Address Satan's Accusations and Agree with the Adversary

Heavenly Father, I know that until the end of the age of sin, satan still has legal access to the Courts of Heaven to level accusations against the children of men; for it is written in the book of Revelation 12:10:

> *Then I heard a loud voice in heaven, saying, "Now the salvation, and the power, and the kingdom (dominion, reign) of our God, and the authority of His Christ have come; for the accuser of our [believing] brothers and sisters has been thrown down [at last], he who accuses them and keeps bringing charges [of sinful behavior] against them before our God day and night."*

Heavenly Father, the Lord Jesus also said in the book of Matthew 5:25:

> *Come to terms quickly [at the earliest opportunity] with your opponent at law while you are with him on the way [to court],*

> *so that your opponent does not hand you over to the judge, and*
> *the judge to the guard, and you are thrown into prison.*

Heavenly Father, in all humility, while renouncing the spirit of pride, I choose to quickly agree with the legal accusations of my adversary, satan. Righteous Judge, every accusation that satan has filed against me and my bloodline in this Court is true.

6. Repent

Heavenly Father, I repent for my personal transgressions, and for the sins and iniquities of my forefathers that opened the door for the spirit and altar of *fear* to oppress my life, in Jesus' name I pray. Lord, every sin of my forefathers that the enemy is using as a legal right to build cases against me and to cause me to live in *fear*, I ask that the blood of Jesus would just wash them away. I repent for idolizing my fears instead of trusting God. I also repent for self-inflicted word curses and all covenants with demons that have existed in my ancestral bloodline. I am asking that every covenant with demonic powers will now be revoked and that their right to claim me and my bloodline would now be dismissed before Your court, in Jesus' name. Thank You, Lord, for revoking these demonic covenants and evil altars in Jesus' mighty name! Heavenly Father, in my heartfelt desire to divorce myself from the spirit and altar of *fear*, I give back everything and anything that the devil would say came from his kingdom. I only want what the blood of Jesus has secured for me.

7. Appeal to the Blood of Jesus to Wipe Out All Sin (Satan's Evidence)

Lord Jesus, thank You for cleansing me by Your blood so satan has no legal footing against me in Your courtroom. It is written in First John 1:9:

> *If we [freely] admit that we have sinned and confess our sins,*
> *He is faithful and just [true to His own nature and promises],*

and will forgive our sins and cleanse us continually from all unrighteousness [our wrongdoing, everything not in conformity with His will and purpose].

Righteous Judge, I appeal to the blood of Jesus to wipe out all my shortcomings, transgressions, and iniquities, in Jesus' name, I pray. I receive by faith the cleansing power of the blood of Jesus.

8. *Ask the Court to Dismiss All of Satan's Accusations and Charges*

Heavenly Father, based upon Jesus' finished work and my heartfelt repentance, I now move on the Court of Heaven to dismiss all of satan's accusations and charges against me and my bloodline in Jesus' name. For it is written that the accuser of the brethren has been cast down. So, I ask You Father to cast down all of satan's accusations against me, in Jesus' name, I pray.

9. *Ask the Lord to Send Angels to Destroy the Evil Altar and Execute the Lord's Judgment Against It*

Heavenly Father, Righteous Judge, I ask that You send high-ranking angelic officers of the Courts who excel in strength to execute the judgment of Your supreme court and destroy the evil altar of *fear* and the idol that sits on it that satan planted in my bloodline, in Jesus' name I pray. By the spirit of prophecy, I prophesy the complete destruction of the evil altar of *fear* in my life, in Jesus' name. For it is written in Psalm 91:11-12, *"For He will command His angels in regard to you, to protect and defend and guard you in all your ways [of obedience and service]. They will lift you up in their hands, so that you do not [even] strike your foot against a stone."* I receive angelic assistance, right now, in Jesus' name.

10. Present Scriptures That Will Be Used in Issuing a Divine Restraining Order

Heavenly Father, I present before Your Supreme Court the following scriptures as my rock-solid evidence against the spirit and altar of *fear* my life. It is written:

> For God did not give us a spirit of timidity or cowardice or fear, but [He has given us a spirit] of power and of love and of sound judgment and personal discipline [abilities that result in a calm, well-balanced mind and self-control] (2 Timothy 1:7).

> But now, this is what the Lord, your Creator says, O Jacob, and He who formed you, O Israel, "Do not fear, for I have redeemed you [from captivity]; I have called you by name; you are Mine!" (Isaiah 43:1)

Righteous Judge, based upon the aforementioned scriptures, it is clear that the spirit and altar of *fear,* if allowed to succeed, would cause great injury to my life, destiny, and also inflict irreparable damage to the purposes of God. I ask that that every legal right the spirit and altar of *fear* is holding be revoked in Jesus' glorious name. Righteous Judge, based upon the aforementioned scriptures, it is clear that I qualify for a divine restraining order against the altar of *fear* and the idol that sits on it, in Jesus' name.

11. Ask the Court to Issue a Divine Restraining Order and Receive the Divine Restraining Order by Faith

Heavenly Father, Righteous Judge, I now ask that a divine restraining order and a permanent injunction against the spirit and altar of *fear* in my life would now be issued by the authority of Your Supreme Court, in Jesus' name. Heavenly Father, I decree and declare that any and all forms of *fear* the devil has issued or is orchestrating against my life are now cancelled in Jesus' glorious name. Heavenly Father, I receive this divine restraining order and permanent injunction by faith, in Jesus' name. For it is written in the Constitution of Your Kingdom in Hebrews 11:6, *"But without faith it is impossible to [walk with God and] please Him, for whoever comes [near] to God must [necessarily] believe that God exists and that He rewards those who [earnestly and diligently] seek Him."* I believe and declare by faith that the spirit and altar of *fear* in my life has been judged, in Jesus' name!

12. Ask the Lord to Seal Your Righteous Verdict and Court Proceedings in the Blood of Jesus

Heavenly Father, Righteous Judge, I now ask You to seal my righteous verdict against the spirit and altar of *fear* in the precious blood of Jesus. May You also cover with the blood of Jesus all my legal proceedings in this Court in Jesus' name. I decree and declare that my righteous verdict of release and breakthrough from the evil altar of *fear* is now secured in the documents of the Courts of Heaven. For it is written in John's Gospel, chapter 8:36, *"So if the Son makes you free, then you are unquestionably free."* I decree and declare that I am free from the evil altar of *fear* in Jesus' name, amen!

Prayer #25

Uprooting the Altar of Trauma

As for those who are left of you, I will bring *despair* (lack of courage, weakness) into their hearts in the lands of their enemies; the sound of a scattered leaf will put them to flight, and they will flee as if [running] from the sword, and will fall even when no one is chasing them.
—Leviticus 26:36

According to the American Psychological Association, "Trauma is an emotional response to a terrible event like an accident, rape, or natural disaster. Immediately after the event, shock and denial are typical. Longer term reactions include unpredictable emotions, flashbacks, strained relationships, and even physical symptoms like headaches or nausea." As a minister of the gospel who travels extensively, especially in the United States, I can attest that I have met many Christians who love Jesus but suffer from trauma. Sometimes the trauma is so severe they end up with a split personality and each of those personalities becomes an alter ego. So in a few hours of being with them, you can easily observe them manifest entirely different personalities. I have observed for the most part victims of trauma usually become attendants to the evil altar of trauma. No matter what they do and say they end up cycling back to the "trauma." They are attendants to the evil altar of trauma that satan planted in their soul when they experienced the traumatic experience. The *dangerous prayer* below is designed to help you break free of the evil altar of trauma and start living again!

Prayer of Activation

1. Address the Father in Praise and Worship

Heavenly Father, holy is Your name and greatly to be praised. I worship and adore You in Jesus' name. May Your Kingdom manifest in my life as it is in Heaven. Plead my cause, O Lord, with those who strive with me; fight against any entity or person who is contending against me. Heavenly Father, it is written in Psalm 27:6, *"And now my head will be lifted up above my enemies around me, in His tent I will offer sacrifices with shouts of joy; I will sing, yes, I will sing praises to the Lord."* Abba, I enjoin my worship to the heavenly chorus of worship of Your holy angels and the crowd of witnesses, in Jesus' name.

2. Ask for the Court to Be Seated

Heavenly Father, Righteous Judge, I ask that the Courts of Heaven be seated according to Daniel 7:9-10. I ask this in Jesus' mighty name. It is written:

> I kept looking until thrones were set up, and the Ancient of Days (God) took His seat; His garment was white as snow and the hair of His head like pure wool. His throne was flames of fire; its wheels were a burning fire. A river of fire was flowing and coming out from before Him; a thousand thousands were attending Him, and ten thousand times ten thousand were standing before Him; the court was seated, and the books were opened.

Heavenly Father, I am requesting the privilege of standing before the courtroom of the Ancient of Days according to what was revealed to the prophet Daniel, in Jesus' name, I pray. Heavenly Father, I stand in Your royal

courtroom because of the blood and finished work of Jesus on the cross. I have come to receive Your righteous judgment over my life against the spirit and altar of *trauma* that satan planted in my generational bloodline. Heavenly Father, I call upon Your holy angels to be witnesses to my lawsuit and righteous prosecution of the evil altar of *trauma*. I decree and declare that this evil altar of *trauma* will not kill me or my family members before our appointed time; neither will it kill the divine relationships I need to achieve my God-given destiny here on earth, in Jesus' name I pray.

3. Surrender Your Rights to Self-Representation to the Lord as Your Advocate

Heavenly Father, Your Word in First John 2:1-2 says, "*My little children, these things I write to you, so that you may not sin. And if anyone sins, we have an Advocate with the Father, Jesus Christ the righteous. And He Himself is the propitiation for our sins, and not for ours only but also for the whole world*" (NKJV). I thank You that Jesus is my faithful Advocate before the Righteous Judge in the Courts of Heaven. Lord Jesus, I surrender my rights to self-representation and summon You as my Advocate to help me plead my case before the Righteous Judge and prosecute the evil of altar of *trauma* that satan planted in my bloodline. I also ask the blessed Holy Spirit, who is the highest officer of the Courts of Heaven here on earth, to make me sensitive to the proceedings of this Court in order to successfully prosecute the evil altar of *trauma* in Jesus' name.

4. Summon the Evil Altar and the Idol That Sits on It to Appear in Court

Heavenly Father, even as I stand in Your royal courtroom I present myself as a living sacrifice, holy and acceptable before You according to Romans 12:1. Heavenly Father, Righteous Judge, I summon the altar of *trauma* in my bloodline and the idol that sits on it to appear in Your royal courtroom

to face prosecution in Jesus' name. For it is written in First Corinthians 6:3, *"Do you not know that we [believers] will judge angels? How much more then [as to] matters of this life?"* Heavenly Father, I exercise my God-given authority in Christ Jesus to judge demons and principalities, in Jesus' name I pray. Righteous Judge, it is also written in the Constitution of Your Kingdom in First John 3:8, *"For this purpose the Son of God was manifested, that He might destroy the works of the devil"* (NKJV).

5. *Address Satan's Accusations and Agree with the Adversary*

Heavenly Father, I know that until the end of the age of sin, satan still has legal access to the Courts of Heaven to level accusations against the children of men; for it is written in the book of Revelation 12:10:

> *Then I heard a loud voice in heaven, saying, "Now the salvation, and the power, and the kingdom (dominion, reign) of our God, and the authority of His Christ have come; for the accuser of our [believing] brothers and sisters has been thrown down [at last], he who accuses them and keeps bringing charges [of sinful behavior] against them before our God day and night."*

Heavenly Father, the Lord Jesus also said in the book of Matthew 5:25:

> *Come to terms quickly [at the earliest opportunity] with your opponent at law while you are with him on the way [to court], so that your opponent does not hand you over to the judge, and the judge to the guard, and you are thrown into prison.*

Heavenly Father, in all humility, while renouncing the spirit of pride, I choose to quickly agree with the legal accusations of my adversary, satan. Righteous Judge, every accusation that satan has filed against me and my bloodline in this Court is true.

6. Repent

Heavenly Father, I repent for my personal transgressions, and for the sins and iniquities of my forefathers that opened the door for the spirit and altar of *trauma* to oppress my life, in Jesus' name I pray. Lord, every sin of my forefathers that the enemy is using as a legal right to build cases against me and to traumatize me, I ask that the blood of Jesus would just wash them away. I forgive anyone involved in traumatizing me. I also repent for self-inflicted word curses and all covenants with demons of *trauma* that have existed in my ancestral bloodline. I am asking that every covenant with demonic powers will now be revoked and that their right to claim me and my bloodline would now be dismissed before Your court, in Jesus' name. Thank You, Lord, for revoking these demonic covenants and evil altars of *trauma* in Jesus' mighty name! Heavenly Father, in my heartfelt desire to divorce myself from the spirit and altar of *trauma*, I give back everything and anything that the devil would say came from his kingdom. I only want what the blood of Jesus has secured for me.

7. Appeal to the Blood of Jesus to Wipe Out All Sin (Satan's Evidence)

Lord Jesus, thank You for cleansing me by Your blood so satan has no legal footing against me in Your courtroom. It is written in First John 1:9:

> *If we [freely] admit that we have sinned and confess our sins,*
> *He is faithful and just [true to His own nature and promises],*
> *and will forgive our sins and cleanse us continually from all*
> *unrighteousness [our wrongdoing, everything not in confor-*
> *mity with His will and purpose].*

Righteous Judge, I appeal to the blood of Jesus to wipe out all my short-comings, transgressions, and iniquities, in Jesus' name, I pray. I receive by faith the cleansing power of the blood of Jesus.

8. *Ask the Court to Dismiss All of Satan's Accusations and Charges*

Heavenly Father, based upon Jesus' finished work and my heartfelt repentance, I now move on the Court of Heaven to dismiss all of satan's accusations and charges against me and my bloodline in Jesus' name. For it is written that the accuser of the brethren has been cast down. So, I ask You Father to cast down all of satan's accusations against me, in Jesus' name, I pray.

9. *Ask the Lord to Send Angels to Destroy the Evil Altar and Execute the Lord's Judgment Against It*

Heavenly Father, Righteous Judge, I ask that You send high-ranking angelic officers of the Courts who excel in strength to execute the judgment of Your supreme court and destroy the evil altar of *trauma* and the idol that sits on it that satan planted in my bloodline, in Jesus' name I pray. By the spirit of prophecy, I prophesy the complete destruction of the evil altar of *trauma* in my life, in Jesus' name. For it is written in Psalm 91:11-12, *"For He will command His angels in regard to you, to protect and defend and guard you in all your ways [of obedience and service]. They will lift you up in their hands, so that you do not [even] strike your foot against a stone."* I receive angelic assistance, right now, in Jesus' name.

10. *Present Scriptures That Will Be Used in Issuing a Divine Restraining Order*

Heavenly Father, I present before Your Supreme Court the following scriptures as my rock-solid evidence against the spirit and altar of *trauma* in my life. It is written:

> *He shall call upon Me, and I will answer him; I will be with him in trouble; I will deliver him and honor him. With long*

> *life I will satisfy him, and show him My salvation* (Psalm 91:15-16 NKJV).
>
> *For the brokenness of the daughter of my people I (Jeremiah) am broken; I mourn, anxiety has gripped me. Is there no balm in Gilead? Is there no physician there? Why then has not the [spiritual] health of the daughter of my people been restored?* (Jeremiah 8:21-22)

Righteous Judge, based upon the aforementioned scriptures, it is clear that the spirit and altar of *trauma,* if allowed to succeed, would cause great injury to my life, destiny, and also inflict irreparable damage to the purposes of God. I ask that that every legal right the spirit and altar of *trauma* is holding be revoked in Jesus' glorious name. Righteous Judge, based upon the aforementioned scriptures, it is clear that I qualify for a divine restraining order against the altar of *trauma* and the idol that sits on it, in Jesus' name.

11. Ask the Court to Issue a Divine Restraining Order and Receive the Divine Restraining Order by Faith

Heavenly Father, Righteous Judge, I now ask that a divine restraining order and a permanent injunction against the spirit and altar of *trauma* in my life would now be issued by the authority of Your Supreme Court, in Jesus' name. Heavenly Father, I decree and declare that any and all forms of *trauma* the devil is and has orchestrated against my life are now cancelled in Jesus' glorious name. Heavenly Father, I receive this divine restraining order and permanent injunction by faith, in Jesus' name. For it is written in the Constitution of Your Kingdom in Hebrews 11:6, *"But without faith it is impossible to [walk with God and] please Him, for whoever comes [near] to God must [necessarily] believe that God exists and that He rewards those who [earnestly and diligently] seek Him."* I believe and declare by faith that the spirit and altar of *trauma* in my life has been judged, in Jesus' name!

12. Ask the Lord to Seal Your Righteous Verdict and Court Proceedings in the Blood of Jesus

Heavenly Father, Righteous Judge, I now ask You to seal my righteous verdict against the spirit and altar of *trauma* in the precious blood of Jesus. May You also cover with the blood of Jesus all my legal proceedings in this Court in Jesus' name. I decree and declare that my righteous verdict of release and breakthrough from the evil altar of *trauma* is now secured in the documents of the Courts of Heaven. For it is written in John's Gospel, chapter 8:36, *"So if the Son makes you free, then you are unquestionably free."* I decree and declare that I am free of the evil altar of *trauma* in Jesus' name, amen!

Prayer #26

Uprooting the Altar of
Your Father's House

Now on that same night the Lord said to Gideon, "Take your father's bull, the second bull seven years old, and tear down the altar of Baal that belongs to your father, and cut down the Asherah that is beside it; and build an altar to the Lord your God on top of this mountain stronghold [with stones laid down] in an orderly way. Then take the second bull and offer a burnt sacrifice using the wood of the Asherah which you shall cut down."
—Judges 6:25-26

Without a shadow of doubt, the most difficult fight you will ever face in your life with idols and evil altars in your bloodline is when the Lord sends you to tear down the evil altars of your father's house in order to dethrone the idol (demon-god) that sits on it! Be warned! Why? This is due to the fact that the idol (familiar spirit) and evil altar of your father's house were planted in the family bloodline by your forefathers. These, for the most part, were men or women in positions of authority over the family bloodline. Consequently, the decisions they made over the family became legally binding in the realm of the spirit and are therefore recognized in the Courts of Heaven. Deceived by the devil, many of our forefathers willingly opened the door of the family bloodline to the idols (familiar spirits) and evil altars that are now firmly planted in your generational bloodline. Gideon could not move forward into his God-given destiny as a deliverer of Israel until he dealt head-on with the altar of Baal which was in his father's house. You have do the same thing Gideon did! The *dangerous prayer* below is designed to help you do just that!

Prayer of Activation

1. Address the Father in Praise and Worship

Heavenly Father, holy is Your name and greatly to be praised. I worship and adore You in Jesus' name. May Your Kingdom manifest in my life as it is in Heaven. Plead my cause, O Lord, with those who strive with me; fight against any entity or person who is contending against me. Heavenly Father, it is written in Psalm 27:6, *"And now my head will be lifted up above my enemies around me, in His tent I will offer sacrifices with shouts of joy; I will sing, yes, I will sing praises to the Lord."* Abba, I enjoin my worship to the heavenly chorus of worship of Your holy angels and the crowd of witnesses, in Jesus' name.

2. Ask for the Court to Be Seated

Heavenly Father, Righteous Judge, I ask that the Courts of Heaven be seated according to Daniel 7:9-10. I ask this in Jesus' mighty name. It is written:

> *I kept looking until thrones were set up, and the Ancient of Days (God) took His seat; His garment was white as snow and the hair of His head like pure wool. His throne was flames of fire; its wheels were a burning fire. A river of fire was flowing and coming out from before Him; a thousand thousands were attending Him, and ten thousand times ten thousand*

were standing before Him; the court was seated, and the books were opened.

Heavenly Father, I am requesting the privilege of standing before the courtroom of the Ancient of Days according to what was revealed to the prophet Daniel, in Jesus' name, I pray. Heavenly Father, I stand in Your royal courtroom because of the blood and finished work of Jesus on the cross. I have come to receive Your righteous judgment over my life against the spirit and altar of *my father's house* that satan planted in my generational bloodline. Heavenly Father, I call upon Your holy angels to be witnesses to my lawsuit and righteous prosecution of the evil altar of *my father's house*. I decree and declare that this evil altar of *my father's house* will not kill me or my family members before our appointed time; neither will it destroy my ability to live a peaceful and prosperous life here on earth, in Jesus' name I pray.

3. *Surrender Your Rights to Self-Representation to the Lord as Your Advocate*

Heavenly Father, Your Word in First John 2:1-2 says, "*My little children, these things I write to you, so that you may not sin. And if anyone sins, we have an Advocate with the Father, Jesus Christ the righteous. And He Himself is the propitiation for our sins, and not for ours only but also for the whole world*" (NKJV). I thank You that Jesus is my faithful Advocate before the Righteous Judge in the Courts of Heaven. Lord Jesus, I surrender my rights to self-representation and summon You as my Advocate to help me plead my case before the Righteous Judge and prosecute the evil of altar of *my father's house* that satan planted in my bloodline. I also ask the blessed Holy Spirit, who is the highest officer of the Courts of Heaven here on earth, to make me sensitive to the proceedings of this Court in order to successfully prosecute the evil altar of *my father's house* in Jesus' name.

4. Summon the Evil Altar and the Idol That Sits on It to Appear in Court

Heavenly Father, even as I stand in Your royal courtroom I present myself as a living sacrifice, holy and acceptable before You according to Romans 12:1. Heavenly Father, Righteous Judge, I summon the altar of *my father's house* in my bloodline and the idol that sits on it to appear in Your royal courtroom to face prosecution in Jesus' name. For it is written in First Corinthians 6:3, *"Do you not know that we [believers] will judge angels? How much more then [as to] matters of this life?"* Heavenly Father, I exercise my God-given authority in Christ Jesus to judge demons and principalities, in Jesus' name I pray. Righteous Judge, it is also written in the Constitution of Your Kingdom in First John 3:8, *"For this purpose the Son of God was manifested, that He might destroy the works of the devil"* (NKJV).

5. Address Satan's Accusations and Agree with the Adversary

Heavenly Father, I know that until the end of the age of sin, satan still has legal access to the Courts of Heaven to level accusations against the children of men; for it is written in the book of Revelation 12:10:

> *Then I heard a loud voice in heaven, saying, "Now the salvation, and the power, and the kingdom (dominion, reign) of our God, and the authority of His Christ have come; for the accuser of our [believing] brothers and sisters has been thrown down [at last], he who accuses them and keeps bringing charges [of sinful behavior] against them before our God day and night."*

Heavenly Father, the Lord Jesus also said in the book of Matthew 5:25:

> *Come to terms quickly [at the earliest opportunity] with your opponent at law while you are with him on the way [to court],*

so that your opponent does not hand you over to the judge, and
the judge to the guard, and you are thrown into prison.

Heavenly Father, in all humility, while renouncing the spirit of pride, I choose to quickly agree with the legal accusations of my adversary, satan. Righteous Judge, every accusation that satan has filed against me and my bloodline in this Court is true.

6. Repent

Heavenly Father, I repent for my personal transgressions, and for the sins and iniquities of my forefathers that opened the door for the spirit and altar of *my father's house* to oppress my life, in Jesus' name I pray. Lord, every sin of my forefathers that the enemy is using as a legal right to build cases against me and to deny me my destiny, I ask that the blood of Jesus would just wash them away. I also repent for self-inflicted word curses and all covenants with demons that have existed in my ancestral bloodline. I am asking that every covenant with demonic powers connected to the evil altar of *my father's house* will now be revoked and that their right to claim me and my bloodline would now be dismissed before Your court, in Jesus' name. Thank You, Lord, for revoking these demonic covenants and evil altars in Jesus' mighty name! Heavenly Father, in my heartfelt desire to divorce myself from the spirit and altar of *my father's house*, I give back everything and anything that the devil would say came from his kingdom. I only want what the blood of Jesus has secured for me.

7. Appeal to the Blood of Jesus to Wipe Out All Sin (Satan's Evidence)

Lord Jesus, thank You for cleansing me by Your blood so satan has no legal footing against me in Your courtroom. It is written in First John 1:9:

If we [freely] admit that we have sinned and confess our sins,
He is faithful and just [true to His own nature and promises],
and will forgive our sins and cleanse us continually from all
unrighteousness [our wrongdoing, everything not in confor-
mity with His will and purpose].

Righteous Judge, I appeal to the blood of Jesus to wipe out all my short-comings, transgressions, and iniquities, in Jesus' name, I pray. I receive by faith the cleansing power of the blood of Jesus.

8. Ask the Court to Dismiss All of Satan's Accusations and Charges

Heavenly Father, based upon Jesus' finished work and my heartfelt repentance, I now move on the Court of Heaven to dismiss all of satan's accusations and charges against me and my bloodline in Jesus' name. For it is written that the accuser of the brethren has been cast down. So, I ask You Father to cast down all of satan's accusations against me, in Jesus' name, I pray.

9. Ask the Lord to Send Angels to Destroy the Evil Altar and Execute the Lord's Judgment Against It

Heavenly Father, Righteous Judge, I ask that You send high-ranking angelic officers of the Courts who excel in strength to execute the judgment of Your supreme court and destroy the evil altar of *my father's house* and the idol that sits on it that satan planted in my bloodline, in Jesus' name I pray. By the spirit of prophecy, I prophesy the complete destruction of the evil altar of *my father's house* in my life, in Jesus' name. For it is written in Psalm 91:11-12, "*For He will command His angels in regard to you, to protect and defend and guard you in all your ways [of obedience and service]. They will lift you up in their hands, so that you do not [even] strike your foot against a stone.*" I receive angelic assistance, right now, in Jesus' name.

10. Present Scriptures That Will Be Used in Issuing a Divine Restraining Order

Heavenly Father, I present before Your Supreme Court the following scriptures as my rock-solid evidence against the spirit and altar of *my father's house* in my life. It is written:

> *Then Elijah said to all the people, "Come near to me." So all the people approached him. And he repaired and rebuilt the [old] altar of the Lord that had been torn down [by Jezebel]* (1 Kings 18:30).

> *Yet do you say, "Why should the son not bear the punishment for the father's sin?" When the son has practiced justice and righteousness and has kept all My statutes and has done them, he shall certainly live. The person who sins [is the one that] will die. The son will not bear the punishment for the sin of the father, nor will the father bear the punishment for the sin of the son; the righteousness of the righteous shall be on himself, and the wickedness of the wicked shall be on himself* (Ezekiel 18:19-20).

Righteous Judge, based upon the aforementioned scriptures, it is clear that the spirit and altar of *my father's house,* if allowed to succeed, would cause great injury to my life, destiny, and also inflict irreparable damage to the purposes of God. I ask that that every legal right the spirit and altar of *my father's house* is holding be revoked in Jesus' glorious name. Righteous Judge, based upon the aforementioned scriptures, it is clear that I qualify for a divine restraining order against the altar of *my father's house* and the idol that sits on it, in Jesus' name.

11. Ask the Court to Issue a Divine Restraining Order and Receive the Divine Restraining Order by Faith

Heavenly Father, Righteous Judge, I now ask that a divine restraining order and a permanent injunction against the spirit and altar of *my father's house* in my life would now be issued by the authority of Your Supreme Court, in Jesus' name. Heavenly Father, I decree and declare that any calamity or misfortune the devil is orchestrating against my life through the evil altar of *my father's house* is now cancelled in Jesus' glorious name. Heavenly Father, I receive this divine restraining order and permanent injunction by faith, in Jesus' name. For it is written in the Constitution of Your Kingdom in Hebrews 11:6, *"But without faith it is impossible to [walk with God and] please Him, for whoever comes [near] to God must [necessarily] believe that God exists and that He rewards those who [earnestly and diligently] seek Him."* I believe and declare by faith that the spirit and altar of *my father's house* in my life has been judged, in Jesus' name!

12. Ask the Lord to Seal Your Righteous Verdict and Court Proceedings in the Blood of Jesus

Heavenly Father, Righteous Judge, I now ask You to seal my righteous verdict against the spirit and altar of *my father's house* in the precious blood of Jesus. May You also cover with the blood of Jesus all my legal proceedings in this Court in Jesus' name. I decree and declare that my righteous verdict of release and breakthrough from the evil altar of *my father's house* is now secured in the documents of the Courts of Heaven. For it is written in John's Gospel, chapter 8:36, *"So if the Son makes you free, then you are unquestionably free."* I decree and declare that I am free of the evil altar of *my father's house* in Jesus' name, amen!

Prayer #27

Uprooting the Altar of Marital Unfaithfulness

Bring charges against your mother, bring charges; for she is not My wife, nor am I her Husband! Let her put away her harlotries from her sight, and her adulteries from between her breasts .

—Hosea 2:2 NKJV

There is no other God-ordained human institution that satan has attacked as viciously as the institution of marriage. The alarming rates of divorce in both the world and the Christian church is deeply troubling. Stats don't lie! Marriage is under demonic and cultural assault. Many of these marriages are victims of what I call the altar of marital unfaithfulness. This altar is usually formed when a married man or woman engages in a sexual or emotional affair with a member of the opposite sex. In the times we live in when marriage, sex, and sexuality have been radically redefined, I know of husbands who lost their wives to other women and vice versa. The biggest victims of this evil altar of marital unfaithfulness are the children who are caught in the crossfire! This is why I am passionate about the following *dangerous prayer.*

Prayer of Activation

1. Address the Father in Praise and Worship

Heavenly Father, holy is Your name and greatly to be praised. I worship and adore You in Jesus' name. May Your Kingdom manifest in my life as it is in Heaven. Plead my cause, O Lord, with those who strive with me; fight against any entity or person who is contending against me. Heavenly Father, it is written in Psalm 27:6, *"And now my head will be lifted up above my enemies around me, in His tent I will offer sacrifices with shouts of joy; I will sing, yes, I will sing praises to the Lord."* Abba, I enjoin my worship to the heavenly chorus of worship of Your holy angels and the crowd of witnesses, in Jesus' name.

2. Ask for the Court to Be Seated

Heavenly Father, Righteous Judge, I ask that the Courts of Heaven be seated according to Daniel 7:9-10. I ask this in Jesus' mighty name. It is written:

> *I kept looking until thrones were set up, and the Ancient of Days (God) took His seat; His garment was white as snow and the hair of His head like pure wool. His throne was flames of fire; its wheels were a burning fire. A river of fire was flowing and coming out from before Him; a thousand thousands were attending Him, and ten thousand times ten thousand were standing before Him; the court was seated, and the books were opened.*

Heavenly Father, I am requesting the privilege of standing before the courtroom of the Ancient of Days according to what was revealed to the prophet Daniel, in Jesus' name, I pray. Heavenly Father, I stand in Your royal

courtroom because of the blood and finished work of Jesus on the cross. I have come to receive Your righteous judgment over my life against the spirit and altar of *marital unfaithfulness* that satan planted in my generational bloodline. Heavenly Father, I call upon Your holy angels to be witnesses to my lawsuit and righteous prosecution of the evil altar of *marital unfaithfulness*. I decree and declare that this evil altar of *marital unfaithfulness* will not destroy my marriage or open a door to an extramarital affair, in Jesus' name I pray.

3. Surrender Your Rights to Self-Representation to the Lord as Your Advocate

Heavenly Father, Your Word in First John 2:1-2 says, "*My little children, these things I write to you, so that you may not sin. And if anyone sins, we have an Advocate with the Father, Jesus Christ the righteous. And He Himself is the propitiation for our sins, and not for ours only but also for the whole world*" (NKJV). I thank You that Jesus is my faithful Advocate before the Righteous Judge in the Courts of Heaven. Lord Jesus, I surrender my rights to self-representation and summon You as my Advocate to help me plead my case before the Righteous Judge and prosecute the evil of altar of *marital unfaithfulness* that satan planted in my bloodline. I also ask the blessed Holy Spirit, who is the highest officer of the Courts of Heaven here on earth, to make me sensitive to the proceedings of this Court in order to successfully prosecute the evil altar of *marital unfaithfulness* in Jesus' name.

4. Summon the Evil Altar and the Idol That Sits on It to Appear in Court

Heavenly Father, even as I stand in Your royal courtroom I present myself as a living sacrifice, holy and acceptable before You according to Romans 12:1. Heavenly Father, Righteous Judge, I summon the altar of *marital unfaithfulness* in my bloodline and the idol that sits on it to appear in

Your royal courtroom to face prosecution in Jesus' name. For it is written in First Corinthians 6:3, *"Do you not know that we [believers] will judge angels? How much more then [as to] matters of this life?"* Heavenly Father, I exercise my God-given authority in Christ Jesus to judge demons and principalities, in Jesus' name I pray. Righteous Judge, it is also written in the Constitution of Your Kingdom in First John 3:8, *"For this purpose the Son of God was manifested, that He might destroy the works of the devil"* (NKJV).

5. Address Satan's Accusations and Agree with the Adversary

Heavenly Father, I know that until the end of the age of sin, satan still has legal access to the Courts of Heaven to level accusations against the children of men; for it is written in the book of Revelation 12:10:

> *Then I heard a loud voice in heaven, saying, "Now the salvation, and the power, and the kingdom (dominion, reign) of our God, and the authority of His Christ have come; for the accuser of our [believing] brothers and sisters has been thrown down [at last], he who accuses them and keeps bringing charges [of sinful behavior] against them before our God day and night."*

Heavenly Father, the Lord Jesus also said in the book of Matthew 5:25:

> *Come to terms quickly [at the earliest opportunity] with your opponent at law while you are with him on the way [to court], so that your opponent does not hand you over to the judge, and the judge to the guard, and you are thrown into prison.*

Heavenly Father, in all humility, while renouncing the spirit of pride, I choose to quickly agree with the legal accusations of my adversary, satan. Righteous Judge, every accusation that satan has filed against me and my bloodline in this Court is true.

6. Repent

Heavenly Father, I repent for my personal transgressions, and for the sins and iniquities of my forefathers that opened the door for the spirit and altar of *marital unfaithfulness* to oppress my life, in Jesus' name I pray. Lord, every sin of my forefathers that the enemy is using as a legal right to build cases against me and to deny me a godly marriage, I ask that the blood of Jesus would just wash them away. I repent for any sexual or emotional affair that I have ever had with persons who are not my spouse. I also repent for self-inflicted word curses and all covenants with demons that have existed in my ancestral bloodline. I am asking that every covenant with demonic powers will now be revoked and that their right to claim me and my bloodline would now be dismissed before Your court, in Jesus' name. Thank You, Lord, for revoking these demonic covenants and evil altars in Jesus' mighty name! Heavenly Father, in my heartfelt desire to divorce myself from the spirit and altar of *marital unfaithfulness*, I give back everything and anything that the devil would say came from his kingdom. I only want what the blood of Jesus has secured for me.

7. Appeal to the Blood of Jesus to Wipe Out All Sin (Satan's Evidence)

Lord Jesus, thank You for cleansing me by Your blood so satan has no legal footing against me in Your courtroom. It is written in First John 1:9:

> *If we [freely] admit that we have sinned and confess our sins, He is faithful and just [true to His own nature and promises], and will forgive our sins and cleanse us continually from all unrighteousness [our wrongdoing, everything not in conformity with His will and purpose].*

Righteous Judge, I appeal to the blood of Jesus to wipe out all my short-comings, transgressions, and iniquities, in Jesus' name, I pray. I receive by faith the cleansing power of the blood of Jesus.

8. *Ask the Court to Dismiss All of Satan's Accusations and Charges*

Heavenly Father, based upon Jesus' finished work and my heartfelt repentance, I now move on the Court of Heaven to dismiss all of satan's accusations and charges against me and my bloodline in Jesus' name. For it is written that the accuser of the brethren has been cast down. So, I ask You Father to cast down all of satan's accusations against me, in Jesus' name, I pray.

9. *Ask the Lord to Send Angels to Destroy the Evil Altar and Execute the Lord's Judgment Against It*

Heavenly Father, Righteous Judge, I ask that You send high-ranking angelic officers of the Courts who excel in strength to execute the judgment of Your supreme court and destroy the evil altar of *marital unfaithfulness* and the idol that sits on it that satan planted in my bloodline, in Jesus' name I pray. By the spirit of prophecy, I prophesy the complete destruction of the evil altar of *marital unfaithfulness* in my life, in Jesus' name. For it is written in Psalm 91:11-12, *"For He will command His angels in regard to you, to protect and defend and guard you in all your ways [of obedience and service]. They will lift you up in their hands, so that you do not [even] strike your foot against a stone."* I receive angelic assistance, right now, in Jesus' name.

10. Present Scriptures That Will Be Used in Issuing a Divine Restraining Order

Heavenly Father, I present before Your Supreme Court the following scriptures as my rock-solid evidence against the spirit and altar of *marital unfaithfulness* in my life. It is written:

> *So they are no longer two, but one flesh. Therefore, what God has joined together, let no one separate* (Matthew 19:6).
>
> *Marriage is to be held in honor among all [that is, regarded as something of great value], and the marriage bed undefiled [by immorality or by any sexual sin]; for God will judge the sexually immoral and adulterous* (Hebrews 13:4).

Righteous Judge, based upon the aforementioned scriptures, it is clear that the spirit and altar of *marital unfaithfulness,* if allowed to succeed, would cause great injury to my life, destiny, and also inflict irreparable damage to the purposes of God. I ask that that every legal right the spirit and altar of *marital unfaithfulness* is holding be revoked in Jesus' glorious name. Righteous Judge, based upon the aforementioned scriptures, it is clear that I qualify for a divine restraining order against the altar of *marital unfaithfulness* and the idol that sits on it, in Jesus' name.

11. Ask the Court to Issue a Divine Restraining Order and Receive the Divine Restraining Order by Faith

Heavenly Father, Righteous Judge, I now ask that a divine restraining order and a permanent injunction against the spirit and altar of *marital unfaithfulness* in my life would now be issued by the authority of Your Supreme Court, in Jesus' name. Heavenly Father, I decree and declare that any and all forms of *marital unfaithfulness* the devil is orchestrating against my life are now cancelled in Jesus' glorious name. Heavenly Father, I receive this divine restraining order and permanent injunction by faith, in Jesus' name. For it is written in the Constitution of Your Kingdom in Hebrews 11:6, *"But without faith it is impossible to [walk with God and] please Him, for whoever comes [near] to God must [necessarily] believe that God exists and that He rewards those who [earnestly and diligently] seek Him."* I believe and declare by faith that the spirit and altar of *marital unfaithfulness* in my life has been judged, in Jesus' name!

12. Ask the Lord to Seal Your Righteous Verdict and Court Proceedings in the Blood of Jesus

Heavenly Father, Righteous Judge, I now ask You to seal my righteous verdict against the spirit and altar of *marital unfaithfulness* in the precious blood of Jesus. May You also cover with the blood of Jesus all my legal proceedings in this Court in Jesus' name. I decree and declare that my righteous verdict of release and breakthrough from the evil altar of *marital unfaithfulness* is now secured in the documents of the Courts of Heaven. For it is written in John's Gospel, chapter 8:36, *"So if the Son makes you free, then you are unquestionably free."* I decree and declare that I am free of the evil altar of *marital unfaithfulness* in Jesus' name, amen!

Prayer #28

Uprooting the Altar of Slumber or Prayerlessness

Israel's watchmen are blind, they are all without knowledge. They are all mute dogs, they cannot bark; panting, lying down, they love to *slumber.*

—Isaiah 56:10

When it comes to the secret art of communion with God, there is nothing more important than the art and practice of prayer. Prayer is very important to a healthy and dynamic spiritual life. The truth of the matter is that when prayer dies in the life of a believer, their intimate relationship with God has already begun to die. Most importantly, it's impossible to draw upon divine resources for manifesting destiny and advancing the kingdom of God without the vehicle of prayer. One of the evil altars satan loves to assign to Christians is what I call the altar of slumber or prayerlessness. According to the Barna research group, it was discovered that many American pastors do not pray more than 15 minutes a day! How tragic! However, it explains the level of powerlessness in the church and in the lives of so many Christians. That said, there are a lot of well-meaning Christians who really want to pray. However, every time they want to pray a spirit of slumber or laziness engulfs them like a dark monsoon cloud and they end up not praying at all. Thankfully, the *dangerous prayer* below was designed to destroy this evil altar of slumber and prayerlessness!

Prayer of Activation

1. Address the Father in Praise and Worship

Heavenly Father, holy is Your name and greatly to be praised. I worship and adore You in Jesus' name. May Your Kingdom manifest in my life as it is in Heaven. Plead my cause, O Lord, with those who strive with me; fight against any entity or person who is contending against me. Heavenly Father, it is written in Psalm 27:6, *"And now my head will be lifted up above my enemies around me, in His tent I will offer sacrifices with shouts of joy; I will sing, yes, I will sing praises to the Lord."* Abba, I enjoin my worship to the heavenly chorus of worship of Your holy angels and the crowd of witnesses, in Jesus' name.

2. Ask for the Court to Be Seated

Heavenly Father, Righteous Judge, I ask that the Courts of Heaven be seated according to Daniel 7:9-10. I ask this in Jesus' mighty name. It is written:

> I kept looking until thrones were set up, and the Ancient of Days (God) took His seat; His garment was white as snow and the hair of His head like pure wool. His throne was flames of fire; its wheels were a burning fire. A river of fire was flowing and coming out from before Him; a thousand thousands were attending Him, and ten thousand times ten thousand were standing before Him; the court was seated, and the books were opened.

Heavenly Father, I am requesting the privilege of standing before the courtroom of the Ancient of Days according to what was revealed to the prophet Daniel, in Jesus' name, I pray. Heavenly Father, I stand in Your royal

courtroom because of the blood and finished work of Jesus on the cross. I have come to receive Your righteous judgment over my life against the spirit and altar of *slumber or prayerlessness* that satan planted in my generational bloodline. Heavenly Father, I call upon Your holy angels to be witnesses to my lawsuit and righteous prosecution of the evil altar of *slumber or prayerlessness*. I decree and declare that this evil altar of *slumber or prayerlessness* will not continue to kill my prayer life or rob me of special times of intimacy with God in the secret place, in Jesus' name I pray.

3. Surrender Your Rights to Self-Representation to the Lord as Your Advocate

Heavenly Father, Your Word in First John 2:1-2 says, "*My little children, these things I write to you, so that you may not sin. And if anyone sins, we have an Advocate with the Father, Jesus Christ the righteous. And He Himself is the propitiation for our sins, and not for ours only but also for the whole world*" (NKJV). I thank You that Jesus is my faithful Advocate before the Righteous Judge in the Courts of Heaven. Lord Jesus, I surrender my rights to self-representation and summon You as my Advocate to help me plead my case before the Righteous Judge and prosecute the evil of altar of *slumber or prayerlessness* that satan planted in my bloodline. I also ask the blessed Holy Spirit, who is the highest officer of the Courts of Heaven here on earth, to make me sensitive to the proceedings of this Court in order to successfully prosecute the evil altar of *slumber and prayerlessness* in Jesus' name.

4. Summon the Evil Altar and the Idol That Sits on It to Appear in Court

Heavenly Father, even as I stand in Your royal courtroom I present myself as a living sacrifice, holy and acceptable before You according to Romans 12:1. Heavenly Father, Righteous Judge, I summon the altar of *slumber or prayerlessness* in my bloodline and the idol that sits on it to appear in Your royal courtroom to face prosecution in Jesus' name. For it is written in First Corinthians 6:3, *"Do you not know that we [believers] will judge angels? How much more then [as to] matters of this life?"* Heavenly Father, I exercise my God-given authority in Christ Jesus to judge demons and principalities, in Jesus' name I pray. Righteous Judge, it is also written in the Constitution of Your Kingdom in First John 3:8, *"For this purpose the Son of God was manifested, that He might destroy the works of the devil"* (NKJV).

5. Address Satan's Accusations and Agree with the Adversary

Heavenly Father, I know that until the end of the age of sin, satan still has legal access to the Courts of Heaven to level accusations against the children of men; for it is written in the book of Revelation 12:10:

> *Then I heard a loud voice in heaven, saying, "Now the salvation, and the power, and the kingdom (dominion, reign) of our God, and the authority of His Christ have come; for the accuser of our [believing] brothers and sisters has been thrown down [at last], he who accuses them and keeps bringing charges [of sinful behavior] against them before our God day and night."*

Heavenly Father, the Lord Jesus also said in the book of Matthew 5:25:

> *Come to terms quickly [at the earliest opportunity] with your opponent at law while you are with him on the way [to court], so that your opponent does not hand you over to the judge, and the judge to the guard, and you are thrown into prison.*

Heavenly Father, in all humility, while renouncing the spirit of pride, I choose to quickly agree with the legal accusations of my adversary, satan. Righteous Judge, every accusation that satan has filed against me and my bloodline in this Court is true.

6. Repent

Heavenly Father, I repent for my personal transgressions, and for the sins and iniquities of my forefathers that opened the door for the spirit and altar of *slumber or prayerlessness* to oppress my life, in Jesus' name I pray. Lord, every sin of my forefathers that the enemy is using as a legal right to build cases against me and to deny me a vibrant prayer life, I ask that the blood of Jesus would just wash them away. I repent for the many times I have to gone about my day or to bed without meeting You in prayer. I also repent for self-inflicted word curses and all covenants with demons that have existed in my ancestral bloodline. I am asking that every covenant with demonic powers will now be revoked and that their right to claim me and my bloodline would now be dismissed before Your court, in Jesus' name. Thank You, Lord, for revoking these demonic covenants and evil altars in Jesus' mighty name! Heavenly Father, in my heartfelt desire to divorce myself from the spirit and altar of *slumber or prayerlessness*, I give back everything and anything that the devil would say came from his kingdom. I only want what the blood of Jesus has secured for me.

7. *Appeal to the Blood of Jesus to Wipe Out All Sin (Satan's Evidence)*

Lord Jesus, thank You for cleansing me by Your blood so satan has no legal footing against me in Your courtroom. It is written in First John 1:9:

> *If we [freely] admit that we have sinned and confess our sins,*
> *He is faithful and just [true to His own nature and promises],*
> *and will forgive our sins and cleanse us continually from all*
> *unrighteousness [our wrongdoing, everything not in confor-*
> *mity with His will and purpose].*

Righteous Judge, I appeal to the blood of Jesus to wipe out all my short-comings, transgressions, and iniquities, in Jesus' name, I pray. I receive by faith the cleansing power of the blood of Jesus.

8. *Ask the Court to Dismiss All of Satan's Accusations and Charges*

Heavenly Father, based upon Jesus' finished work and my heartfelt repentance, I now move on the Court of Heaven to dismiss all of satan's accusations and charges against me and my bloodline in Jesus' name. For it is written that the accuser of the brethren has been cast down. So, I ask You Father to cast down all of satan's accusations against me, in Jesus' name, I pray.

9. *Ask the Lord to Send Angels to Destroy the Evil Altar and Execute the Lord's Judgment Against It*

Heavenly Father, Righteous Judge, I ask that You send high-ranking angelic officers of the Courts who excel in strength to execute the judgment of Your supreme court and destroy the evil altar of *slumber or prayerlessness* and the idol that sits on it that satan planted in my bloodline, in Jesus' name I pray. By the spirit of prophecy, I prophesy the complete destruction of the evil altar of *slumber or prayerlessness* in my life, in Jesus' name. For it is written in Psalm 91:11-12, *"For He will command His angels in regard to you, to protect and defend and guard you in all your ways [of obedience and service]. They will lift you up in their hands, so that you do not [even] strike your foot against a stone."* I receive angelic assistance, right now, in Jesus' name.

10. Present Scriptures That Will Be Used in Issuing a Divine Restraining Order

Heavenly Father, I present before Your Supreme Court the following scriptures as my rock-solid evidence against the spirit and altar of *slumber or prayerlessness* in my life. It is written:

> Now Jesus was telling the disciples a parable to make the point that at all times they ought to pray and not give up and lose heart (Luke 18:1).

> For this reason He says, "Awake, sleeper, and arise from the dead, and Christ will shine [as dawn] upon you and give you light" (Ephesians 5:14).

Righteous Judge, based upon the aforementioned scriptures, it is clear that the spirit and altar of *slumber or prayerlessness,* if allowed to succeed, would cause great injury to my life, destiny, and also inflict irreparable damage to the purposes of God. I ask that that every legal right the spirit and altar of *slumber or prayerlessness* is holding be revoked in Jesus' glorious name. Righteous Judge, based upon the aforementioned scriptures, it is clear that I qualify for a divine restraining order against the altar of *slumber or prayerlessness* and the idol that sits on it, in Jesus' name.

11. Ask the Court to Issue a Divine Restraining Order and Receive the Divine Restraining Order by Faith

Heavenly Father, Righteous Judge, I now ask that a divine restraining order and a permanent injunction against the spirit and altar of *slumber or prayerlessness* in my life would now be issued by the authority of Your Supreme Court, in Jesus' name. Heavenly Father, I decree and declare that any form of *slumber or prayerlessness* the devil has issued or is orchestrating against my life is now cancelled in Jesus' glorious name. Heavenly Father,

I receive this divine restraining order and permanent injunction by faith, in Jesus' name. For it is written in the Constitution of Your Kingdom in Hebrews 11:6, *"But without faith it is impossible to [walk with God and] please Him, for whoever comes [near] to God must [necessarily] believe that God exists and that He rewards those who [earnestly and diligently] seek Him."* I believe and declare by faith that the spirit and altar of *slumber or prayerlessness* in my life has been judged, in Jesus' name!

12. Ask the Lord to Seal Your Righteous Verdict and Court Proceedings in the Blood of Jesus

Heavenly Father, Righteous Judge, I now ask You to seal my righteous verdict against the spirit and altar of *slumber or prayerlessness* in the precious blood of Jesus. May You also cover with the blood of Jesus all my legal proceedings in this Court in Jesus' name. I decree and declare that my righteous verdict of release and breakthrough from the evil altar of *slumber or prayerlessness* is now secured in the documents of the Courts of Heaven. For it is written in John's Gospel, chapter 8:36, *"So if the Son makes you free, then you are unquestionably free."* I decree and declare that I am free of the evil altar of *slumber and prayerlessness* in Jesus' name, amen!

Prayer #29

Uprooting the Altar of Your Mother's House

Against You, You only, have I sinned and done that which is evil in Your sight, so that You are justified when You speak [Your sentence] and faultless in Your judgment. I was brought forth in [a state of] wickedness; in sin my mother conceived me [and from my beginning I, too, was sinful].

—Psalm 51:4-5

I t's not just the evil altar of our father's house that we must all deal with; we also have to face the evil altar of our mother's house or bloodline. The truth is that our spiritual ancestry comes from both our father and mother. This means that both spiritually and genetically we are deeply influenced, whether we know it or not, by both the spiritual and genetic tendencies of our mother's bloodline. This is why King David declares in Psalm 51:5, "*I was brought forth in [a state of] wickedness; in sin my mother conceived me [and from my beginning I, too, was sinful].*" David is clearly acknowledging that some of the iniquity he dealt with in his life was due to the spiritual corruption inherent in his mother's bloodline. Just like we prosecuted and destroyed the evil altar of our father's house, it's time to do the same with all the evil altars of our mother's bloodline.

Prayer of Activation

1. Address the Father in Praise and Worship

Heavenly Father, holy is Your name and greatly to be praised. I worship and adore You in Jesus' name. May Your Kingdom manifest in my life as it is in Heaven. Plead my cause, O Lord, with those who strive with me; fight against any entity or person who is contending against me. Heavenly Father, it is written in Psalm 27:6, *"And now my head will be lifted up above my enemies around me, in His tent I will offer sacrifices with shouts of joy; I will sing, yes, I will sing praises to the Lord."* Abba, I enjoin my worship to the heavenly chorus of worship of Your holy angels and the crowd of witnesses, in Jesus' name.

2. Ask for the Court to Be Seated

Heavenly Father, Righteous Judge, I ask that the Courts of Heaven be seated according to Daniel 7:9-10. I ask this in Jesus' mighty name. It is written:

> *I kept looking until thrones were set up, and the Ancient of Days (God) took His seat; His garment was white as snow and the hair of His head like pure wool. His throne was flames of fire; its wheels were a burning fire. A river of fire was flowing and coming out from before Him; a thousand thousands were attending Him, and ten thousand times ten thousand were standing before Him; the court was seated, and the books were opened.*

Heavenly Father, I am requesting the privilege of standing before the courtroom of the Ancient of Days according to what was revealed to the prophet Daniel, in Jesus' name, I pray. Heavenly Father, I stand in Your royal

courtroom because of the blood and finished work of Jesus on the cross. I have come to receive Your righteous judgment over my life against the spirit and altar of *my mother's house* that satan planted in my generational bloodline. Heavenly Father, I call upon Your holy angels to be witnesses to my lawsuit and righteous prosecution of the evil altar of *my mother's house*. I decree and declare that this evil altar of *my mother's house* will not kill me or my family members before our appointed time; neither will it stop me from living a peaceful and prosperous life here on earth, in Jesus' name I pray.

3. Surrender Your Rights to Self-Representation to the Lord as Your Advocate

Heavenly Father, Your Word in First John 2:1-2 says, "*My little children, these things I write to you, so that you may not sin. And if anyone sins, we have an Advocate with the Father, Jesus Christ the righteous. And He Himself is the propitiation for our sins, and not for ours only but also for the whole world*" (NKJV). I thank You that Jesus is my faithful Advocate before the Righteous Judge in the Courts of Heaven. Lord Jesus, I surrender my rights to self-representation and summon You as my Advocate to help me plead my case before the Righteous Judge and prosecute the evil of altar of *my mother's house* that satan planted in my bloodline. I also ask the blessed Holy Spirit, who is the highest officer of the Courts of Heaven here on earth, to make me sensitive to the proceedings of this Court in order to successfully prosecute the evil altar of *my mother's house* in Jesus' name.

4. Summon the Evil Altar and the Idol That Sits on It to Appear in Court

Heavenly Father, even as I stand in Your royal courtroom I present myself as a living sacrifice, holy and acceptable before You according to Romans 12:1. Heavenly Father, Righteous Judge, I summon the altar of *my mother's house* in my bloodline and the idol that sits on it to appear in

Your royal courtroom to face prosecution in Jesus' name. For it is written in First Corinthians 6:3, *"Do you not know that we [believers] will judge angels? How much more then [as to] matters of this life?"* Heavenly Father, I exercise my God-given authority in Christ Jesus to judge demons and principalities, in Jesus' name I pray. Righteous Judge, it is also written in the Constitution of Your Kingdom in First John 3:8, *"For this purpose the Son of God was manifested, that He might destroy the works of the devil"* (NKJV).

5. Address Satan's Accusations and Agree with the Adversary

Heavenly Father, I know that until the end of the age of sin, satan still has legal access to the Courts of Heaven to level accusations against the children of men; for it is written in the book of Revelation 12:10:

> *Then I heard a loud voice in heaven, saying, "Now the salvation, and the power, and the kingdom (dominion, reign) of our God, and the authority of His Christ have come; for the accuser of our [believing] brothers and sisters has been thrown down [at last], he who accuses them and keeps bringing charges [of sinful behavior] against them before our God day and night."*

Heavenly Father, the Lord Jesus also said in the book of Matthew 5:25:

> *Come to terms quickly [at the earliest opportunity] with your opponent at law while you are with him on the way [to court], so that your opponent does not hand you over to the judge, and the judge to the guard, and you are thrown into prison.*

Heavenly Father, in all humility, while renouncing the spirit of pride, I choose to quickly agree with the legal accusations of my adversary, satan. Righteous Judge, every accusation that satan has filed against me and my bloodline in this Court is true.

6. Repent

Heavenly Father, I repent for my personal transgressions, and for the sins and iniquities of my forefathers that opened the door for the spirit and altar of *my mother's house* to oppress my life, in Jesus' name I pray. Lord, every sin of my forefathers that the enemy is using as a legal right to build cases against me and to deny me my destiny, I ask that the blood of Jesus would just wash them away. I repent for anything I have in common with the iniquity of my mother's bloodline. I also repent for self-inflicted word curses and all covenants with demons that have existed in my ancestral bloodline. I am asking that every covenant with demonic powers will now be revoked and that their right to claim me and my bloodline would now be dismissed before Your court, in Jesus' name. Thank You, Lord, for revoking these demonic covenants and evil altars of *my mother's house* in Jesus' mighty name! Heavenly Father, in my heartfelt desire to divorce myself from the spirit and altar of *my mother's house*, I give back everything and anything that the devil would say came from his kingdom. I only want what the blood of Jesus has secured for me.

7. Appeal to the Blood of Jesus to Wipe Out All Sin (Satan's Evidence)

Lord Jesus, thank You for cleansing me by Your blood so satan has no legal footing against me in Your courtroom. It is written in First John 1:9:

> *If we [freely] admit that we have sinned and confess our sins, He is faithful and just [true to His own nature and promises], and will forgive our sins and cleanse us continually from all unrighteousness [our wrongdoing, everything not in conformity with His will and purpose].*

Righteous Judge, I appeal to the blood of Jesus to wipe out all my short-comings, transgressions, and iniquities, in Jesus' name, I pray. I receive by faith the cleansing power of the blood of Jesus.

8. Ask the Court to Dismiss All of Satan's Accusations and Charges

Heavenly Father, based upon Jesus' finished work and my heartfelt repentance, I now move on the Court of Heaven to dismiss all of satan's accusations and charges against me and my bloodline in Jesus' name. For it is written that the accuser of the brethren has been cast down. So, I ask You Father to cast down all of satan's accusations against me, in Jesus' name, I pray.

9. Ask the Lord to Send Angels to Destroy the Evil Altar and Execute the Lord's Judgment Against It

Heavenly Father, Righteous Judge, I ask that You send high-ranking angelic officers of the Courts who excel in strength to execute the judgment of Your supreme court and destroy the evil altar of *my mother's house* and the idol that sits on it that satan planted in my bloodline, in Jesus' name I pray. By the spirit of prophecy, I prophesy the complete destruction of the evil altar of *my mother's house* in my life, in Jesus' name. For it is written in Psalm 91:11-12, *"For He will command His angels in regard to you, to protect and defend and guard you in all your ways [of obedience and service]. They will lift you up in their hands, so that you do not [even] strike your foot against a stone."* I receive angelic assistance, right now, in Jesus' name.

10. Present Scriptures That Will Be Used in Issuing a Divine Restraining Order

Heavenly Father, I present before Your Supreme Court the following scriptures as my rock-solid evidence against the spirit and altar of *my mother's house* in my life. It is written:

> *When I passed by you and saw you squirming in your [newborn] blood, I said to you while you were there in your blood, "Live!" Yes, I said to you while you were there in your blood, "Live!"* (Ezekiel 16:6)
>
> *The thief does not come except to steal, and to kill, and to destroy. I have come that they may have life, and that they may have it more abundantly* (John 10:10 NKJV).

Righteous Judge, based upon the aforementioned scriptures, it is clear that the spirit and altar of *my mother's house,* if allowed to succeed, would cause great injury to my life, destiny, and also inflict irreparable damage to the purposes of God. I ask that that every legal right the spirit and altar of *my mother's house* is holding be revoked in Jesus' glorious name. Righteous Judge, based upon the aforementioned scriptures, it is clear that I qualify for a divine restraining order against the altar of *my mother's house* and the idol that sits on it, in Jesus' name.

11. Ask the Court to Issue a Divine Restraining Order and Receive the Divine Restraining Order by Faith

Heavenly Father, Righteous Judge, I now ask that a divine restraining order and a permanent injunction against the spirit and altar of *my mother's house* in my life would now be issued by the authority of Your Supreme Court, in Jesus' name. Heavenly Father, I decree and declare that anything the devil has issued or is orchestrating against my life using the evil altar of *my mother's house* is now cancelled in Jesus' glorious name. Heavenly Father, I receive this divine restraining order and permanent injunction by faith, in Jesus' name. For it is written in the Constitution of Your Kingdom in Hebrews 11:6, *"But without faith it is impossible to [walk with God and] please Him, for whoever comes [near] to God must [necessarily] believe that God exists and that He rewards those who [earnestly and diligently] seek Him."* I believe and declare by faith that the spirit and altar of *my mother's house* in my life has been judged, in Jesus' name!

12. Ask the Lord to Seal Your Righteous Verdict and Court Proceedings in the Blood of Jesus

Heavenly Father, Righteous Judge, I now ask You to seal my righteous verdict against the spirit and altar of *my mother's house* in the precious blood of Jesus. May You also cover with the blood of Jesus all my legal proceedings in this Court in Jesus' name. I decree and declare that my righteous verdict of release and breakthrough from the evil altar of *my mother's house* is now secured in the documents of the Courts of Heaven. For it is written in John's Gospel, chapter 8:36, *"So if the Son makes you free, then you are unquestionably free."* I decree and declare that I am free from the evil altar of *my mother's house* in Jesus' name, amen!

Prayer #30

Uprooting the Altar of Barrenness

Then the men of the city said to Elisha, "Look, this city is in a pleasant place, as my lord [Elisha] sees; but the water is bad and the land is *barren*."

—**2 Kings 2:19**

When I researched words that are synonymous with the word *barrenness* using the online thesaurus, the following words quickly came up:

1. childlessness

2. fruitlessness

3. impotence

4. infertility

5. unproductiveness

6. infecundity

When I looked at the meaning of all of these words, one thing was clear! None of them represent the will of God for mankind. There are many marriages right now that are headed toward the divorce court because of the absence of children in the marriage. There are husbands who have justified sexual affairs with their mistresses in search of children because, for whatever reason, their lawful wedded wife is barren. Nevertheless, as the words above suggest, *barrenness* goes beyond not having children in marriage to encompass a lack of productivity or fruitfulness in any human endeavor, especially in business. Thankfully, the *dangerous prayer* below is designed to help you destroy the evil altar of *barrenness!*

Prayer of Activation

1. Address the Father in Praise and Worship

Heavenly Father, holy is Your name and greatly to be praised. I worship and adore You in Jesus' name. May Your Kingdom manifest in my life as it is in Heaven. Plead my cause, O Lord, with those who strive with me; fight against any entity or person who is contending against me. Heavenly Father, it is written in Psalm 27:6, *"And now my head will be lifted up above my enemies around me, in His tent I will offer sacrifices with shouts of joy; I will sing, yes, I will sing praises to the Lord."* Abba, I enjoin my worship to the heavenly chorus of worship of Your holy angels and the crowd of witnesses, in Jesus' name.

2. Ask for the Court to Be Seated

Heavenly Father, Righteous Judge, I ask that the Courts of Heaven be seated according to Daniel 7:9-10. I ask this in Jesus' mighty name. It is written:

> *I kept looking until thrones were set up, and the Ancient of Days (God) took His seat; His garment was white as snow and the hair of His head like pure wool. His throne was flames of fire; its wheels were a burning fire. A river of fire was flowing and coming out from before Him; a thousand thousands were attending Him, and ten thousand times ten thousand*

were standing before Him; the court was seated, and the books were opened.

Heavenly Father, I am requesting the privilege of standing before the courtroom of the Ancient of Days according to what was revealed to the prophet Daniel, in Jesus' name, I pray. Heavenly Father, I stand in Your royal courtroom because of the blood and finished work of Jesus on the cross. I have come to receive Your righteous judgment over my life against the spirit and altar of *barrenness* that satan planted in my generational bloodline. Heavenly Father, I call upon Your holy angels to be witnesses to my lawsuit and righteous prosecution of the evil altar of *barrenness*. I decree and declare that this evil altar of *barrenness* will not steal my God-given opportunity to give birth to children of my own; neither will it make barren my business and career endeavors, in Jesus' name I pray.

3. Surrender Your Rights to Self-Representation to the Lord as Your Advocate

Heavenly Father, Your Word in First John 2:1-2 says, "*My little children, these things I write to you, so that you may not sin. And if anyone sins, we have an Advocate with the Father, Jesus Christ the righteous. And He Himself is the propitiation for our sins, and not for ours only but also for the whole world*" (NKJV). I thank You that Jesus is my faithful Advocate before the Righteous Judge in the Courts of Heaven. Lord Jesus, I surrender my rights to self-representation and summon You as my Advocate to help me plead my case before the Righteous Judge and prosecute the evil of altar of *barrenness* that satan planted in my bloodline. I also ask the blessed Holy Spirit, who is the highest officer of the Courts of Heaven here on earth, to make me sensitive to the proceedings of this Court in order to successfully prosecute the evil altar of *barrenness* in Jesus' name.

4. Summon the Evil Altar and the Idol That Sits on It to Appear in Court

Heavenly Father, even as I stand in Your royal courtroom I present myself as a living sacrifice, holy and acceptable before You according to Romans 12:1. Heavenly Father, Righteous Judge, I summon the altar of *barrenness* in my bloodline and the idol that sits on it to appear in Your royal courtroom to face prosecution in Jesus' name. For it is written in First Corinthians 6:3, *"Do you not know that we [believers] will judge angels? How much more then [as to] matters of this life?"* Heavenly Father, I exercise my God-given authority in Christ Jesus to judge demons and principalities, in Jesus' name I pray. Righteous Judge, it is also written in the Constitution of Your Kingdom in First John 3:8, *"For this purpose the Son of God was manifested, that He might destroy the works of the devil"* (NKJV).

5. Address Satan's Accusations and Agree with the Adversary

Heavenly Father, I know that until the end of the age of sin, satan still has legal access to the Courts of Heaven to level accusations against the children of men; for it is written in the book of Revelation 12:10:

> *Then I heard a loud voice in heaven, saying, "Now the salvation, and the power, and the kingdom (dominion, reign) of our God, and the authority of His Christ have come; for the accuser of our [believing] brothers and sisters has been thrown down [at last], he who accuses them and keeps bringing charges [of sinful behavior] against them before our God day and night."*

Heavenly Father, the Lord Jesus also said in the book of Matthew 5:25:

> *Come to terms quickly [at the earliest opportunity] with your opponent at law while you are with him on the way [to court],*

so that your opponent does not hand you over to the judge, and the judge to the guard, and you are thrown into prison.

Heavenly Father, in all humility, while renouncing the spirit of pride, I choose to quickly agree with the legal accusations of my adversary, satan. Righteous Judge, every accusation that satan has filed against me and my bloodline in this Court is true.

6. Repent

Heavenly Father, I repent for my personal transgressions, and for the sins and iniquities of my forefathers that opened the door for the spirit and altar of *barrenness* to oppress my life, in Jesus' name I pray. Lord, every sin of my forefathers that the enemy is using as a legal right to build cases against me and to deny me my destiny through *barrenness*, I ask that the blood of Jesus would just wash them away. I also repent for self-inflicted word curses and all covenants with demons of *barrenness* that have existed in my ancestral bloodline. I am asking that every covenant with demonic powers will now be revoked and that their right to claim me and my bloodline would now be dismissed before Your court, in Jesus' name. Thank You, Lord, for revoking these demonic covenants and evil altars of *barrenness* in Jesus' mighty name! Heavenly Father, in my heartfelt desire to divorce myself from the spirit and altar of *barrenness,* I give back everything and anything that the devil would say came from his kingdom. I only want what the blood of Jesus has secured for me.

7. Appeal to the Blood of Jesus to Wipe Out All Sin (Satan's Evidence)

Lord Jesus, thank You for cleansing me by Your blood so satan has no legal footing against me in Your courtroom. It is written in First John 1:9:

If we [freely] admit that we have sinned and confess our sins,
He is faithful and just [true to His own nature and promises],
and will forgive our sins and cleanse us continually from all
unrighteousness [our wrongdoing, everything not in confor-
mity with His will and purpose].

Righteous Judge, I appeal to the blood of Jesus to wipe out all my short-comings, transgressions, and iniquities, in Jesus' name, I pray. I receive by faith the cleansing power of the blood of Jesus.

8. Ask the Court to Dismiss All of Satan's Accusations and Charges

Heavenly Father, based upon Jesus' finished work and my heartfelt repentance, I now move on the Court of Heaven to dismiss all of satan's accusations and charges against me and my bloodline in Jesus' name. For it is written that the accuser of the brethren has been cast down. So, I ask You Father to cast down all of satan's accusations against me, in Jesus' name, I pray.

9. Ask the Lord to Send Angels to Destroy the Evil Altar and Execute the Lord's Judgment Against It

Heavenly Father, Righteous Judge, I ask that You send high-ranking angelic officers of the Courts who excel in strength to execute the judgment of Your supreme court and destroy the evil altar of *barrenness* and the idol that sits on it that satan planted in my bloodline, in Jesus' name I pray. By the spirit of prophecy, I prophesy the complete destruction of the evil altar of *barrenness* in my life, in Jesus' name. For it is written in Psalm 91:11-12, *"For He will command His angels in regard to you, to protect and defend and guard you in all your ways [of obedience and service]. They will lift you up in their hands, so that you do not [even] strike your foot against a stone."* I receive angelic assistance, right now, in Jesus' name.

10. Present Scriptures That Will Be Used in Issuing a Divine Restraining Order

Heavenly Father, I present before Your Supreme Court the following scriptures as my rock-solid evidence against the spirit and altar of *barrenness* in my life. It is written:

> *No one shall suffer miscarriage or be **barren** in your land; I will fulfill the number of your days* (Exodus 23:26).

> *Then Elisha went to the spring of water and threw the salt in it and said, "Thus says the Lord: 'I [not the salt] have purified and healed these waters; there shall no longer be death or **barrenness** because of it'"* (2 Kings 2:21).

Righteous Judge, based upon the aforementioned scriptures, it is clear to me that the spirit and altar of *barrenness,* if allowed to succeed, would cause great injury to my life, destiny, and also inflict irreparable damage to the purposes of God. I ask that that every legal right the spirit and altar of *barrenness* is holding be revoked in Jesus' glorious name. Righteous Judge, based upon the aforementioned scriptures, it is clear that I qualify for a divine restraining order against the altar of *barrenness* and the idol that sits on it, in Jesus' name.

11. Ask the Court to Issue a Divine Restraining Order and Receive the Divine Restraining Order by Faith

Heavenly Father, Righteous Judge, I now ask that a divine restraining order and a permanent injunction against the spirit and altar of *barrenness* in my life would now be issued by the authority of Your Supreme Court, in Jesus' name. Heavenly Father, I decree and declare that every form of *barrenness* the devil has issued or is orchestrating against my life is now cancelled in Jesus' glorious name. Heavenly Father, I receive this divine restraining order and permanent injunction by faith, in Jesus' name. For it is written in the Constitution of Your Kingdom in Hebrews 11:6, *"But without faith it is impossible to [walk with God and] please Him, for whoever comes [near] to God must [necessarily] believe that God exists and that He rewards those who [earnestly and diligently] seek Him."* I believe and declare by faith that the spirit and altar of *barrenness* in my life has been judged, in Jesus' name!

12. Ask the Lord to Seal Your Righteous Verdict and Court Proceedings in the Blood of Jesus

Heavenly Father, Righteous Judge, I now ask You to seal my righteous verdict against the spirit and altar of *barrenness* in the precious blood of Jesus. May You also cover with the blood of Jesus all my legal proceedings in this Court in Jesus' name. I decree and declare that my righteous verdict of release and breakthrough from the evil altar of *barrenness* is now secured in the documents of the Courts of Heaven. For it is written in John's Gospel, chapter 8:36, *"So if the Son makes you free, then you are unquestionably free."* I decree and declare that I am free from the evil altar of *barrenness* in Jesus' name, amen!

Prayer #31

Uprooting the Altar of Unfruitfulness

Seeing a lone fig tree at the roadside, He went to it and found nothing but leaves on it; and He said to it, "Never again will fruit come from you." And at once the fig tree withered.
—**Matthew 21:19**

O ne of the first commandments that God gave to man in the garden of Eden was to be fruitful! So fruitfulness is an essential part of man's existence here on earth. When we are being fruitful, we are honoring our true purpose for being. Many people have passed the test of existence but have failed the test of essence because they are not being fruitful in what God called them to be. Fruitfulness is tied to our essence, so satan loves to assign altars of unfruitfulness to people's lives, especially Christians. Fruitfulness is so important that Jesus cursed the fig tree for failing to produce fruit. May you not end up like the fig tree! Please use the *dangerous prayer* below to uproot and destroy the evil altar of unfruitfulness.

Prayer of Activation

1. Address the Father in Praise and Worship

Heavenly Father, holy is Your name and greatly to be praised. I worship and adore You in Jesus' name. May Your Kingdom manifest in my life as it is in Heaven. Plead my cause, O Lord, with those who strive with me; fight against any entity or person who is contending against me. Heavenly Father, it is written in Psalm 27:6, *"And now my head will be lifted up above my enemies around me, in His tent I will offer sacrifices with shouts of joy; I will sing, yes, I will sing praises to the Lord."* Abba, I enjoin my worship to the heavenly chorus of worship of Your holy angels and the crowd of witnesses, in Jesus' name.

2. Ask for the Court to Be Seated

Heavenly Father, Righteous Judge, I ask that the Courts of Heaven be seated according to Daniel 7:9-10. I ask this in Jesus' mighty name. It is written:

> *I kept looking until thrones were set up, and the Ancient of Days (God) took His seat; His garment was white as snow and the hair of His head like pure wool. His throne was flames of fire; its wheels were a burning fire. A river of fire was flowing and coming out from before Him; a thousand thousands were attending Him, and ten thousand times ten thousand were standing before Him; the court was seated, and the books were opened.*

Heavenly Father, I am requesting the privilege of standing before the courtroom of the Ancient of Days according to what was revealed to the prophet Daniel, in Jesus' name, I pray. Heavenly Father, I stand in Your royal

courtroom because of the blood and finished work of Jesus on the cross. I have come to receive Your righteous judgment over my life against the spirit and altar of *unfruitfulness* that satan planted in my generational bloodline. Heavenly Father, I call upon Your holy angels to be witnesses to my lawsuit and righteous prosecution of the evil altar of *unfruitfulness*. I decree and declare that this evil altar of *unfruitfulness* will not kill my ability to be fruitful in all my ministry or business endeavors, in Jesus' name I pray.

3. Surrender Your Rights to Self-Representation to the Lord as Your Advocate

Heavenly Father, Your Word in First John 2:1-2 says, "*My little children, these things I write to you, so that you may not sin. And if anyone sins, we have an Advocate with the Father, Jesus Christ the righteous. And He Himself is the propitiation for our sins, and not for ours only but also for the whole world*" (NKJV). I thank You that Jesus is my faithful Advocate before the Righteous Judge in the Courts of Heaven. Lord Jesus, I surrender my rights to self-representation and summon You as my Advocate to help me plead my case before the Righteous Judge and prosecute the evil of altar of *unfruitfulness* that satan planted in my bloodline. I also ask the blessed Holy Spirit, who is the highest officer of the Courts of Heaven here on earth, to make me sensitive to the proceedings of this Court in order to successfully prosecute the evil altar of *unfruitfulness* in Jesus' name.

4. Summon the Evil Altar and the Idol That Sits on It to Appear in Court

Heavenly Father, even as I stand in Your royal courtroom I present myself as a living sacrifice, holy and acceptable before You according to Romans 12:1. Heavenly Father, Righteous Judge, I summon the altar of *unfruitfulness* in my bloodline and the idol that sits on it to appear in Your royal courtroom to face prosecution in Jesus' name. For it is written in First

Corinthians 6:3, *"Do you not know that we [believers] will judge angels? How much more then [as to] matters of this life?"* Heavenly Father, I exercise my God-given authority in Christ Jesus to judge demons and principalities, in Jesus' name I pray. Righteous Judge, it is also written in the Constitution of Your Kingdom in First John 3:8, *"For this purpose the Son of God was manifested, that He might destroy the works of the devil"* (NKJV).

5. Address Satan's Accusations and Agree with the Adversary

Heavenly Father, I know that until the end of the age of sin, satan still has legal access to the Courts of Heaven to level accusations against the children of men; for it is written in the book of Revelation 12:10:

> *Then I heard a loud voice in heaven, saying, "Now the salvation, and the power, and the kingdom (dominion, reign) of our God, and the authority of His Christ have come; for the accuser of our [believing] brothers and sisters has been thrown down [at last], he who accuses them and keeps bringing charges [of sinful behavior] against them before our God day and night."*

Heavenly Father, the Lord Jesus also said in the book of Matthew 5:25:

> *Come to terms quickly [at the earliest opportunity] with your opponent at law while you are with him on the way [to court], so that your opponent does not hand you over to the judge, and the judge to the guard, and you are thrown into prison.*

Heavenly Father, in all humility, while renouncing the spirit of pride, I choose to quickly agree with the legal accusations of my adversary, satan. Righteous Judge, every accusation that satan has filed against me and my bloodline in this Court is true.

6. Repent

Heavenly Father, I repent for my personal transgressions, and for the sins and iniquities of my forefathers that opened the door for the spirit and altar of *unfruitfulness* to oppress my life, in Jesus' name I pray. Lord, every sin of my forefathers that the enemy is using as a legal right to build cases against me and to deny me my destiny, I ask that the blood of Jesus would just wash them away. I repent for not tapping into my God-given potential. I also repent for self-inflicted word curses and all covenants with demons that have existed in my ancestral bloodline. I am asking that every covenant with demonic powers will now be revoked and that their right to claim me and my bloodline would now be dismissed before Your court, in Jesus' name. Thank You, Lord, for revoking these demonic covenants and evil altars of *unfruitfulness* in Jesus' mighty name! Heavenly Father, in my heartfelt desire to divorce myself from the spirit and altar of *unfruitfulness*, I give back everything and anything that the devil would say came from his kingdom. I only want what the blood of Jesus has secured for me.

7. Appeal to the Blood of Jesus to Wipe Out All Sin (Satan's Evidence)

Lord Jesus, thank You for cleansing me by Your blood so satan has no legal footing against me in Your courtroom. It is written in First John 1:9:

> *If we [freely] admit that we have sinned and confess our sins,*
> *He is faithful and just [true to His own nature and promises],*
> *and will forgive our sins and cleanse us continually from all*
> *unrighteousness [our wrongdoing, everything not in confor-*
> *mity with His will and purpose].*

Righteous Judge, I appeal to the blood of Jesus to wipe out all my shortcomings, transgressions, and iniquities, in Jesus' name, I pray. I receive by faith the cleansing power of the blood of Jesus.

8. *Ask the Court to Dismiss All of Satan's Accusations and Charges*

Heavenly Father, based upon Jesus' finished work and my heartfelt repentance, I now move on the Court of Heaven to dismiss all of satan's accusations and charges against me and my bloodline in Jesus' name. For it is written that the accuser of the brethren has been cast down. So, I ask You Father to cast down all of satan's accusations against me, in Jesus' name, I pray.

9. *Ask the Lord to Send Angels to Destroy the Evil Altar and Execute the Lord's Judgment Against It*

Heavenly Father, Righteous Judge, I ask that You send high-ranking angelic officers of the Courts who excel in strength to execute the judgment of Your supreme court and destroy the evil altar of *unfruitfulness* and the idol that sits on it that satan planted in my bloodline, in Jesus' name I pray. By the spirit of prophecy, I prophesy the complete destruction of the evil altar of *unfruitfulness* in my life, in Jesus' name. For it is written in Psalm 91:11-12, *"For He will command His angels in regard to you, to protect and defend and guard you in all your ways [of obedience and service]. They will lift you up in their hands, so that you do not [even] strike your foot against a stone."* I receive angelic assistance, right now, in Jesus' name.

10. *Present Scriptures That Will Be Used in Issuing a Divine Restraining Order*

Heavenly Father, I present before Your Supreme Court the following scriptures as my rock-solid evidence against the spirit and altar of *unfruitfulness* in my life. It is written:

The righteous will flourish like the date palm [long-lived, upright and useful]; they will grow like a cedar in Lebanon [majestic and stable] (Psalm 92:12).

You have not chosen Me, but I have chosen you and I have appointed and placed and purposefully planted you, so that you would go and bear fruit and keep on bearing, and that your fruit will remain and be lasting, so that whatever you ask of the Father in My name [as My representative] He may give to you (John 15:16).

Righteous Judge, based upon the aforementioned scriptures, it is clear that the spirit and altar of *unfruitfulness,* if allowed to succeed, would cause great injury to my life, destiny, and also inflict irreparable damage to the purposes of God. I ask that that every legal right the spirit and altar of *unfruitfulness* is holding be revoked in Jesus' glorious name. Righteous Judge, based upon the aforementioned scriptures, it is clear that I qualify for a divine restraining order against the altar of *unfruitfulness* and the idol that sits on it, in Jesus' name.

11. Ask the Court to Issue a Divine Restraining Order and Receive the Divine Restraining Order by Faith

Heavenly Father, Righteous Judge, I now ask that a divine restraining order and a permanent injunction against the spirit and altar of *unfruitfulness* in my life would now be issued by the authority of Your Supreme Court, in Jesus' name. Heavenly Father, I decree and declare that any and all forms of *unfruitfulness* the devil has and is orchestrating against my life is now cancelled in Jesus' glorious name. Heavenly Father, I receive this divine restraining order and permanent injunction by faith, in Jesus' name. For it is written in the Constitution of Your Kingdom in Hebrews 11:6, *"But without faith it is impossible to [walk with God and] please Him, for whoever comes [near] to God must [necessarily] believe that God exists and that He rewards those who [earnestly and diligently] seek Him.*" I believe and declare by faith that the spirit and altar of *unfruitfulness* in my life has been judged, in Jesus' name!

12. Ask the Lord to Seal Your Righteous Verdict and Court Proceedings in the Blood of Jesus

Heavenly Father, Righteous Judge, I now ask You to seal my righteous verdict against the spirit and altar of *unfruitfulness* in the precious blood of Jesus. May You also cover with the blood of Jesus all my legal proceedings in this Court in Jesus' name. I decree and declare that my righteous verdict of release and breakthrough from the evil altar of *unfruitfulness* is now secured in the documents of the Courts of Heaven. For it is written in John's Gospel, chapter 8:36, *"So if the Son makes you free, then you are unquestionably free."* I decree and declare that I am free of the evil altar of *unfruitfulness* in Jesus' name, amen!

Prayer #32

Uprooting the Altar of Hopelessness

But they will say, "That is **hopeless**! For we are going to follow our own plans, and each of us will act in accordance with the stubbornness of his evil heart."
—Jeremiah 18:12

There is no spiritual force more powerful than hope. Hope actually gives substance to our faith according to Hebrews 11:1. Hope is the essential ingredient in the human soul that allows the human spirit to rise above any tragedy or difficult circumstance. Hope is the sustaining power that rises in the human heart to say, "Tomorrow will be better than yesterday." Without, it rates of suicides shoot through the roof. Much of the social pandemic of homelessness in America can be traced to a loss of hope more than an addiction to a narcotic. I have come across so many people, and the moment I look in their eyes I can easily discern when they have given up on life or on their God-given dream. They have surrendered and have become unwitting attendants to an evil altar of hopelessness. I declare this will not be your portion in Jesus' name. Please use the *dangerous prayer* below to destroy this evil and malicious altar!

Prayer of Activation

1. Address the Father in Praise and Worship

Heavenly Father, holy is Your name and greatly to be praised. I worship and adore You in Jesus' name. May Your Kingdom manifest in my life as it is in Heaven. Plead my cause, O Lord, with those who strive with me; fight against any entity or person who is contending against me. Heavenly Father, it is written in Psalm 27:6, *"And now my head will be lifted up above my enemies around me, in His tent I will offer sacrifices with shouts of joy; I will sing, yes, I will sing praises to the Lord."* Abba, I enjoin my worship to the heavenly chorus of worship of Your holy angels and the crowd of witnesses, in Jesus' name.

2. Ask for the Court to Be Seated

Heavenly Father, Righteous Judge, I ask that the Courts of Heaven be seated according to Daniel 7:9-10. I ask this in Jesus' mighty name. It is written:

> *I kept looking until thrones were set up, and the Ancient of Days (God) took His seat; His garment was white as snow and the hair of His head like pure wool. His throne was flames of fire; its wheels were a burning fire. A river of fire was flowing and coming out from before Him; a thousand thousands were attending Him, and ten thousand times ten thousand were standing before Him; the court was seated, and the books were opened.*

Heavenly Father, I am requesting the privilege of standing before the courtroom of the Ancient of Days according to what was revealed to the prophet Daniel, in Jesus' name, I pray. Heavenly Father, I stand in Your royal

courtroom because of the blood and finished work of Jesus on the cross. I have come to receive Your righteous judgment over my life against the spirit and altar of *hopelessness* that satan planted in my generational bloodline. Heavenly Father, I call upon Your holy angels to be witnesses to my lawsuit and righteous prosecution of the evil altar of *hopelessness*. I decree and declare that this evil altar of *hopelessness* will not continue to control me or kill my optimism for a better and brighter future, in Jesus' name I pray.

3. Surrender Your Rights to Self-Representation to the Lord as Your Advocate

Heavenly Father, Your Word in First John 2:1-2 says, "*My little children, these things I write to you, so that you may not sin. And if anyone sins, we have an Advocate with the Father, Jesus Christ the righteous. And He Himself is the propitiation for our sins, and not for ours only but also for the whole world*" (NKJV). I thank You that Jesus is my faithful Advocate before the Righteous Judge in the Courts of Heaven. Lord Jesus, I surrender my rights to self-representation and summon You as my Advocate to help me plead my case before the Righteous Judge and prosecute the evil of altar of *hopelessness* that satan planted in my bloodline. I also ask the blessed Holy Spirit, who is the highest officer of the Courts of Heaven here on earth, to make me sensitive to the proceedings of this Court in order to successfully prosecute the evil altar of *hopelessness* in Jesus' name.

4. Summon the Evil Altar and the Idol That Sits on It to Appear in Court

Heavenly Father, even as I stand in Your royal courtroom I present myself as a living sacrifice, holy and acceptable before You according to Romans 12:1. Heavenly Father, Righteous Judge, I summon the altar of *hopelessness* in my bloodline and the idol that sits on it to appear in Your royal courtroom to face prosecution in Jesus' name. For it is written in

First Corinthians 6:3, *"Do you not know that we [believers] will judge angels? How much more then [as to] matters of this life?"* Heavenly Father, I exercise my God-given authority in Christ Jesus to judge demons and principalities, in Jesus' name I pray. Righteous Judge, it is also written in the Constitution of Your Kingdom in First John 3:8, *"For this purpose the Son of God was manifested, that He might destroy the works of the devil"* (NKJV).

5. *Address Satan's Accusations and Agree with the Adversary*

Heavenly Father, I know that until the end of the age of sin, satan still has legal access to the Courts of Heaven to level accusations against the children of men; for it is written in the book of Revelation 12:10:

> *Then I heard a loud voice in heaven, saying, "Now the salvation, and the power, and the kingdom (dominion, reign) of our God, and the authority of His Christ have come; for the accuser of our [believing] brothers and sisters has been thrown down [at last], he who accuses them and keeps bringing charges [of sinful behavior] against them before our God day and night."*

Heavenly Father, the Lord Jesus also said in the book of Matthew 5:25:

> *Come to terms quickly [at the earliest opportunity] with your opponent at law while you are with him on the way [to court], so that your opponent does not hand you over to the judge, and the judge to the guard, and you are thrown into prison.*

Heavenly Father, in all humility, while renouncing the spirit of pride, I choose to quickly agree with the legal accusations of my adversary, satan. Righteous Judge, every accusation that satan has filed against me and my bloodline in this Court is true.

6. Repent

Heavenly Father, I repent for my personal transgressions, and for the sins and iniquities of my forefathers that opened the door for the spirit and altar of *hopelessness* to oppress my life, in Jesus' name I pray. Lord, every sin of my forefathers that the enemy is using as a legal right to build cases against me and to deny me hope, I ask that the blood of Jesus would just wash them away. I repent for giving up on life and my God-given dream. I also repent for self-inflicted word curses and all covenants with demons of *hopelessness* that have existed in my ancestral bloodline. I am asking that every covenant with demonic powers will now be revoked and that their right to claim me and my bloodline would now be dismissed before Your court, in Jesus' name. Thank You, Lord, for revoking these demonic covenants and evil altars of *hopelessness* in Jesus' mighty name! Heavenly Father, in my heartfelt desire to divorce myself from the spirit and altar of *hopelessness*, I give back everything and anything that the devil would say came from his kingdom. I only want what the blood of Jesus has secured for me.

7. Appeal to the Blood of Jesus to Wipe Out All Sin (Satan's Evidence)

Lord Jesus, thank You for cleansing me by Your blood so satan has no legal footing against me in Your courtroom. It is written in First John 1:9:

> If we [freely] admit that we have sinned and confess our sins,
> He is faithful and just [true to His own nature and promises],
> and will forgive our sins and cleanse us continually from all
> unrighteousness [our wrongdoing, everything not in confor-
> mity with His will and purpose].

Righteous Judge, I appeal to the blood of Jesus to wipe out all my shortcomings, transgressions, and iniquities, in Jesus' name, I pray. I receive by faith the cleansing power of the blood of Jesus.

8. Ask the Court to Dismiss All of Satan's Accusations and Charges

Heavenly Father, based upon Jesus' finished work and my heartfelt repentance, I now move on the Court of Heaven to dismiss all of satan's accusations and charges against me and my bloodline in Jesus' name. For it is written that the accuser of the brethren has been cast down. So, I ask You Father to cast down all of satan's accusations against me, in Jesus' name, I pray.

9. Ask the Lord to Send Angels to Destroy the Evil Altar and Execute the Lord's Judgment Against It

Heavenly Father, Righteous Judge, I ask that You send high-ranking angelic officers of the Courts who excel in strength to execute the judgment of Your supreme court and destroy the evil altar of *hopelessness* and the idol that sits on it that satan planted in my bloodline, in Jesus' name I pray. By the spirit of prophecy, I prophesy the complete destruction of the evil altar of *hopelessness* in my life, in Jesus' name. For it is written in Psalm 91:11-12, *"For He will command His angels in regard to you, to protect and defend and guard you in all your ways [of obedience and service]. They will lift you up in their hands, so that you do not [even] strike your foot against a stone."* I receive angelic assistance, right now, in Jesus' name.

10. Present Scriptures That Will Be Used in Issuing a Divine Restraining Order

Heavenly Father, I present before Your Supreme Court the following scriptures as my rock-solid evidence against the spirit and altar of *hopelessness* in my life. It is written:

> *And now, Lord, for what do I expectantly wait? My hope [my confident expectation] is in You* (Psalm 39:7).

*Behold, the eye of the Lord is on those who fear Him, on those who **hope** in His mercy* (Psalm 33:18 NKJV).

Righteous Judge, based upon the aforementioned scriptures, it is clear that the spirit and altar of *hopelessness,* if allowed to succeed, would cause great injury to my life, destiny, and also inflict irreparable damage to the purposes of God. I ask that that every legal right the spirit and altar of *hopelessness* is holding be revoked in Jesus' glorious name. Righteous Judge, based upon the aforementioned scriptures, it is clear that I qualify for a divine restraining order against the altar of *hopelessness* and the idol that sits on it, in Jesus' name.

11. Ask the Court to Issue a Divine Restraining Order and Receive the Divine Restraining Order by Faith

Heavenly Father, Righteous Judge, I now ask that a divine restraining order and a permanent injunction against the spirit and altar of *hopelessness* in my life would now be issued by the authority of Your Supreme Court, in Jesus' name. Heavenly Father, I decree and declare that any and all forms of *hopelessness* the devil has issued or is orchestrating against my life are now cancelled in Jesus' glorious name. Heavenly Father, I receive this divine restraining order and permanent injunction by faith, in Jesus' name. For it is written in the Constitution of Your Kingdom in Hebrews 11:6, *"But without faith it is impossible to [walk with God and] please Him, for whoever comes [near] to God must [necessarily] believe that God exists and that He rewards those who [earnestly and diligently] seek Him."* I believe and declare by faith that the spirit and altar of *hopelessness* in my life has been judged, in Jesus' name!

12. Ask the Lord to Seal Your Righteous Verdict and Court Proceedings in the Blood of Jesus

Heavenly Father, Righteous Judge, I now ask You to seal my righteous verdict against the spirit and altar of *hopelessness* in the precious blood of Jesus. May You also cover with the blood of Jesus all my legal proceedings in this Court in Jesus' name. I decree and declare that my righteous verdict of release and breakthrough from the evil altar of *hopelessness* is now secured in the documents of the Courts of Heaven. For it is written in John's Gospel, chapter 8:36, *"So if the Son makes you free, then you are unquestionably free."* I decree and declare that I am free of the evil altar of *hopelessness* in Jesus' name, amen!

Prayer #33

Uprooting the Altar of Restlessness

When I lie down I say, "When shall I arise [and the night be gone]?" But the night continues, and I am continually tossing until the dawning of day.

—Job 7:4

It goes without saying or contradiction that God has called us to a life of rest. Jesus admonishes us in Matthew 11:29 to come to Him and He will give us rest for our souls. Nevertheless, many of God's children live restless lives. Even *bedtime* is a massive struggle. For whatever reason they cannot bring themselves to relax to enjoy a restful sleep. Unfortunately for many of these people, even the daytimes are just as restless as the nighttimes. Job experienced the menacing power of this evil altar of restlessness when satan came after his family and everything he owned. Pharmaceutical companies are making billions of dollars all over the world prescribing Prozac to a population of restless people. But a pharmaceutical pill cannot get rid of a spiritual problem, only mask it temporarily. God wants to permanently destroy the evil altar of restlessness that has been harassing you. Please use the *dangerous prayer* below to destroy this evil altar!

Prayer of Activation

1. Address the Father in Praise and Worship

Heavenly Father, holy is Your name and greatly to be praised. I worship and adore You in Jesus' name. May Your Kingdom manifest in my life as it is in Heaven. Plead my cause, O Lord, with those who strive with me; fight against any entity or person who is contending against me. Heavenly Father, it is written in Psalm 27:6, *"And now my head will be lifted up above my enemies around me, in His tent I will offer sacrifices with shouts of joy; I will sing, yes, I will sing praises to the Lord."* Abba, I enjoin my worship to the heavenly chorus of worship of Your holy angels and the crowd of witnesses, in Jesus' name.

2. Ask for the Court to Be Seated

Heavenly Father, Righteous Judge, I ask that the Courts of Heaven be seated according to Daniel 7:9-10. I ask this in Jesus' mighty name. It is written:

> *I kept looking until thrones were set up, and the Ancient of Days (God) took His seat; His garment was white as snow and the hair of His head like pure wool. His throne was flames of fire; its wheels were a burning fire. A river of fire was flowing and coming out from before Him; a thousand thousands were attending Him, and ten thousand times ten thousand were standing before Him; the court was seated, and the books were opened.*

Heavenly Father, I am requesting the privilege of standing before the courtroom of the Ancient of Days according to what was revealed to the prophet Daniel, in Jesus' name, I pray. Heavenly Father, I stand in Your royal

courtroom because of the blood and finished work of Jesus on the cross. I have come to receive Your righteous judgment over my life against the spirit and altar of *restlessness* that satan planted in my generational bloodline. Heavenly Father, I call upon Your holy angels to be witnesses to my lawsuit and righteous prosecution of the evil altar of *restlessness*. I decree and declare that this evil altar of *restlessness* will not continue to control me or kill my optimism for a better and brighter future, in Jesus' name I pray.

3. Surrender Your Rights to Self-Representation to the Lord as Your Advocate

Heavenly Father, Your Word in First John 2:1-2 says, "*My little children, these things I write to you, so that you may not sin. And if anyone sins, we have an Advocate with the Father, Jesus Christ the righteous. And He Himself is the propitiation for our sins, and not for ours only but also for the whole world*" (NKJV). I thank You that Jesus is my faithful Advocate before the Righteous Judge in the Courts of Heaven. Lord Jesus, I surrender my rights to self-representation and summon You as my Advocate to help me plead my case before the Righteous Judge and prosecute the evil of altar of *restlessness* that satan planted in my bloodline. I also ask the blessed Holy Spirit, who is the highest officer of the Courts of Heaven here on earth, to make me sensitive to the proceedings of this Court in order to successfully prosecute the evil altar of *restlessness* in Jesus' name.

4. Summon the Evil Altar and the Idol That Sits on It to Appear in Court

Heavenly Father, even as I stand in Your royal courtroom I present myself as a living sacrifice, holy and acceptable before You according to Romans 12:1. Heavenly Father, Righteous Judge, I summon the altar of *restlessness* in my bloodline and the idol that sits on it to appear in Your royal courtroom to face prosecution in Jesus' name. For it is written in First Corinthians 6:3,

"Do you not know that we [believers] will judge angels? How much more then [as to] matters of this life?" Heavenly Father, I exercise my God-given authority in Christ Jesus to judge demons and principalities, in Jesus' name I pray. Righteous Judge, it is also written in the Constitution of Your Kingdom in First John 3:8, *"For this purpose the Son of God was manifested, that He might destroy the works of the devil"* (NKJV).

5. *Address Satan's Accusations and Agree with the Adversary*

Heavenly Father, I know that until the end of the age of sin, satan still has legal access to the Courts of Heaven to level accusations against the children of men; for it is written in the book of Revelation 12:10:

> *Then I heard a loud voice in heaven, saying, "Now the salvation, and the power, and the kingdom (dominion, reign) of our God, and the authority of His Christ have come; for the accuser of our [believing] brothers and sisters has been thrown down [at last], he who accuses them and keeps bringing charges [of sinful behavior] against them before our God day and night."*

Heavenly Father, the Lord Jesus also said in the book of Matthew 5:25:

> *Come to terms quickly [at the earliest opportunity] with your opponent at law while you are with him on the way [to court], so that your opponent does not hand you over to the judge, and the judge to the guard, and you are thrown into prison.*

Heavenly Father, in all humility, while renouncing the spirit of pride, I choose to quickly agree with the legal accusations of my adversary, satan. Righteous Judge, every accusation that satan has filed against me and my bloodline in this Court is true.

6. Repent

Heavenly Father, I repent for my personal transgressions, and for the sins and iniquities of my forefathers that opened the door for the spirit and altar of *restlessness* to oppress my life, in Jesus' name I pray. Lord, every sin of my forefathers that the enemy is using as a legal right to build cases against me and to deny me a restful life, I ask that the blood of Jesus would just wash them away. I also repent for self-inflicted word curses and all covenants with demons of *restlessness* that have existed in my ancestral bloodline. I am asking that every covenant with demonic powers will now be revoked and that their right to claim me and my bloodline would now be dismissed before Your court, in Jesus' name. Thank You, Lord, for revoking these demonic covenants and evil altars of *restlessness* in Jesus' mighty name! Heavenly Father, in my heartfelt desire to divorce myself from the spirit and altar of *restlessness*, I give back everything and anything that the devil would say came from his kingdom. I only want what the blood of Jesus has secured for me.

7. Appeal to the Blood of Jesus to Wipe Out All Sin (Satan's Evidence)

Lord Jesus, thank You for cleansing me by Your blood so satan has no legal footing against me in Your courtroom. It is written in First John 1:9:

> *If we [freely] admit that we have sinned and confess our sins, He is faithful and just [true to His own nature and promises], and will forgive our sins and cleanse us continually from all unrighteousness [our wrongdoing, everything not in conformity with His will and purpose].*

Righteous Judge, I appeal to the blood of Jesus to wipe out all my shortcomings, transgressions, and iniquities, in Jesus' name, I pray. I receive by faith the cleansing power of the blood of Jesus.

8. Ask the Court to Dismiss All of Satan's Accusations and Charges

Heavenly Father, based upon Jesus' finished work and my heartfelt repentance, I now move on the Court of Heaven to dismiss all of satan's accusations and charges against me and my bloodline in Jesus' name. For it is written that the accuser of the brethren has been cast down. So, I ask You Father to cast down all of satan's accusations against me, in Jesus' name, I pray.

9. Ask the Lord to Send Angels to Destroy the Evil Altar and Execute the Lord's Judgment Against It

Heavenly Father, Righteous Judge, I ask that You send high-ranking angelic officers of the Courts who excel in strength to execute the judgment of Your supreme court and destroy the evil altar of *restlessness* and the idol that sits on it that satan planted in my bloodline, in Jesus' name I pray. By the spirit of prophecy, I prophesy the complete destruction of the evil altar of *restlessness* in my life, in Jesus' name. For it is written in Psalm 91:11-12, *"For He will command His angels in regard to you, to protect and defend and guard you in all your ways [of obedience and service]. They will lift you up in their hands, so that you do not [even] strike your foot against a stone."* I receive angelic assistance, right now, in Jesus' name.

10. Present Scriptures That Will Be Used in Issuing a Divine Restraining Order

Heavenly Father, I present before Your Supreme Court the following scriptures as my rock-solid evidence against the spirit and altar of *restlessness* in my life. It is written:

> *Come to Me, all who are weary and heavily burdened [by religious rituals that provide no peace], and I will give you rest*

[refreshing your souls with salvation]. Take My yoke upon you and learn from Me [following Me as My disciple], for I am gentle and humble in heart, and you will find rest (renewal, blessed quiet) for your souls (Matthew 11:28-29).

Righteous Judge, based upon the aforementioned scriptures, it is clear that the spirit and altar of *restlessness,* if allowed to succeed, would cause great injury to my life, destiny, and also inflict irreparable damage to the purposes of God. I ask that that every legal right the spirit and altar of *restlessness* is holding be revoked in Jesus' glorious name. Righteous Judge, based upon the aforementioned scriptures, it is clear that I qualify for a divine restraining order against the altar of *restlessness* and the idol that sits on it, in Jesus' name.

11. Ask the Court to Issue a Divine Restraining Order and Receive the Divine Restraining Order by Faith

Heavenly Father, Righteous Judge, I now ask that a divine restraining order and a permanent injunction against the spirit and altar of *restlessness* in my life would now be issued by the authority of Your Supreme Court, in Jesus' name. Heavenly Father, I decree and declare that any and all forms of *restlessness* the devil has issued or is orchestrating against my life are now cancelled in Jesus' glorious name. Heavenly Father, I receive this divine restraining order and permanent injunction by faith, in Jesus' name. For it is written in the Constitution of Your Kingdom in Hebrews 11:6, *"But without faith it is impossible to [walk with God and] please Him, for whoever comes [near] to God must [necessarily] believe that God exists and that He rewards those who [earnestly and diligently] seek Him."* I believe and declare by faith that the spirit and altar of *restlessness* in my life has been judged, in Jesus' name!

12. Ask the Lord to Seal Your Righteous Verdict and Court Proceedings in the Blood of Jesus

Heavenly Father, Righteous Judge, I now ask You to seal my righteous verdict against the spirit and altar of *restlessness* in the precious blood of Jesus. May You also cover with the blood of Jesus all my legal proceedings in this Court in Jesus' name. I decree and declare that my righteous verdict of release and breakthrough from the evil altar of *restlessness* is now secured in the documents of the Courts of Heaven. For it is written in John's Gospel, chapter 8:36, *"So if the Son makes you free, then you are unquestionably free."* I decree and declare that I am free of the evil altar of *restlessness* in Jesus' name, amen!

Prayer #34

Uprooting the Altar of Sexual Molestation

When she brought them to him to eat, he took hold of her and said, "Come, lie with me, my sister." She replied, "No, my brother! Do not violate me, for such a thing is not done in Israel; do not do this disgraceful thing! As for me, how could I get rid of my shame and disgrace? And you, you will be considered one of the fools in Israel. So now, just speak to the king [about taking me as your wife], for he will not withhold me from you." But he would not listen to her; and since he was stronger than she, he violated her and lay with her.
—2 Samuel 13:11-14

You need not look further than social media to see how sexualized our modern culture has become. It seems like everything on social media and television, not to mention movies, have become highly sexualized. I've never seen a culture that is so obsessed with sex and sexual orientation than the culture we are living in. It is therefore not surprising why some sex crimes all over the world, especially in the United States, are on the rise. The American foster care system, which was designed to shelter abandoned children, is itself a victim of this highly sexualized culture we live in. Child Protection Services (CPS) reports many instances of sexual molestation of foster children by the very people who are supposed to be protecting them. Without a doubt the biggest cancer on the soul of nations is the rapid rise in the sex trafficking of little boys and girls for the sexual satisfaction of adult sexual deviants from around the world.

When I was living in Texas, in the church that I pastored, a brother was arrested by the police for molesting two of his nieces. They were both below the age of nine years old. We were completely shocked, not to mention angry! From our vantage point this brother loved Jesus and had a great family. I could never have imagined him on his worst day being arrested for the sexual molestation of two minors. Unfortunately, that is exactly what happened. He is now serving a 45-year sentence at a correctional facility in the state of Texas. How tragic! When I asked him, "What happened?" tears of sorrow and regret flooded his face. He told me he had been off his prescription drugs that were designed to suppress his feelings of pedophilia. Apparently, pedophilia was rampant in his family bloodline. According to him, his bloodline was an unending cycle of the sexual molestation of family members by family members. It was an open secret. Unfortunately, at that time I did not know that any evil ritual in any family that forms a predictable pattern is due to the presence of an evil altar in that bloodline, which feeds on that repeating ritual. Thankfully, the *dangerous prayer* below is designed to help anyone who has ever been sexually molested to break free of this vicious stigma and oppressive altar.

Prayer of Activation

1. Address the Father in Praise and Worship

Heavenly Father, holy is Your name and greatly to be praised. I worship and adore You in Jesus' name. May Your Kingdom manifest in my life as it is in Heaven. Plead my cause, O Lord, with those who strive with me; fight against any entity or person who is contending against me. Heavenly Father, it is written in Psalm 27:6, *"And now my head will be lifted up above my enemies around me, in His tent I will offer sacrifices with shouts of joy; I will sing, yes, I will sing praises to the Lord."* Abba, I enjoin my worship to the heavenly chorus of worship of Your holy angels and the crowd of witnesses, in Jesus' name.

2. Ask for the Court to Be Seated

Heavenly Father, Righteous Judge, I ask that the Courts of Heaven be seated according to Daniel 7:9-10. I ask this in Jesus' mighty name. It is written:

> *I kept looking until thrones were set up, and the Ancient of Days (God) took His seat; His garment was white as snow and the hair of His head like pure wool. His throne was flames of fire; its wheels were a burning fire. A river of fire was flowing and coming out from before Him; a thousand thousands were attending Him, and ten thousand times ten thousand were standing before Him; the court was seated, and the books were opened.*

Heavenly Father, I am requesting the privilege of standing before the courtroom of the Ancient of Days according to what was revealed to the prophet Daniel, in Jesus' name, I pray. Heavenly Father, I stand in Your royal courtroom because of the blood and finished work of Jesus on the cross. I have come to receive Your righteous judgment over my life against the spirit and altar of *sexual molestation* that satan planted in my generational bloodline. Heavenly Father, I call upon Your holy angels to be witnesses to my lawsuit and righteous prosecution of the evil altar of *sexual molestation*. I decree and declare that this evil altar of *sexual molestation* will not continue to traumatize and control me, nor will it poison or stop me from having a godly view of sex and sexuality, in Jesus' name I pray.

3. Surrender Your Rights to Self-Representation to the Lord as Your Advocate

Heavenly Father, Your Word in First John 2:1-2 says, *"My little children, these things I write to you, so that you may not sin. And if anyone sins, we have an Advocate with the Father, Jesus Christ the righteous. And He Himself is the propitiation for our sins, and not for ours only but also for the whole world"* (NKJV). I thank You that Jesus is my faithful Advocate before the Righteous Judge in the Courts of Heaven. Lord Jesus, I surrender my rights to self-representation and summon You as my Advocate to help me plead my case before the Righteous Judge and prosecute the evil of altar of *sexual molestation* that satan planted in my bloodline. I also ask the blessed Holy Spirit, who is the highest officer of the Courts of Heaven here on earth, to make me sensitive to the proceedings of this Court in order to successfully prosecute the evil altar of *sexual molestation* in Jesus' name.

4. Summon the Evil Altar and the Idol That Sits on It to Appear in Court

Heavenly Father, even as I stand in Your royal courtroom I present myself as a living sacrifice, holy and acceptable before You according to Romans 12:1. Heavenly Father, Righteous Judge, I summon the altar of *sexual molestation* in my bloodline and the idol that sits on it to appear in Your royal courtroom to face prosecution in Jesus' name. For it is written in First Corinthians 6:3, *"Do you not know that we [believers] will judge angels? How much more then [as to] matters of this life?"* Heavenly Father, I exercise my God-given authority in Christ Jesus to judge demons and principalities, in Jesus' name I pray. Righteous Judge, it is also written in the Constitution of Your Kingdom in First John 3:8, *"For this purpose the Son of God was manifested, that He might destroy the works of the devil"* (NKJV).

5. Address Satan's Accusations and Agree with the Adversary

Heavenly Father, I know that until the end of the age of sin, satan still has legal access to the Courts of Heaven to level accusations against the children of men; for it is written in the book of Revelation 12:10:

> *Then I heard a loud voice in heaven, saying, "Now the salvation, and the power, and the kingdom (dominion, reign) of our God, and the authority of His Christ have come; for the accuser of our [believing] brothers and sisters has been thrown down [at last], he who accuses them and keeps bringing charges [of sinful behavior] against them before our God day and night."*

Heavenly Father, the Lord Jesus also said in the book of Matthew 5:25:

> *Come to terms quickly [at the earliest opportunity] with your opponent at law while you are with him on the way [to court], so that your opponent does not hand you over to the judge, and the judge to the guard, and you are thrown into prison.*

Heavenly Father, in all humility, while renouncing the spirit of pride, I choose to quickly agree with the legal accusations of my adversary, satan. Righteous Judge, every accusation that satan has filed against me and my bloodline in this Court is true.

6. Repent

Heavenly Father, I repent for my personal transgressions, and for the sins and iniquities of my forefathers that opened the door for the spirit and altar of *sexual molestation* to oppress my life, in Jesus' name I pray. Lord, every sin of my forefathers that the enemy is using as a legal right to build cases against me and to deny me my destiny, I ask that the blood of Jesus would just wash them away. I also repent for self-inflicted word curses and all covenants with demons that have existed in my ancestral bloodline. I am asking that every covenant with demonic powers will now be revoked and that their right to claim me and my bloodline would now be dismissed before Your court, in Jesus' name. Thank You, Lord, for revoking these demonic covenants and evil altars in Jesus' mighty name! Heavenly Father, in my heartfelt desire to divorce myself from the spirit and altar of *sexual molestation*, I give back everything and anything that the devil would say came from his kingdom. I only want what the blood of Jesus has secured for me.

7. *Appeal to the Blood of Jesus to Wipe Out All Sin (Satan's Evidence)*

Lord Jesus, thank You for cleansing me by Your blood so satan has no legal footing against me in Your courtroom. It is written in First John 1:9:

> *If we [freely] admit that we have sinned and confess our sins, He is faithful and just [true to His own nature and promises], and will forgive our sins and cleanse us continually from all unrighteousness [our wrongdoing, everything not in conformity with His will and purpose].*

Righteous Judge, I appeal to the blood of Jesus to wipe out all my shortcomings, transgressions, and iniquities, in Jesus' name, I pray. I receive by faith the cleansing power of the blood of Jesus.

8. *Ask the Court to Dismiss All of Satan's Accusations and Charges*

Heavenly Father, based upon Jesus' finished work and my heartfelt repentance, I now move on the Court of Heaven to dismiss all of satan's accusations and charges against me and my bloodline in Jesus' name. For it is written that the accuser of the brethren has been cast down. So, I ask You

Father to cast down all of satan's accusations against me, in Jesus' name, I pray.

9. Ask the Lord to Send Angels to Destroy the Evil Altar and Execute the Lord's Judgment Against It

Heavenly Father, Righteous Judge, I ask that You send high-ranking angelic officers of the Courts who excel in strength to execute the judgment of Your supreme court and destroy the evil altar of *sexual molestation* and the idol that sits on it that satan planted in my bloodline, in Jesus' name I pray. By the spirit of prophecy, I prophesy the complete destruction of the evil altar of *sexual molestation* in my life, in Jesus' name. For it is written in Psalm 91:11-12, *"For He will command His angels in regard to you, to protect and defend and guard you in all your ways [of obedience and service]. They will lift you up in their hands, so that you do not [even] strike your foot against a stone."* I receive angelic assistance, right now, in Jesus' name.

10. Present Scriptures That Will Be Used in Issuing a Divine Restraining Order

Heavenly Father, I present before Your Supreme Court the following scriptures as my rock-solid evidence against the spirit and altar of *sexual molestation* in my life. It is written:

> *The Spirit of the Lord God is upon me, because the Lord has anointed and commissioned me to bring good news to the humble and afflicted; He has sent me to bind up [the wounds of] the brokenhearted, to proclaim release [from confinement and condemnation] to the [physical and spiritual] captives and freedom to prisoners* (Isaiah 61:1).

> *He lets me lie down in green pastures; He leads me beside the still and quiet waters. He refreshes and restores my soul (life);*

He leads me in the paths of righteousness for His name's sake (Psalm 23:2-3).

Righteous Judge, based upon the aforementioned scriptures, it is clear that the spirit and altar of *sexual molestation,* if allowed to succeed, would cause great injury to my life, destiny, and also inflict irreparable damage to the purposes of God. I ask that that every legal right the spirit and altar of *sexual molestation* is holding be revoked in Jesus' glorious name. Righteous Judge, based upon the aforementioned scriptures, it is clear that I qualify for a divine restraining order against the altar of *sexual molestation* and the idol that sits on it, in Jesus' name.

11. Ask the Court to Issue a Divine Restraining Order and Receive the Divine Restraining Order by Faith

Heavenly Father, Righteous Judge, I now ask that a divine restraining order and a permanent injunction against the spirit and altar of *sexual molestation* in my life would now be issued by the authority of Your Supreme Court, in Jesus' name. Heavenly Father, I decree and declare that any and all forms of *sexual molestation* the devil has issued or is orchestrating against my life are now cancelled in Jesus' glorious name. Heavenly Father, I receive this divine restraining order and permanent injunction by faith, in Jesus' name. For it is written in the Constitution of Your Kingdom in Hebrews 11:6, *"But without faith it is impossible to [walk with God and] please Him, for whoever comes [near] to God must [necessarily] believe that God exists and that He rewards those who [earnestly and diligently] seek Him."* I believe and declare by faith that the spirit and altar of *sexual molestation* in my life has been judged, in Jesus' name!

12. Ask the Lord to Seal Your Righteous Verdict and Court Proceedings in the Blood of Jesus

Heavenly Father, Righteous Judge, I now ask You to seal my righteous verdict against the spirit and altar of *sexual molestation* in the precious blood of Jesus. May You also cover with the blood of Jesus all my legal proceedings in this Court in Jesus' name. I decree and declare that my righteous verdict of release and breakthrough from the evil altar of *sexual molestation* is now secured in the documents of the Courts of Heaven. For it is written in John's Gospel, chapter 8:36, *"So if the Son makes you free, then you are unquestionably free."* I decree and declare that I am free of the evil altar of *sexual molestation* in Jesus' name, amen!

Prayer #35

Uprooting the Altar of Freemasonry

The carpenter stretches out a measuring line, he marks out the shape [of the idol] with red chalk; he works it with planes and out-lines it with the compass; and he makes it like the form of a man, like the beauty of man, that it may sit in a house.

—Isaiah 44:13

I have been involved in the deliverance ministry for at least three decades, ever since I was introduced to the ministry of Derek Prince. His books on spiritual warfare and deliverance, such as *They Shall Expel Demons,* dras-tically changed my life. In most serious deliverance cases Derek Prince ran into and I ran into, there was usually a common root of involvement in *free-masonry.* The "Free Masons" are a secret society that look docile and inno-cent at the lowest levels of membership. However, many women and men, now former Masons who reached the 32nd degree and above, can attest that they were initiated into the direct and intimate worship of lucifer (satan). So in essence, *freemasonry* is a religion of satan worship and anyone who carries the evil altar of *freemasonry* in their bloodline needs to be delivered or face very severe spiritual consequences.

Jack Harris, author of *Freemasonry* and a former "worshipful master" of a Masonic lodge, authoritatively speaks about one of the most deceptive cults in the United States today. "Freemasonry is a false religion, teaching that men can approach God not through the finished work of Jesus Christ but through their own abilities. This secret organization has entangled ministers, elders, deacons, trustees, Sunday school teachers, and people all over the world in a web of lies and satanic rituals—all of which are veiled with the language of the Bible!" The *dangerous prayer* below was designed to help you silence and destroy this evil altar in the Courts of Heaven.

Prayer of Activation

1. Address the Father in Praise and Worship

Heavenly Father, holy is Your name and greatly to be praised. I worship and adore You in Jesus' name. May Your Kingdom manifest in my life as it is in Heaven. Plead my cause, O Lord, with those who strive with me; fight against any entity or person who is contending against me. Heavenly Father, it is written in Psalm 27:6, *"And now my head will be lifted up above my enemies around me, in His tent I will offer sacrifices with shouts of joy; I will sing, yes, I will sing praises to the Lord."* Abba, I enjoin my worship to the heavenly chorus of worship of Your holy angels and the crowd of witnesses, in Jesus' name.

2. Ask for the Court to Be Seated

Heavenly Father, Righteous Judge, I ask that the Courts of Heaven be seated according to Daniel 7:9-10. I ask this in Jesus' mighty name. It is written:

> I kept looking until thrones were set up, and the Ancient of Days (God) took His seat; His garment was white as snow and the hair of His head like pure wool. His throne was flames of fire; its wheels were a burning fire. A river of fire was flowing and coming out from before Him; a thousand thousands

were attending Him, and ten thousand times ten thousand were standing before Him; the court was seated, and the books were opened.

Heavenly Father, I am requesting the privilege of standing before the courtroom of the Ancient of Days according to what was revealed to the prophet Daniel, in Jesus' name, I pray. Heavenly Father, I stand in Your royal courtroom because of the blood and finished work of Jesus on the cross. I have come to receive Your righteous judgment over my life against the spirit and altar of *freemasonry* that satan planted in my generational bloodline. Heavenly Father, I call upon Your holy angels to be witnesses to my lawsuit and righteous prosecution of the evil altar of *freemasonry*. I decree and declare that this evil altar of *freemasonry* will not continue to control me or force me into becoming a member of the secret society of freemasons, in Jesus' name I pray.

3. Surrender Your Rights to Self-Representation to the Lord as Your Advocate

Heavenly Father, Your Word in First John 2:1-2 says, *"My little children, these things I write to you, so that you may not sin. And if anyone sins, we have an Advocate with the Father, Jesus Christ the righteous. And He Himself is the propitiation for our sins, and not for ours only but also for the whole world"* (NKJV). I thank You that Jesus is my faithful Advocate before the Righteous Judge in the Courts of Heaven. Lord Jesus, I surrender my rights to self-representation and summon You as my Advocate to help me plead my case before the Righteous Judge and prosecute the evil of altar of *freemasonry* that satan planted in my bloodline. I also ask the blessed Holy Spirit, who is the highest officer of the Courts of Heaven here on earth, to make me sensitive to the proceedings of this Court in order to successfully prosecute the evil altar of *freemasonry* in Jesus' name.

4. Summon the Evil Altar and the Idol That Sits on It to Appear in Court

Heavenly Father, even as I stand in Your royal courtroom I present myself as a living sacrifice, holy and acceptable before You according to Romans 12:1. Heavenly Father, Righteous Judge, I summon the altar of *freemasonry* in my bloodline and the idol that sits on it to appear in Your royal courtroom to face prosecution in Jesus' name. For it is written in First Corinthians 6:3, *"Do you not know that we [believers] will judge angels? How much more then [as to] matters of this life?"* Heavenly Father, I exercise my God-given authority in Christ Jesus to judge demons and principalities, in Jesus' name I pray. Righteous Judge, it is also written in the Constitution of Your Kingdom in First John 3:8, *"For this purpose the Son of God was manifested, that He might destroy the works of the devil"* (NKJV).

5. Address Satan's Accusations and Agree with the Adversary

Heavenly Father, I know that until the end of the age of sin, satan still has legal access to the Courts of Heaven to level accusations against the children of men; for it is written in the book of Revelation 12:10:

> *Then I heard a loud voice in heaven, saying, "Now the salvation, and the power, and the kingdom (dominion, reign) of our God, and the authority of His Christ have come; for the accuser of our [believing] brothers and sisters has been thrown down [at last], he who accuses them and keeps bringing charges [of sinful behavior] against them before our God day and night."*

Heavenly Father, the Lord Jesus also said in the book of Matthew 5:25:

> *Come to terms quickly [at the earliest opportunity] with your opponent at law while you are with him on the way [to court],*

so that your opponent does not hand you over to the judge, and
the judge to the guard, and you are thrown into prison.

Heavenly Father, in all humility, while renouncing the spirit of pride, I choose to quickly agree with the legal accusations of my adversary, satan. Righteous Judge, every accusation that satan has filed against me and my bloodline in this Court is true.

6. *Repent*

Heavenly Father, I repent for my personal transgressions, and for the sins and iniquities of my forefathers that opened the door for the spirit and altar of *freemasonry* to oppress my life, in Jesus' name I pray. Lord, every sin of my forefathers that the enemy is using as a legal right to build cases against me and to deny me my destiny, I ask that the blood of Jesus would just wash them away. I repent for any secret societies I have ever been part of. I also repent for self-inflicted word curses and all covenants with demons behind *freemasonry* that have existed in my ancestral bloodline. I am asking that every covenant with demonic powers will now be revoked and that their right to claim me and my bloodline would now be dismissed before Your court, in Jesus' name. Thank You, Lord, for revoking these demonic covenants and evil altars in Jesus' mighty name! Heavenly Father, in my heartfelt desire to divorce myself from the spirit and altar of *freemasonry,* I give back everything and anything that the devil would say came from his kingdom. I only want what the blood of Jesus has secured for me.

7. *Appeal to the Blood of Jesus to Wipe Out All Sin (Satan's Evidence)*

Lord Jesus, thank You for cleansing me by Your blood so satan has no legal footing against me in Your courtroom. It is written in First John 1:9:

*If we [freely] admit that we have sinned and confess our sins,
He is faithful and just [true to His own nature and promises],
and will forgive our sins and cleanse us continually from all
unrighteousness [our wrongdoing, everything not in conformity with His will and purpose].*

Righteous Judge, I appeal to the blood of Jesus to wipe out all my short-
comings, transgressions, and iniquities, in Jesus' name, I pray. I receive by
faith the cleansing power of the blood of Jesus.

8. *Ask the Court to Dismiss All of Satan's Accusations and Charges*

Heavenly Father, based upon Jesus' finished work and my heartfelt
repentance, I now move on the Court of Heaven to dismiss all of satan's
accusations and charges against me and my bloodline in Jesus' name. For it
is written that the accuser of the brethren has been cast down. So, I ask You
Father to cast down all of satan's accusations against me, in Jesus' name, I
pray.

9. *Ask the Lord to Send Angels to Destroy the Evil Altar and Execute the Lord's Judgment Against It*

Heavenly Father, Righteous Judge, I ask that You send high-ranking
angelic officers of the Courts who excel in strength to execute the judgment
of Your supreme court and destroy the evil altar of *freemasonry* and the idol
that sits on it that satan planted in my bloodline, in Jesus' name I pray. By
the spirit of prophecy, I prophesy the complete destruction of the evil altar
of *freemasonry* in my life, in Jesus' name. For it is written in Psalm 91:11-12,
*"For He will command His angels in regard to you, to protect and defend and
guard you in all your ways [of obedience and service]. They will lift you up in
their hands, so that you do not [even] strike your foot against a stone."* I receive
angelic assistance, right now, in Jesus' name.

10. Present Scriptures That Will Be Used in Issuing a Divine Restraining Order

Heavenly Father, I present before Your Supreme Court the following scriptures as my rock-solid evidence against the spirit and altar of *freemasonry* in my life. It is written:

> *See to it that no one takes you captive through philosophy and empty deception [pseudo-intellectual babble], according to the tradition [and musings] of mere men, following the elementary principles of this world, rather than following [the truth—the teachings of] Christ* (Colossians 2:8).

> *Jesus asked them, "Have you never read in the Scriptures: 'The [very] Stone which the builders rejected and threw away, has become the chief Cornerstone; this is the Lord's doing, and it is marvelous and wonderful in our eyes'?"* (Matthew 21:42)

Righteous Judge, based upon the aforementioned scriptures, it is clear that the spirit and altar of *freemasonry*, if allowed to succeed, would cause great injury to my life, destiny, and also inflict irreparable damage to the purposes of God. I ask that that every legal right the spirit and altar of *freemasonry* is holding be revoked in Jesus' glorious name. Righteous Judge, based upon the aforementioned scriptures, it is clear that I qualify for a divine restraining order against the altar of *freemasonry* and the idol that sits on it, in Jesus' name.

11. Ask the Court to Issue a Divine Restraining Order and Receive the Divine Restraining Order by Faith

Heavenly Father, Righteous Judge, I now ask that a divine restraining order and a permanent injunction against the spirit and altar of *freemasonry* in my life would now be issued by the authority of Your Supreme Court, in

Jesus' name. Heavenly Father, I decree and declare that any and all forms of *freemasonry* the devil is orchestrating against my life are now cancelled in Jesus' glorious name. Heavenly Father, I receive this divine restraining order and permanent injunction by faith, in Jesus' name. For it is written in the Constitution of Your Kingdom in Hebrews 11:6, *"But without faith it is impossible to [walk with God and] please Him, for whoever comes [near] to God must [necessarily] believe that God exists and that He rewards those who [earnestly and diligently] seek Him."* I believe and declare by faith that the spirit and altar of *freemasonry* in my life has been judged, in Jesus' name!

12. Ask the Lord to Seal Your Righteous Verdict and Court Proceedings in the Blood of Jesus

Heavenly Father, Righteous Judge, I now ask You to seal my righteous verdict against the spirit and altar of *freemasonry* in the precious blood of Jesus. May You also cover with the blood of Jesus all my legal proceedings in this Court in Jesus' name. I decree and declare that my righteous verdict of release and breakthrough from the evil altar of *freemasonry* is now secured in the documents of the Courts of Heaven. For it is written in John's Gospel, chapter 8:36, *"So if the Son makes you free, then you are unquestionably free."* I decree and declare that I am free of the evil altar of *freemasonry* in Jesus' name, amen!

Prayer #35

Uprooting the Altar That Scatters

Then I raised my eyes and looked, and there were four horns. And I said to the angel who talked with me, "What are these?" So he answered me, "These are the horns that have scattered Judah, Israel, and Jerusalem."
—**Zechariah 1:18-19 NKJV**

The biblical pattern is that God uses what His servants have struggled with or suffered from to unlock spiritual mysteries that are remedies to those same challenges. In other words, God turns our "mess" into our message, our "pain" into our "power," and so forth. This is certainly the case for me, in reference to what I now know about the evil altar of the scatterer. I suffered terribly under the oppressive power of this evil altar for 28 years! Even though I loved Jesus and gave Him my whole life without reservation, most of the ministry and business projects for advancement that came my way ended up being scattered into a thousand pieces of broken dreams and aspirations. I cannot tell you how many times I cried myself to sleep as I helplessly stood by as satan tore my best-laid plans to pieces! This is why I am so passionate about the book you are now holding in your hand.

During those very frustrating 28 years, I came across Christians of all races and social statuses who were also fighting this evil and wicked altar of the scatterer! Unfortunately for me, at the time I had very limited revelation concerning the nature and operational dynamics of altars! When God began to teach on altars, I self-published a book on the subject called *The Battle of Altars*, mostly to help myself wrap my mind around what I was fighting. When my young sister Judy was given a prophetic dream revealing that the evil altar that was oppressing our family was the altar of the scatterer, the lightbulb went on! The Holy Spirit showed me that this was the evil altar of my father's house that had to be destroyed if I wanted to receive everything God had ordained for my life. The *dangerous prayer* below came as a result of that experience. Believe you me! I hate the evil altar of the scatterer with a passion!

Prayer of Activation

1. Address the Father in Praise and Worship

Heavenly Father, holy is Your name and greatly to be praised. I worship and adore You in Jesus' name. May Your Kingdom manifest in my life as it is in Heaven. Plead my cause, O Lord, with those who strive with me; fight against any entity or person who is contending against me. Heavenly Father, it is written in Psalm 27:6, *"And now my head will be lifted up above my enemies around me, in His tent I will offer sacrifices with shouts of joy; I will sing, yes, I will sing praises to the Lord."* Abba, I enjoin my worship to the heavenly chorus of worship of Your holy angels and the crowd of witnesses, in Jesus' name.

2. Ask for the Court to Be Seated

Heavenly Father, Righteous Judge, I ask that the Courts of Heaven be seated according to Daniel 7:9-10. I ask this in Jesus' mighty name. It is written:

I kept looking until thrones were set up, and the Ancient of Days (God) took His seat; His garment was white as snow and the hair of His head like pure wool. His throne was flames of fire; its wheels were a burning fire. A river of fire was flowing and coming out from before Him; a thousand thousands were attending Him, and ten thousand times ten thousand were standing before Him; the court was seated, and the books were opened.

Heavenly Father, I am requesting the privilege of standing before the courtroom of the Ancient of Days according to what was revealed to the prophet Daniel, in Jesus' name, I pray. Heavenly Father, I stand in Your royal courtroom because of the blood and finished work of Jesus on the cross. I have come to receive Your righteous judgment over my life against the spirit and altar of *the scatterer* that satan planted in my generational bloodline. Heavenly Father, I call upon Your holy angels to be witnesses to my lawsuit and righteous prosecution of the evil altar of *the scatterer*. I decree and declare that this evil altar of *the scatterer* will not continue to control me or scatter my God-given blessings and force me to live below my God-given rights and privileges, in Jesus' name I pray.

3. Surrender Your Rights to Self-Representation to the Lord as Your Advocate

Heavenly Father, Your Word in First John 2:1-2 says, "*My little children, these things I write to you, so that you may not sin. And if anyone sins, we have an Advocate with the Father, Jesus Christ the righteous. And He Himself is the propitiation for our sins, and not for ours only but also for the whole world*" (NKJV). I thank You that Jesus is my faithful Advocate before the Righteous Judge in the Courts of Heaven. Lord Jesus, I surrender my rights to self-representation and summon You as my Advocate to help me plead my case before the Righteous Judge and prosecute the evil of altar of *the scatterer* that satan planted in my bloodline. I also ask the blessed Holy Spirit, who is the highest officer of the Courts of Heaven here on earth, to make me sensitive to the proceedings of this Court in order to successfully prosecute the evil altar of *the scatterer* in Jesus' name.

4. Summon the Evil Altar and the Idol That Sits on It to Appear in Court

Heavenly Father, even as I stand in Your royal courtroom I present myself as a living sacrifice, holy and acceptable before You according to Romans 12:1. Heavenly Father, Righteous Judge, I summon the altar of *the scatterer* in my bloodline and the idol that sits on it to appear in Your royal courtroom to face prosecution in Jesus' name. For it is written in First Corinthians 6:3, *"Do you not know that we [believers] will judge angels? How much more then [as to] matters of this life?"* Heavenly Father, I exercise my God-given authority in Christ Jesus to judge demons and principalities, in Jesus' name I pray. Righteous Judge, it is also written in the Constitution of Your Kingdom in First John 3:8, *"For this purpose the Son of God was manifested, that He might destroy the works of the devil"* (NKJV).

5. Address Satan's Accusations and Agree with the Adversary

Heavenly Father, I know that until the end of the age of sin, satan still has legal access to the Courts of Heaven to level accusations against the children of men; for it is written in the book of Revelation 12:10:

> *Then I heard a loud voice in heaven, saying, "Now the salvation, and the power, and the kingdom (dominion, reign) of our God, and the authority of His Christ have come; for the accuser of our [believing] brothers and sisters has been thrown down [at last], he who accuses them and keeps bringing charges [of sinful behavior] against them before our God day and night."*

Heavenly Father, the Lord Jesus also said in the book of Matthew 5:25:

Come to terms quickly [at the earliest opportunity] with your opponent at law while you are with him on the way [to court], so that your opponent does not hand you over to the judge, and the judge to the guard, and you are thrown into prison.

Heavenly Father, in all humility, while renouncing the spirit of pride, I choose to quickly agree with the legal accusations of my adversary, satan. Righteous Judge, every accusation that satan has filed against me and my bloodline in this Court is true.

6. Repent

Heavenly Father, I repent for my personal transgressions, and for the sins and iniquities of my forefathers that opened the door for the spirit and altar of *the scatterer* to oppress my life, in Jesus' name I pray. Lord, every sin of my forefathers that the enemy is using as a legal right to build cases against me and to deny me my destiny, I ask that the blood of Jesus would just wash them away. I repent for any time I have been an agent of scattering other people's resources. I also repent for self-inflicted word curses and all covenants with demons of *scattering* that have existed in my ancestral bloodline. I am asking that every covenant with demonic powers will now be revoked and that their right to claim me and my bloodline would now be dismissed before Your court, in Jesus' name. Thank You, Lord, for revoking these demonic covenants and evil altars in Jesus' mighty name! Heavenly Father, in my heartfelt desire to divorce myself from the spirit and altar of *the scatterer,* I give back everything and anything that the devil would say came from his kingdom. I only want what the blood of Jesus has secured for me.

7. *Appeal to the Blood of Jesus to Wipe Out All Sin (Satan's Evidence)*

Lord Jesus, thank You for cleansing me by Your blood so satan has no legal footing against me in Your courtroom. It is written in First John 1:9:

> *If we [freely] admit that we have sinned and confess our sins,*
> *He is faithful and just [true to His own nature and promises],*
> *and will forgive our sins and cleanse us continually from all*
> *unrighteousness [our wrongdoing, everything not in confor-*
> *mity with His will and purpose].*

Righteous Judge, I appeal to the blood of Jesus to wipe out all my short-comings, transgressions, and iniquities, in Jesus' name, I pray. I receive by faith the cleansing power of the blood of Jesus.

8. *Ask the Court to Dismiss All of Satan's Accusations and Charges*

Heavenly Father, based upon Jesus' finished work and my heartfelt repentance, I now move on the Court of Heaven to dismiss all of satan's accusations and charges against me and my bloodline in Jesus' name. For it is written that the accuser of the brethren has been cast down. So, I ask You Father to cast down all of satan's accusations against me, in Jesus' name, I pray.

9. *Ask the Lord to Send Angels to Destroy the Evil Altar and Execute the Lord's Judgment Against It*

Heavenly Father, Righteous Judge, I ask that You send high-ranking angelic officers of the Courts who excel in strength to execute the judgment of Your supreme court and destroy the evil altar of *the scatterer* and the idol that sits on it that satan planted in my bloodline, in Jesus' name I pray. By the spirit of prophecy, I prophesy the complete destruction of the evil altar of *the scatterer* in my life, in Jesus' name. For it is written in Psalm 91:11-12, *"For He will command His angels in regard to you, to protect and defend and guard you in all your ways [of obedience and service]. They will lift you up in their hands, so that you do not [even] strike your foot against a stone."* I receive angelic assistance, right now, in Jesus' name.

10. Present Scriptures That Will Be Used in Issuing a Divine Restraining Order

Heavenly Father, I present before Your Supreme Court the following scriptures as my rock-solid evidence against the spirit and altar of *the scatterer* in my life. It is written:

> *Then the Lord showed me four craftsmen. And I said, "What are these coming to do?" So he said, "These are the horns that scattered Judah, so that no one could lift up his head; but the craftsmen are coming to terrify them, to cast out the horns of the nations that lifted up their horn against the land of Judah to scatter it"* (Zechariah 1:20-21 NKJV).

> *And I will compensate you for the years that the swarming locust has eaten, the creeping locust, the stripping locust, and the gnawing locust—My great army which I sent among you. You will have plenty to eat and be satisfied and praise the name of the Lord your God who has dealt wondrously with you; and My people shall never be put to shame* (Joel 2:25-26 NKJV).

Righteous Judge, based upon the aforementioned scriptures, it is clear that the spirit and altar of *the scatterer,* if allowed to succeed, would cause great injury to my life, destiny, and also inflict irreparable damage to the purposes of God. I ask that that every legal right the spirit and altar of *the scatterer* is holding be revoked in Jesus' glorious name. Righteous Judge, based upon the aforementioned scriptures, it is clear that I qualify for a divine restraining order against the altar of *the scatterer* and the idol that sits on it, in Jesus' name.

11. Ask the Court to Issue a Divine Restraining Order and Receive the Divine Restraining Order by Faith

Heavenly Father, Righteous Judge, I now ask that a divine restraining order and a permanent injunction against the spirit and altar of *the scatterer* in my life would now be issued by the authority of Your Supreme Court, in Jesus' name. Heavenly Father, I decree and declare that any and all activities of *the scatterer* the devil is orchestrating against my life are now cancelled in Jesus' glorious name. Heavenly Father, I receive this divine restraining order and permanent injunction by faith, in Jesus' name. For it is written in the Constitution of Your Kingdom in Hebrews 11:6, *"But without faith it is impossible to [walk with God and] please Him, for whoever comes [near] to God must [necessarily] believe that God exists and that He rewards those who [earnestly and diligently] seek Him."* I believe and declare by faith that the spirit and altar of *the scatterer* in my life has been judged, in Jesus' name!

12. Ask the Lord to Seal Your Righteous Verdict and Court Proceedings in the Blood of Jesus

Heavenly Father, Righteous Judge, I now ask You to seal my righteous verdict against the spirit and altar of *the scatterer* in the precious blood of Jesus. May You also cover with the blood of Jesus all my legal proceedings in this Court in Jesus' name. I decree and declare that my righteous verdict of release and breakthrough from the evil altar of *the scatterer* is now secured in the documents of the Courts of Heaven. For it is written in John's Gospel, chapter 8:36, *"So if the Son makes you free, then you are unquestionably free."* I decree and declare that I am free of the evil altar of *the scatterer* in Jesus' name, amen!

Prayer #36

Uprooting the Altar of Suicide

When Judas, His betrayer, saw that Jesus was condemned, he was gripped with remorse and returned the thirty pieces of silver to the chief priests and the elders, saying, "I have sinned by betraying innocent blood." They replied, "What is that to us? See to that yourself!" And throwing the pieces of silver into the temple sanctuary, he left; and went away and hanged himself.
—**Matthew 27:3-5**

In my humble opinion there is no death more tragic than suicide! It's the only death in which the deceased is their own murderer. Over two decades ago I lost one of my favorite cousins by the name of Chungu, may his spirit rest in peace! He had just graduated high school at the top of his class and was headed to a prestigious university. We were all very happy for him. While he was waiting for his first university semester to start, he decided to visit his elder brother. During his visit, his elder brother's Jezebel wife falsely accused him of stealing something he had no knowledge of. He was so upset about this unfortunate turn of events. He quickly became despondent, went outside at night while everyone was sleeping, climbed a tall tree, and hung himself. His elder brother discovered his lifeless body hanging from the tree in the morning. Chungu's suicide death changed all our lives and broke his elder brother's spirit. Since then I am very sympathetic to families who have experienced this tragedy.

According to the CDC (Centers for Disease Control), "Suicide is a large and growing public health problem. Suicide rates increased 33% between 1999 and 2019, with a small decline in 2019. Suicide is the 10th leading cause of death in the United States. It was responsible for more than 47,500 deaths in 2019, which is about one death every 11 minutes." I want this stat to sink into your heart—one death every 11 minutes! In my study of evil altars, I am convinced that the altar of suicide remains satan's favorite weapon for shortening people's lives and dragging their souls to hell. This is not to say that I believe that everyone who commits suicide goes to hell. Only God knows. But you can use the *dangerous prayer* below to destroy this evil altar in your life and bloodline. If you know anyone who struggles with suicidal thoughts use this prayer on them.

Prayer of Activation

1. Address the Father in Praise and Worship

Heavenly Father, holy is Your name and greatly to be praised. I worship and adore You in Jesus' name. May Your Kingdom manifest in my life as it is in Heaven. Plead my cause, O Lord, with those who strive with me; fight against any entity or person who is contending against me. Heavenly Father, it is written in Psalm 27:6, *"And now my head will be lifted up above my enemies around me, in His tent I will offer sacrifices with shouts of joy; I will sing, yes, I will sing praises to the Lord."* Abba, I enjoin my worship to the heavenly chorus of worship of Your holy angels and the crowd of witnesses, in Jesus' name.

2. Ask for the Court to Be Seated

Heavenly Father, Righteous Judge, I ask that the Courts of Heaven be seated according to Daniel 7:9-10. I ask this in Jesus' mighty name. It is written:

> *I kept looking until thrones were set up, and the Ancient of Days (God) took His seat; His garment was white as snow and the hair of His head like pure wool. His throne was flames of fire; its wheels were a burning fire. A river of fire was flowing and coming out from before Him; a thousand thousands were attending Him, and ten thousand times ten thousand were standing before Him; the court was seated, and the books were opened.*

Heavenly Father, I am requesting the privilege of standing before the courtroom of the Ancient of Days according to what was revealed to the prophet Daniel, in Jesus' name, I pray. Heavenly Father, I stand in Your royal courtroom because of the blood and finished work of Jesus on the cross. I have come to receive Your righteous judgment over my life against the spirit and altar of *suicide* that satan planted in my generational bloodline. Heavenly Father, I call upon Your holy angels to be witnesses to my lawsuit and righteous prosecution of the evil altar of *suicide*. I decree and declare that this evil altar of *suicide* will not continue to control me with suicidal thoughts or kill me or members of my family before our appointed time of death, in Jesus' name I pray.

3. Surrender Your Rights to Self-Representation to the Lord as Your Advocate

Heavenly Father, Your Word in First John 2:1-2 says, "*My little children, these things I write to you, so that you may not sin. And if anyone sins, we have an Advocate with the Father, Jesus Christ the righteous. And He Himself is the propitiation for our sins, and not for ours only but also for the whole world"* (NKJV). I thank You that Jesus is my faithful Advocate before the Righteous Judge in the Courts of Heaven. Lord Jesus, I surrender my rights to self-representation and summon You as my Advocate to help me plead my case before the Righteous Judge and prosecute the evil of altar of *suicide* that satan planted in my soul or bloodline. I also ask the blessed Holy Spirit, who is the highest officer of the Courts of Heaven here on earth, to make me sensitive to the proceedings of this Court in order to successfully prosecute the evil altar of *suicide* in Jesus' name.

4. Summon the Evil Altar and the Idol That Sits on It to Appear in Court

Heavenly Father, even as I stand in Your royal courtroom I present myself as a living sacrifice, holy and acceptable before You according to Romans 12:1. Heavenly Father, Righteous Judge, I summon the altar of *suicide* in my bloodline and the idol that sits on it to appear in Your royal courtroom to face prosecution in Jesus' name. For it is written in First Corinthians 6:3, *"Do you not know that we [believers] will judge angels? How much more then [as to] matters of this life?"* Heavenly Father, I exercise my God-given authority in Christ Jesus to judge demons and principalities, in Jesus' name I pray. Righteous Judge, it is also written in the constitution of Your Kingdom in First John 3:8, *"For this purpose the Son of God was manifested, that He might destroy the works of the devil"* (NKJV).

5. Address Satan's Accusations and Agree with the Adversary

Heavenly Father, I know that until the end of the age of sin, satan still has legal access to the Courts of Heaven to level accusations against the children of men; for it is written in the book of Revelation 12:10:

> Then I heard a loud voice in heaven, saying, "Now the salvation, and the power, and the kingdom (dominion, reign)

*of our God, and the authority of His Christ have come; for
the accuser of our [believing] brothers and sisters has been
thrown down [at last], he who accuses them and keeps bringing charges [of sinful behavior] against them before our God
day and night."*

Heavenly Father, the Lord Jesus also said in the book of Matthew 5:25:

*Come to terms quickly [at the earliest opportunity] with your
opponent at law while you are with him on the way [to court],
so that your opponent does not hand you over to the judge, and
the judge to the guard, and you are thrown into prison.*

Heavenly Father, in all humility, while renouncing the spirit of pride,
I choose to quickly agree with the legal accusations of my adversary, satan.
Righteous Judge, every accusation that satan has filed against me and my
bloodline in this Court is true.

6. Repent

Heavenly Father, I repent for my personal transgressions, and for the
sins and iniquities of my forefathers that opened the door for the spirit and
altar of *suicide* to oppress my life, in Jesus' name I pray. Lord, every sin of
my forefathers that the enemy is using as a legal right to build cases against
me and to oppress my mind with suicidal thoughts, I ask that the blood of
Jesus would just wash them away. I repent for any time I have ever fantasied about committing suicide. I also repent for self-inflicted word curses
and all covenants with demons of *suicide* that have existed in my ancestral
bloodline. I am asking that every covenant with demonic powers will now
be revoked and that their right to claim me and my bloodline would now
be dismissed before Your court, in Jesus' name. Thank You, Lord, for revoking these demonic covenants and destroying the evil altar of *suicide* in Jesus'
mighty name! Heavenly Father, in my heartfelt desire to divorce myself from

the spirit and altar of *suicide,* I give back everything and anything that the devil would say came from his kingdom. I only want what the blood of Jesus has secured for me.

7. *Appeal to the Blood of Jesus to Wipe Out All Sin (Satan's Evidence)*

Lord Jesus, thank You for cleansing me by Your blood so satan has no legal footing against me in Your courtroom. It is written in First John 1:9:

> *If we [freely] admit that we have sinned and confess our sins, He is faithful and just [true to His own nature and promises], and will forgive our sins and cleanse us continually from all unrighteousness [our wrongdoing, everything not in conformity with His will and purpose].*

Righteous Judge, I appeal to the blood of Jesus to wipe out all my shortcomings, transgressions, and iniquities, in Jesus' name, I pray. I receive by faith the cleansing power of the blood of Jesus.

8. *Ask the Court to Dismiss All of Satan's Accusations and Charges*

Heavenly Father, based upon Jesus' finished work and my heartfelt repentance, I now move on the Court of Heaven to dismiss all of satan's accusations and charges against me and my bloodline in Jesus' name. For it is written that the accuser of the brethren has been cast down. So, I ask You Father to cast down all of satan's accusations against me, in Jesus' name, I pray.

9. Ask the Lord to Send Angels to Destroy the Evil Altar and Execute the Lord's Judgment Against It

Heavenly Father, Righteous Judge, I ask that You send high-ranking angelic officers of the Courts who excel in strength to execute the judgment of Your supreme court and destroy the evil altar of *suicide* and the idol that sits on it that satan planted in my bloodline, in Jesus' name I pray. By the spirit of prophecy, I prophesy the complete destruction of the evil altar of *suicide* in my life, in Jesus' name. For it is written in Psalm 91:11-12, *"For He will command His angels in regard to you, to protect and defend and guard you in all your ways [of obedience and service]. They will lift you up in their hands, so that you do not [even] strike your foot against a stone."* I receive angelic assistance, right now, in Jesus' name.

10. Present Scriptures That Will Be Used in Issuing a Divine Restraining Order

Heavenly Father, I present before Your Supreme Court the following scriptures as my rock-solid evidence against the spirit and altar of *suicide* in my life. It is written:

> *Then the Lord showed me four craftsmen. And I said, "What are these coming to do?" So he said, "These are the horns that scattered Judah, so that no one could lift up his head; but the craftsmen are coming to terrify them, to cast out the horns of the nations that lifted up their horn against the land of Judah to scatter it"* (Zechariah 1:20-21 NKJV).

> *And I will compensate you for the years that the swarming locust has eaten, the creeping locust, the stripping locust, and the gnawing locust—My great army which I sent among you. You will have plenty to eat and be satisfied and praise the name of the Lord your God who has dealt wondrously with*

you; and My people shall never be put to shame (Joel 2:25-26 NKJV).

Righteous Judge, based upon the aforementioned scriptures, it is clear that the spirit and altar of *suicide,* if allowed to succeed in its mission, would cause great injury to my life, destiny, and also inflict irreparable damage to the purposes of God. I ask that that every legal right the spirit and altar of *suicide* is holding be revoked in Jesus' glorious name. Righteous Judge, based upon the aforementioned scriptures, it is clear that I qualify for a divine restraining order against the altar of *suicide* and the idol that sits on it, in Jesus' name.

11. Ask the Court to Issue a Divine Restraining Order and Receive the Divine Restraining Order by Faith

Heavenly Father, Righteous Judge, I now ask that a divine restraining order and a permanent injunction against the spirit and altar of *suicide* in my life would now be issued by the authority of Your Supreme Court, in Jesus' name. Heavenly Father, I decree and declare that any and all activities of *suicide* the devil is orchestrating against my life are now cancelled in Jesus' glorious name. Heavenly Father, I receive this divine restraining order and permanent injunction by faith, in Jesus' name. For it is written in the Constitution of Your Kingdom in Hebrews 11:6, *"But without faith it is impossible to [walk with God and] please Him, for whoever comes [near] to God must [necessarily] believe that God exists and that He rewards those who [earnestly and diligently] seek Him."* I believe and declare by faith that the spirit and altar of *suicide* in my life has been judged, in Jesus' name!

12. Ask the Lord to Seal Your Righteous Verdict and Court Proceedings in the Blood of Jesus

Heavenly Father, Righteous Judge, I now ask You to seal my righteous verdict against the spirit and altar of *suicide* in the precious blood of Jesus.

May You also cover with the blood of Jesus all my legal proceedings in this Court in Jesus' name. I decree and declare that my righteous verdict of release and breakthrough from the evil altar of *suicide* is now secured in the documents of the Courts of Heaven. For it is written in John's Gospel, chapter 8:36, *"So if the Son makes you free, then you are unquestionably free."* I decree and declare that I am free of the altar of *suicide* in Jesus' name, amen!

About Dr. Francis Myles

Dr. Francis Myles is a multi-gifted international motivational speaker, business consultant, and apostle to the nations. Senior pastor of Lovefest Church International in Lusaka, Zambia. He is also the creator and founder of the world's first Marketplace Bible™ and founder of Francis Myles International, a TV and multimedia ministry based in Atlanta. He is a sought-after conference speaker in both ministerial and marketplace seminars. He is also a spiritual life coach to movers and shakers in the marketplace and political arena. He has appeared on TBN, GodTV, and Daystar. He has been a featured guest on Sid Roth's *It's Supernatural!* TV show and "This Is Your Day" with Pastor Benny Hinn. He is happily married to the love of his life, Carmela Real Myles, and they reside in McDonough, a suburb on the outskirts of Atlanta, in the state of Georgia.